Herman 5/14

THE GLOBAL WAR FOR INTERNET GOVERNANCE

LAURA DENARDIS

The Global War for Internet Governance

Yale UNIVERSITY PRESS

NEW HAVEN AND LONDON

Yale University Press books may be purchased in quantity for educational, business, or promotional use. For information, please e-mail sales.press@yale.edu (U.S. office) or sales@yaleup.co.uk (U.K. office).

Set in Scala type by Westchester Publishing Services.
Printed in the United States of America.

Library of Congress Cataloging-in-Publication Data

DeNardis, Laura, 1966–
    The global war for internet governance / Laura DeNardis.
        pages cm
    Includes bibliographical references and index.
    ISBN 978-0-300-18135-7 (cloth : alk. paper)   1. Internet governance—Law and legislation.   I. Title.
    K4345.D46 2013
    384.3'3—dc23   2013017552

A catalogue record for this book is available from the British Library.

This paper meets the requirements of ANSI/NISO Z39.48–1992 (Permanence of Paper).

10 9 8 7 6 5 4 3 2 1

For Deborah Rebecca Smith

CONTENTS

CHAPTER ONE

The Internet Governance Oxymoron

INTERNET GOVERNANCE CONFLICTS are the new spaces where political and economic power is unfolding in the twenty-first century. Technologies of Internet governance increasingly mediate civil liberties such as freedom of expression and individual privacy. They are entangled with the preservation of national security and the arbitration of digital commerce and innovation. The diffuse nature of Internet governance technologies is shifting historic control over these public interest areas from traditional nation-state bureaucracy to private ordering and new global institutions. Many of these governance functions are technically and institutionally complicated and therefore out of public view. Yet how conflicts over Internet governance are settled will determine some of the most important public interest issues of our time.

The term "Internet governance" conjures up a host of seemingly unrelated global controversies such as the prolonged Internet outage in Egypt during political turmoil or Google's decision not to acquiesce to U.S. government requests to completely remove an incendiary political video from YouTube. It invokes media narratives about the United Nations trying to "take over" the Internet, cybersecurity concerns such as denial of service attacks, and the mercurial privacy policies of social media companies. These issues exist only at the surface of a technologically concealed and institutionally complex ecosystem of governance.

The escalation of Internet control debates into the public consciousness presents a unique moment of opportunity for a treatise on Internet governance. One objective of this book is to explain how the Internet is already governed, particularly through the sinews of power that exist in the architectures and global institutions of Internet governance. There are significant discontinuities between media and policymaker accounts of Internet control and how the Internet is run in practice. Written from the standpoint of an engineer, this book provides the requisite technical and historical background for understanding these practices. Also written from the standpoint of a scholar of science and technology studies (STS), this book constructs a conceptual framework of Internet governance that extends well beyond traditional institution-bound accounts of the policies of sovereign nation states and international agreements to account for the rising privatization of global power and the embedded politics of technical architecture. Questions of governance at these control points are questions of technical and economic efficiency but also expressions of mediation over societal values such as security, individual liberty, innovation policy, and intellectual property rights. Global Internet governance controversies are brewing over how to balance these values. A primary impetus for this book is the need to bring these controversies into the public consciousness and explain the connection between the future of Internet governance and the future of expressive and economic liberty.

Most Internet governance struggles are very complex, even those that have exploded in full view of the mainstream media or have involved mass online collective action. One such episode featured a massive online boycott led by Internet technology companies. Thousands of web sites went dark or altered their opening screens to protest antipiracy legislation moving through the U.S. Congress. Wikipedia blacked out its popular English-language site for twenty-four hours, instead displaying a banner reading "Imagine a World without Free Knowledge." Reddit, Boing Boing, and thousands of other popular sites blocked access to their content. Google blacked out its famous doodle logo on its opening search screen. Internet advocacy efforts cumulatively gathered more than ten million petition signatures, and Congress was inundated with phone calls. This historic protest and mass Internet boycott was a response to two proposed bills, the "Stop Online Piracy Act" (SOPA) and the "Preventing Real Online Threats to Economic Creativity and Theft of Intellectual Property Act" (PROTECT IP Act, or PIPA). These legislative efforts targeted the illegal online trafficking of copyrighted media and counterfeit goods. Their antipiracy objectives initially garnered broad bipartisan support in the House and Senate. The bills would heighten criminal penalties for intellectual property rights violations such as illegally streaming pirated movies. The proposed legislation would also enable law enforcement and intellectual property rights holders to demand that search engines cease providing links to infringing web sites, that Internet service providers block access to these sites, and that financial services companies and advertising firms cease directing payments or serving ads to these sites.

Popular domain name registrar Go Daddy had been one of the Internet companies publicly supporting SOPA. This support triggered its own global backlash against Go Daddy, with a number of customers initiating domain name transfers to other registrars. The company eventually reversed its position and deleted previously released company blog postings supporting the legislation.[1]

The object of the Internet boycott was not the antipiracy intent of the proposed legislation. Rather, the boycotts challenged the mechanisms of how the antipiracy goals would be executed. The bills would have altered various aspects of the Internet's technical, cultural, and institutional norms. Some Internet freedom advocates warned that the bill might make companies like Google liable for copyright infringement on their sites and enable law enforcement to order the removal of web sites containing nothing more than a hyperlink to other sites hosting pirated content. Reddit cofounder Alexis Ohanian warned that the legislation would "obliterate an entire tech industry."[2] Other concerns focused on economic trade freedom, such as the provisions that would have required financial intermediaries including credit card companies and advertisers to cease doing business with a site that a content company claimed was violating its intellectual property rights.

The legislative effort also raised technical concerns by proposing enforcement mechanisms that might alter the Internet's technical operation and possibly compromise its security and stability. This concern involved one of the fundamental technologies of Internet governance, the Domain Name System (DNS) that translates between the alphanumeric names that humans use, such as twitter.com, and the binary addresses computers use to route information to its destination. The universally consistent resolution of unique names into unique numbers is a basic mechanism keeping the Internet operational. This resolution process is overseen by institutions called Internet registries. An authoritative registry manages the centralized database mapping names into numbers for each top-level domain such as .com or .edu. For example, the corporation VeriSign operates the .com domain, among others. The registry propagates an authoritative file mapping names into numbers to other so-called "recursive servers" of network operators, such as Internet service providers, to create a universal and standardized mechanism for consistently resolving domain names into Internet addresses regardless of physical geography or jurisdiction.

The proposed legislation included DNS filtering provisions that would have required Internet service providers to filter and redirect traffic away from web sites by altering the authoritative information it receives from registries. In other words, an Internet service provider would be obliged to resolve a domain name into a different binary address than the global Internet universally dictates, presumably redirecting it to a web site with a law enforcement message. National governments already have the ability to order authoritative registries under their jurisdictions to block access to the domain names under their control. But they do not have this jurisdiction in a top-level domain controlled by a foreign registry. Hence, governments have an interest in ordering network operators within their own jurisdictions to modify the standard domain name resolution process to block web sites. This modification from a hierarchical and consistent system to a series of inconsistent resolution approaches would erode the traditional universality of domain names and potentially complicate the global security and administration of the Internet's infrastructure, transforming the Internet from a universal infrastructure to one that varies from country to country.

During the legislative deliberations about the proposed modifications to Internet governance structures, it became clear that some policymakers were unfamiliar both with how basic technologies of Internet governance work and with how global coordination works among the institutions that manage these systems. Considering the complexity of these technological and institutional frameworks, this might not be surprising. But legislators also dismissed the concerns of leading technical experts. *Roll Call* reported that one of the sponsors of SOPA was generally dismissive of criticism of the bill as "completely hypothetical" and suggested that "none of it is based in reality."[3]

Eighty-three prominent Internet engineers, including TCP/IP inventor Vinton Cerf, Paul Vixie, the author of BIND (DNS server software), and other respected technologists who have contributed to essential Internet protocols, submitted a letter to Congress warning that the potentially catastrophic bill would "risk fragmenting the Internet's Domain Name System," "engender censorship," create "fear and uncertainty for technological innovation," and "seriously harm the credibility of the United States in its role as a steward of key Internet infrastructure."[4] Some of the most respected Internet security experts, including Internet pioneer Steve Crocker, had also written a white paper entitled "Security and Other Technical Concerns Raised by the DNS Filtering Requirements in the PROTECT IP Bill" asserting that the web site redirection provisions were inconsistent with an important security protocol known as Domain Name System Security Extensions (DNSSEC).

The concerns expressed by Internet engineering experts were in themselves insufficient to stop the progression of SOPA and PIPA, which retained bipartisan support and had the vocal backing of mainstream media corporations and powerful lobbies from pharmaceutical, motion picture, and music industries. But opposition to the bills continued to gather momentum. Leading Internet engineers opposed the bills. Advocacy groups such as the Center for Democracy and Technology, the Electronic Frontier Foundation (EFF), and Public Knowledge, among others, vocally opposed the bills and conducted forceful information dissemination campaigns. Media coverage escalated, first in the tech media and eventually in more mainstream media sources. Opposition to the bills finally escalated into the online blackouts of prominent Internet companies and the weight of millions of citizens enlisted by private companies and advocacy groups to sign petitions.

Cumulatively, these efforts changed the framing of the debate from bipartisan antipiracy objectives to two different framings: a "don't break the Internet" framing and an "Internet freedom" framing concerned about censorship and prior restraint on speech. This Internet governance confrontation was grounded in a real technological and social concern but was also culturally constructed and discursively escalated by forces with a significant interest in the outcome.

In response to online petitions, the White House issued an official response stating, "We will not support legislation that reduces freedom of expression, increases cybersecurity risk, or undermines the dynamic, innovative global internet." The statement further noted that laws "must not tamper with the technical architecture of the Internet through manipulation of the Domain Name System (DNS), a foundation of Internet security. Our analysis of the DNS filtering provisions in some proposed legislation suggests that they pose a real risk to cybersecurity and yet leave contraband goods and services accessible online."[5]

Also in the wake of unprecedented online protests and blackouts, several sponsors of the legislation withdrew their support. Ultimately, leaders in the House and Senate decided to table action on the previously fast-moving bills until open issues could be resolved. SOPA and PIPA were killed, at least for the time being.

This Internet governance affair was atypical in playing out on a public stage but was typical in that it involved multiple stakeholders—media industries, Internet industries, private citizens, traditional governance structures, Internet registries, engineers from standards-setting institutions, and cybersecurity experts. It played out locally in the United States but would have had sweeping global implications. Topically, it touched on many of the issues this book addresses: freedom of expression online, Internet infrastructure security and stability, the policy role of Internet companies, the efficacy of Internet protocols, globally coordinated Internet control systems such as the DNS, and the relationship between intellectual property rights enforcement and Internet architecture. These are the issues at the heart of global Internet governance.

GLOBAL INTERNET GOVERNANCE IN THEORY

The primary task of Internet governance involves the design and administration of the technologies necessary to keep the Internet operational and the enactment of substantive policy around these technologies. This technical architecture includes layer upon layer of systems including Internet technical standards; critical Internet resources such as the binary addresses necessary to access the Internet; the DNS; systems of information intermediation such as search engines and financial transaction networks; and network-level systems such as Internet access, Internet exchange points, and Internet security intermediaries. The following sections suggest five features of global Internet governance that will serve as a conceptual framework for this book: how arrangements of technical architecture are arrangements of power; the propensity to use Internet governance technologies as a proxy for content control; the privatization of Internet governance; how Internet points of control serve as sites of global conflict over competing values; and the tension between local geopolitics and collective action problems in Internet globalization.

Arrangements of Technical Architecture as Arrangements of Power
The complex institutional and technical scaffolding of Internet governance is somewhat behind the scenes and not visible to users in the same way applications and content are visible. Although these technologies lie beneath content, they nevertheless instantiate political and cultural tensions. They embed design decisions that shape social and economic structures ranging from individual civil liberties to global innovation policy. Geoffrey Bowker and Susan Leigh Star have explained that "Inverting our commonsense notion of infrastructure means taking what have often been seen as behind the scenes, boring, background processes to the real work of politics and knowledge production and bringing their contribution to the foreground."[6] Bringing infrastructures of Internet governance to the foreground reveals the politics of this architecture.

An influential collection of scholarship has examined large-scale technological systems through the lens of the politics of technical architecture, beginning at least in 1980 with political theorist Langdon Winner's avant-garde piece "Do Artifacts Have Politics?" Winner explained, "At issue is the claim that the machines, structures, and systems of modern material culture can be accurately judged not only for their contributions to efficiency and productivity and their positive and negative environmental side effects, but also for the ways in which they can embody specific forms of power and authority."[7]

A naive view of technology governance would suggest that public authorities establish objectives for large-scale systems and then technical experts and coordinators implement these social goals in the design and administration of systems. This view of governance fails to consider the direct influence of forces with an economic or political stake in the design and administration of technologies, the influence of user communities and markets, and the inevitable unintended outcomes of systems of design and administration. Sheila Jasanoff's theory of co-production has emphasized how technology and social order are produced contemporaneously. This is a useful model that avoids the extremes of both technological and social determinism. Technology "embeds and is embedded in social practices, identities, norms, conventions, discourses, instruments, and institutions—in short, in all the building blocks of what we term the social."[8]

Internet governance decisions involve both scientific reasoning and social considerations of power and authority. For example, the design of the Internet address space (the collection of all available Internet addresses) and the domain name space specified a technical requirement for each name and number to be globally unique. Whereas this requirement for global uniqueness has necessitated forms of centralized coordination, control of names and numbers has been a fundamental global struggle of Internet governance since the 1990s.

Internet protocols, also called standards, are often political in both their design and effects. A protocol such as BitTorrent serves a straightforward technical function of providing peer-to-peer file sharing, but is intractably embroiled in conflicts over media piracy. The Do Not Track protocol normatively provides privacy for individuals wishing to opt out of online advertising-based behavioral tracking. Even routine technologies of bandwidth management are value-laden when they rely on invasive content-inspection techniques like deep packet inspection.

Internet governance also involves the establishment of policies about how these architectures are used to regulate and control content. The SOPA/PIPA legislation would have required modifications to Internet governance technologies, changes with direct implications for security and freedom. It could have also created different possibilities for content mediation apart from intellectual property rights enforcement, effectively creating an infrastructure aimed primarily toward the blocking of content rather than the free flow of information. Traditional governance mechanisms, whether statutory frameworks or international treaties, must consider existing architectural design and the ways in which this design already constructs governance.

Changing the technology's architecture changes the politics it constructs and creates possibilities for both different forms of governance and unanticipated outcomes. The sometimes esoteric nature of these technical governance mechanisms that keep the Internet operational belies the substantive public policy decisions embedded in these mechanisms. An overarching theme of this book is how arrangements of technical architecture are also arrangements of power.

Internet Governance Infrastructure as a Proxy for Content Control
Viewing Internet governance through a theoretical framework of the politics of technical architecture is important not only because of the inherent values designed into this architecture but because traditional power structures increasingly view Internet governance technologies as mechanisms for controlling global information flows. One Internet governance theme is the escalating use of Internet governance technologies as a proxy for content control, whether for enforcing intellectual property rights or other law enforcement functions or for government censorship of citizens.

Social science inquiry can sometimes overlook "inanimate" intermediation points or else view them as neutral actors while focusing on content analysis or the dynamics of social actors or governing institutions. Focusing on intermediation points leads to a set of different governance questions.[9] These intermediaries include financial services companies that facilitate online monetary transactions; web hosting companies that house other entities' content on their servers; search engines; registrars that assign domain names to Internet users; registries that perform domain name resolution processes; entities that run Internet exchange points connecting networks; and the institutions that operate the Internet's routing and addressing infrastructure.

These intermediaries, *ex ante*, establish Internet policies but they also are being used for content mediation functions for which they were not originally designed. This turn to infrastructure intermediaries for content control exists in the context of larger global vicissitudes of political and economic power.

Traditionally dominant institutions of power—whether nation states, religious institutions, or multinational corporations—have lost some of their historic control over information flows. Forces of globalization, technology, and media market diffusion have reduced the ability of these institutions to both contain and maximally profit from this content. Corporate media content producers have lost some control over the monetization of their own content. Revenue models for the cultural production of movies, music, and video games, as well as journalistic enterprises, have been destabilized by content sharing sites, competition from citizen produced news and entertainment, and the low cost of duplication, storage, and distribution of content over digital networks. Traditional intellectual property rights enforcement, based on taking down specific content or suing individuals, has done little to stop global piracy practices. Not surprisingly, interest has turned to terminating Internet access, blocking entire web sites via the DNS, or blocking financial flows, if any, to these sites.

Governments have also experienced a loss of information control, whether the ability to stop the leaking of sensitive national security information or the ability of regimes with restrictive information policies to contain the global exportation of media accounts. An extreme example of government turning to Internet infrastructure for information containment was the Egyptian Internet outage of January 2011, when citizens experienced a government-ordered blackout of Internet access and cell phone service. Egyptian president Hosni Mubarak ordered communications companies to block services during a period of political uprisings. Massive Internet outages have occurred in other countries including Burma and Libya.

The same technologies that improve citizen communication and information diffusion are also used by many types of governments to filter and censor information, to create systems of surveillance, and to disseminate misinformation. The inability of governments to control the flow of information via laws and other mechanisms of traditional authority has shifted political battles into the technical domain of Internet infrastructure and governance.

Another rationale for this interest in infrastructure-based content control relates to cross-border jurisdictional complexities. This was the case in the SOPA/PIPA example mentioned earlier. U.S. legislative interest in ordering DNS blocking of foreign sites via Internet service providers arose from jurisdictional limitations. Infringing sites often use top-level domains controlled by entities outside of the United States, and therefore outside of U.S. jurisdiction. Whereas national laws and, in many cases, international treaties have jurisdictional boundaries that complicate cross-border enforcement, the Internet's intermediating infrastructures transcend these borders and are targets of intervention for content control not possible via traditional governance mechanisms.

Finally, interest in intermediary-based content control arises from the technical and institutional condition that global Internet choke points do exist. Despite the decentralized physical geography of the Internet and the diversity of institutions overseeing this infrastructure, there are centralized points of control. Some are virtual; some are physical; some are virtually centralized and physically distributed. All are increasingly recognized as points of control over Internet infrastructure or points of control over content mediation. This book identifies and examines these technological and institutional control points and the political and economic interest in controlling content at these interstices.

The Privatization of Internet Governance
Internet governance is about governance, not governments. Governance is traditionally understood as the efforts of sovereign nation states to regulate activities within or through national boundaries. Governments oversee many Internet governance functions, whether enforcing child protection measures, enacting privacy laws, enforcing computer fraud and abuse statutes, regulating antitrust, or generally developing national or regional statutes related to information policy. From the standpoint of global Internet governance, some sovereign governments also unfortunately censor information or enact surveillance over citizens. Most Internet governance functions have historically not been the domain of governments but have been executed via private ordering, technical design, and new institutional forms, all enacted in historically specific contexts of technological and social change.

Understanding how the Internet is governed and shaped by these diverse actors is an exercise in bricolage. In the arts, bricolage is the construction of a creative work such as a sculpture from a diverse array of materials at hand. Each individual component has a unique history, material architecture, and economic worth. Combined into a unified whole, the materials assume a different meaning and are ascribed a heightened cultural value.

Much of Internet governance is enacted by private corporations and nongovernmental entities. For example, the particulars of individual privacy online are set via social media end user agreements and the data collection and retention practices of the online advertising industry, search engines, and other information intermediaries. As evident in the Internet protest example introduced earlier, the collective action of private citizens, as well as high-profile boycotts by private companies, can also exert influence on Internet governance decisions. In this sense, private industry not only exerts influence via the policies corporations set for usage of their products and services; it also influences traditional governmental actions. Private companies like VeriSign serve as domain name registries running vital Internet governance operations. Private telecommunications companies make up the majority of the Internet's backbone and conjoin via private contractual agreements at exchange points.

Private corporations enact policy not only in carrying out their core functions but also as actors responding to events on a larger political stage. Private corporations, rather than a government entity, made the determination to cut off services to WikiLeaks after it began releasing sensitive diplomatic correspondences. The company providing WikiLeaks with free DNS resolution services decided to stop providing these services, temporarily erasing its online presence. Amazon stopped hosting WikiLeaks sites on its computers, citing a violation of its terms of service. Financial companies severed the flow of money to WikiLeaks. The WikiLeaks saga serves as an exemplar of the political power of private intermediaries. Where governments could be, and are, constrained by constitutional protections of free press and free speech, private industry is not necessarily subject to these same confinements.

Other forms of privatized Internet governance are directly delegated from government authorities to corporations. In the field of STS, actor-network theory would perhaps refer to this phenomenon as regimes of delegation carried out by technical intermediaries that are often "black-boxed" and overlooked by end users.[10] Delegated governance is particularly prevalent in the Internet context because private companies, rather than public entities, serve as information intermediaries. Governments wanting to enact Internet surveillance, censor information, block unlawful information, or obtain personal data are usually unable to directly execute these tasks. They rely on private industry. Governments ask search engines to remove links. They approach social media companies to delete defamatory material. Governments ask Internet service providers to relinquish personal information about their subscribers for law enforcement or political reasons. Delegated censorship, delegated surveillance, delegated copyright enforcement, and delegated law enforcement have shifted governance—for better or worse—to private intermediaries. These companies assume the challenging and resource-intensive task of arbitrating these government requests in different jurisdictions, cultural contexts, and technical environments.

This phenomenon of privatization and delegation is not unique to Internet control issues but is part of broader political conditions. One condition is the global phenomenon of the privatization of functions traditionally performed by the state, whether the use of private contractors in military combat environments or the outsourcing of federal bureaucratic functions.

There is a notable distinction between forms of privatization of military and bureaucratic state functions and examples of Internet governance privatization. Whereas the outsourcing of law enforcement functions or bureaucratic tasks normally involves financial compensation to the private entity delegated these functions, a unique feature in Internet governance is the expectation that some private entities, whether information intermediaries, or financial and transactional intermediaries, should be compelled to carry out law enforcement functions traditionally performed by the state without compensation and often with additional expense and possibly even liability exposure.

Another broader context is the global influence of multinational corporations on regulatory decisions across industries including pharmaceuticals, telecommunications, entertainment, and energy. In the SOPA/PIPA context, media content industries invested heavily in advancing legislation and the Internet industry spent considerable lobbying money opposing the legislation. Influence also involves knowledge levers in that regulatory areas requiring a great deal of esoteric knowledge rely on the input of industry professionals as well as outside experts, often funded by industry. Another lever was the influence Internet companies had in mobilizing their user bases into political action and capturing the attention of politicians with unprecedented Internet blackouts.

Transnational corporations operating in a variety of industries set de facto global public policy via their approaches to labor practices, environmental impacts, health care for employees, fair trade, and human rights. Multinational corporations, via this cross-cultural decision making, enact global governance. In this broader milieu, the relevant question involves the basis on which nongovernmental entities derive the legitimacy to make technical governance decisions with public policy impacts. In the online context, freedom of expression is mediated by private actors as much as by national laws or international treaties. Various countries' constitutional and statutory protections do not necessarily apply to private actors.

This confluence of issues—governmental privatization of some state functions, the increasing influence of industry on esoteric areas of regulation, and the ways multinational corporations have a de facto global policymaking function—has called attention to corporations as forces of public policy interventions. Recognition of the governance effects of private ordering has led some individual corporations and industry coalitions to develop voluntary and self-regulatory business practices that adhere to certain ethical standards and social values. The latest incarnation of this interest has been broadly termed "corporate social responsibility." Hence, there is a rich body of literature, studies, and initiatives devoted to the topic of corporate social responsibility in global political contexts.[11]

One such effort in the Internet industry is the "Global Network Initiative" (GNI), founded in 2008 as a coalition of information technology companies, advocacy groups, and academics to protect human rights of freedom of expression and privacy in the face of escalating requests from governments for delegated censorship and surveillance. The idea behind GNI was to provide participating companies with a shared framework of principles for privacy and freedom of expression that could be integrated into corporate culture and procedures when faced with governmental requests related to the speech or privacy rights of their users. The principles were drawn from international human rights laws and standards, such as the Universal Declaration of Human Rights (UDHR), the International Covenant on Civil and Political Rights (ICCPR), and the International Covenant on Economic, Social and Cultural Rights (ICESCR). For example, the principles state that companies will protect the freedom of expression of their users "except in narrowly defined circumstances based on internationally recognized laws or standards."[12] The principles also stress the obligations of companies to be held accountable to the public via transparent practices.

Noting this diffusion and privatization of governance, and private reactions to governance delegation, does not in any way suggest the demise of territorial states in regulating the Internet. Indeed, state control of Internet governance functions via private intermediaries has equipped states with new forms of sometimes unaccountable and nontransparent power over information flows. State delegation of governance to industry also raises concerns about the economic and reputational exposure of private entities such as search engine companies and financial intermediaries when carrying out content governance requests. Private industry obligations to carry out content control functions, such as intellectual property rights enforcement, can significantly increase the cost of doing business. Questions about the privatization of Internet governance are not only about freedom of expression but about economic liberty for private companies offering Internet services as well as for individuals relying on these private infrastructures.

Internet Control Points as Sites of Global Conflict over Competing Values
Decisions at Internet control points directly reflect tensions among global information policy norms. These control points are spaces that resolve global tensions via technical design, policy formulation, and nongovernmental administration negotiations. It is tempting to romanticize Internet architecture and governance as innately embodying democratic values of equality, participatory openness, and multistakeholder oversight but there are several problems with this narrative. In a significant portion of the world, Internet governance control structures do not embody democratic values but involve systems of repression, media censorship, and totalitarian surveillance of citizens. In parts of the world that do privilege freedom of expression online, there are nevertheless all-pervasive systems of data collection, retention, and sharing that serve as the underlying business models enabling free email, search, social

media, news, and other forms of complementary information intermediation. This digital shadow of trading privacy for free private goods
serves as an agonistic check on notions of democratic online governance. There are limits to the effects of democratic values even when
these principles are embodied in administrative processes, such as the
participatory and informational openness of some standards-setting processes like the Internet Engineering Task Force. Unintentional barriers
to participation exist even in procedurally open administrative structures.
Most areas of Internet governance require arcane technical knowledge.
Participation is often uncompensated activity, thereby requiring the financial backing of an employer or other funding sources. Cultural barriers of social norms, access, and language always exist. The question is
not whose voices are *allowed* to participate but whose voices are *able* to
participate. Technocracy and democracy often diverge, even when governance processes embody values of openness and inclusion.

Values in Internet architecture and governance structures are not
fixed but are continually negotiated. Some of the most intractable Internet governance questions involve conflicts among competing global values: freedom of expression versus law enforcement objectives; access to
knowledge versus intellectual property rights enforcement; media freedom versus national security; individual privacy versus online business
models based on data collection; and authoritarian regimes seeking
to preserve absolute control over information versus democratic values of openness and freedom. How these conflicts resolve in the design
of technical architecture and the policies of governments and private institutions will have a significant bearing on global innovation policy, national security, and freedom of expression.

Regional Geopolitics versus Collective Action Problems of
  Internet Globalization

The preservation of the Internet's stability and security parallels other
global collective action problems that have cumulative effects on all nations. Some of these global problems obviously include environmental
protection, the prevention of terrorism, the eradication of infectious
diseases, and the protection of human rights. Similar to these global collective action problems, the regional value of Internet infrastructure is
dependent on the network effects afforded by globally coordinated Inter-

net governance functions. Universal and consistent technical standards are the common denominator enabling interoperability among computing devices. The international coordination of Internet names and numbers ensures that each is globally unique. Cooperation at Internet interconnection points collectively creates the Internet's global backbone. Globally coordinated responses to Internet worms and viruses collectively minimize the impact of new cybersecurity threats. International trade agreements provide coordinated enforcement of intellectual property rights.

The local value of stable and secure global Internet governance is inestimable in contemporary societies dependent on networked technologies to handle basic business transactions, the movement of currency, and the exchange of financial securities. The amount of money changing hands electronically measures in the trillions range annually.[13] Social life is also intertwined with digital life. Reputation systems serve as social currency. Couples meet in online dating sites and social life materializes in social media platforms. Press freedom and individual freedom of expression alike are dependent on online infrastructures and the policies enacted to preserve both liberty and infrastructure reliability. Political campaigns rely on Internet-based fundraising and communication with voters. Law enforcement and national security efforts use digital infrastructures for data gathering and information warfare. No less than economic security, modern social life, culture, political discourse, and national security are at stake in keeping the Internet globally operational and secure.

Global Internet stability is just as dependent on local Internet conditions. Local oversight and local infrastructure bottlenecks can serve as "obligatory passage points" for international traffic.[14] This global dependence on local action exists in several respects. First, the Internet has a material architecture as much as a virtual one. The pertinent negative of successful global Internet governance is the absence of disruptions to this physical infrastructure. Widespread disruptions can occur when undersea cables are cut or during power outages that affect the buildings housing Internet exchange points or the Internet's root DNS servers.

As later examples will explain, local institutional disruptions can create very specific Internet governance problems, such as when autonomous systems (for now, think of them as network operators) advertise incorrect Internet routes and disrupt the global routing of traffic or when an interconnection dispute between telecommunications companies results in the disconnection of Internet services for subscribers. Local governmental actions that fragment the Internet's DNS or create cybersecurity problems or even information warfare can have sweeping global effects. Whereas successful global Internet governance functioning is necessary for localities to reap the network effects of Internet architecture, local actions or inactions also can have significant global effects.

Given the public interest issues that lie in the balance, one might assume that the structures of governance overseeing the Internet's technical architecture have been judiciously calibrated and executed. The rapid pace of innovation and social dependence on the Internet's architecture has not afforded this luxury of a carefully planned global governance framework. Multistakeholder control has occurred nevertheless, establishing policies that determine how information is exchanged. Who is doing the governing and what are they deciding? The constellation of actors cumulatively coordinating or ordering various aspects of the Internet's architecture has developed over a long period of time. Internet governance structures were originally based on familiarity, trust, and expertise and on "rough consensus and running code." Things have changed.

DEFINING THE SCOPE OF GLOBAL INTERNET GOVERNANCE

Demarcating Internet governance as a field of inquiry and policy is paradoxical because Internet governance practice historically predates the nomenclature of Internet governance, never mind questions about what constitutes the study of Internet governance.[15] As Milton Mueller explains in *Networks and States* (2010), "Internet governance is the simplest, most direct, and inclusive label for the ongoing set of disputes and deliberations over how the Internet is coordinated, managed, and shaped to reflect policies."[16]

Governance of the Internet and its predecessor networks (for example, ARPANET, NSFNET) has existed since 1969. Someone has had to establish the standards for how computing devices interoperate. Someone has coordinated the distribution of the unique Internet addresses necessary for devices to exchange information over the Internet. Someone has responded to Internet security problems. Someone has selected the values that would be designed into various parts of the network. This governance of technological infrastructure, even if largely out of public view, has always been an arena for public interest problems as well as a site of competition among companies and countries with a stake in the outcome of these decisions.

The study of Internet governance is a subset of the broader realm of Internet research and Internet studies, which William Dutton explains "draws on multiple disciplines—from the social sciences and humanities to computer sciences and engineering—to focus theory and research on questions concerning the social implications of the widespread diffusion and diverse uses of the Internet, Web, and related media, information and communication technologies."[17] Internet researchers who study these intersections among information, technology, and society are often concentrated in interdisciplinary academic centers—such as the Berkman Center for Internet and Society at Harvard, the Centre for Internet and Society in Bangalore, India, the Oxford Internet Institute, and the Yale Information Society Project—as well as university programs in communication and media studies; information science; computer science and engineering; science and technology studies; and law.

The study of Internet governance is a much narrower scholarly field of inquiry within the realm of Internet research just as the practice of Internet governance is narrower than the broader area of information and communication technology policies. To draw these boundaries, it helps to explain what the field addresses versus what it typically does not address.

Keeping in mind that there is nothing rigidly fixed about these boundaries, this book's definition of Internet governance suggests four parameters: (1) the study of Internet governance is distinct from the study of Internet usage; (2) issues of Internet governance relate to Internet-unique technical architecture rather than the larger sphere of information and communication technology design and policy; (3) the practice of Internet governance extends beyond institutions such as the Internet Corporation for Assigned Names and Numbers (ICANN) and standards-setting organizations to include private industry policies, national policies, international treaties, and the design of technical architecture; and (4) Internet governance includes forms of architectural control geared toward promoting interoperability and access to knowledge but unfortunately also includes those techniques geared toward restricting Internet freedom.

These boundaries are narrower than the capacious topics addressed in some venues, such as the United Nations Internet Governance Forum (IGF), which have included topics on the digital divide, digital education, and how the Internet is used generally. Conversely, these boundaries are also broader than legal examinations that focus only on institutional mechanisms of national law or international treaties, or social science approaches that focus on a subset of institutions of Internet governance (especially ICANN) but not on private governance, traditional governmental policies, or technologically mediated policy enactment.

Internet Governance Not Explicitly about Content and Usage
Internet governance questions address technological design and administration, issues generally distinct from questions about content. Inquiry is concerned with how the flow of information is designed and mediated via infrastructure rather than the content and usage of the actual information. Much Internet research and policy focuses on Internet content and usage. This approach addresses the user-centric experience of content interactions and how these interactions affect political discourse or economic and social life.

A few examples of content-related topics generally outside the field of Internet governance include the economic and political implications of user-generated content, the politics of citizen journalism and blog content, new networked models of knowledge production, the political implications of the digital public sphere, and regulations about pornography.[18] Other content-related issues outside the specific realm of Internet governance include the politics of online visual representation or the effects of virtual worlds and online gaming on behavior and sociability. These works address the production of knowledge or the political and economic effects of online content rather than control of the technologies over which this content flows.

Some examinations of the Internet focus on how traditional political actors or citizens use the Internet. For example, eGovernance involves the use of the Internet by governments but does not involve governance of the Internet. Excellent scholarship addresses societal usage issues including digital equality, social media communities, or identity formation and human interconnectedness. Research on Internet usage also examines the implications of Internet consumption patterns for economic development, and new business models for media industries. Global Internet governance concerns generally do not address patterns of Internet usage by various constituencies.

Internet governance scholars, rather than studying Internet usage at the content level, examine the political and economic implications of the design and administration of the Internet's virtual and material architecture. This architecture is usually extraneous to the Internet user's field of view or the meaning of specific content but nevertheless affects access to knowledge, the pace of innovation, and individual rights. The objects of Internet governance inquiry are technical architecture, the private and public entities and rules that control this architecture, and policies about this architecture. Studying Internet governance generally does not address the effects of Internet use or the meaning of content but does address the technologically mediated control of content or the rights of users in accessing this content. As an example of how the work of Internet governance is beneath the layer of content, consider cybersecurity governance techniques that authenticate users, protect the integrity of content, and respond to denial of service attacks, worms, and other security problems. These mechanisms are vital for protecting and securing content but are agnostic to the meaning and usage of this content.

Internet-Unique Technical Architecture Rather than Broader Information and Communication Policies

Issues involved in governance of the Internet are also distinct from the larger sphere of governance of information and communication technologies (ICTs). This distinction helps narrow the field to technologies that are predominantly unique to the Internet, such as cybersecurity, Internet intermediaries, critical Internet resources like Internet addresses, systems of routing and addressing, infrastructure management techniques, interconnection agreements among network operators at Internet exchange points, and the development of standards on which the Internet operates. Global Internet governance generally views these necessary and Internet-unique technical and institutional systems as the primary object of inquiry. Technical resources that are not Internet specific, including electromagnetic spectrum, are typically not part of global Internet governance discourses. Standards for the design of computers are not usually considered an issue of Internet governance, but the standards for interconnecting these computers are. Open source software is a technology and policy issue that is not unique to the Internet so is not a specific concern of global Internet governance. Internet governance usually addresses technologies that are unique to the Internet and deal with interoperability among devices and the management of networked information flows between these devices.

Distributed Governance

Internet governance scholarship has historically focused close attention on two areas: national regulatory frameworks and the governance role of ICANN and associated institutions that manage critical Internet resources. The functions and critical Internet resources that ICANN oversees have been a central struggle of Internet governance. ICANN's administrative framework for administering Internet names and numbers includes the Internet Assigned Numbers Authority (IANA), Internet registrars, and regional Internet registries (RIRs). There has been a great deal of scholarly and press attention to this institutional framework, possibly because domain names are one of the areas of Internet governance that are actually visible to Internet users and because of the controversy surrounding the formation of ICANN and the ensuing international concerns about the United States' historic connection to this institution. Other important institutions of Internet governance include standards-setting organizations such as the World Wide Web Consortium (W3C), the Internet Engineering Task Force (IETF), the International Telecommunication Union (ITU), the Institute of Electrical and Electronics Engineers (IEEE), and many others.

There has also been an emphasis on the question of the appropriate role of government in controlling aspects of Internet architecture and policy. This is a natural lens for legal scholars, primarily focused on a particular nation's laws (for example, Brazil, China, India, the United States). It is also a natural framework for studies and advocacy concerned primarily with how repressive governments "govern" the Internet through filtering, blocking, and other restraints on expression. But this framework can miss much of the actual global Internet governance landscape.

Internet governance is enacted via various routes:

- technical design decisions
- private corporate policies
- global institutions
- national laws and policies
- international treaties.

A significant question of Internet governance addresses the appropriate balance of power between sovereign nation-state governance and non-territorial and privatized mechanisms. A related question asks to what extent problems of Internet governance have created new global institutions and what are the implications for prevailing political structures. Understanding distributed Internet governance requires a basic understanding of Internet technical architecture and of the institutional and industry framework that administers this architecture. It also requires a more expansive lens of inquiry than that offered by fields such as political science, which primarily addresses national jurisdictional issues or international treaties, or economics, which can focus on markets and institutions but miss the role of technology and the cultural and political context in which contemporary Internet policy controversies arise.

The Internet's architecture and governance cannot be adequately studied *sui generis* or through limited lenses of national legal jurisprudence or institutional economics. The very definition of Internet governance is that it is distributed and networked multistakeholder governance, involving traditional public authorities and international agreements, new institutions, and information governance functions enacted via private ordering and arrangements of technical architecture.

Internet Governance—Good and Bad
Governance is the exercise of power to enact a certain set of public interest goals. Judging this power through the lens of history is all the reminder one needs that governance is not always a positive social force. In the global context, retrospectively and presently, some arrangements of governance have been mechanisms for oppression, corruption, and

exploitation. So it is with Internet governance. Many coordinating efforts have produced the overall salutary network effects of interoperability, economic competition and innovation, relative security, and freedom of expression. Other efforts to govern the Internet's infrastructure have resulted in harm to individuals, such as cracking down on political dissent or using personally identifying information to enact surveillance or limit communication.

The same exact technologies and mechanisms of coordination that enable the free flow of information can be used to block access and engage in invasive surveillance of individuals. Without social context, it is not possible to normatively evaluate the merits of any particular mechanism of Internet control. For example, the ability to use filtering technologies to block child pornography is quite different from the use of filtering technologies to block political speech critical of governments. At the same time, there are certain characteristics of technical design and governance—such as interoperable standards—that have, generally, enabled the free flow of information on the Internet.

Studies of Internet governance usually examine questions either of "good" governance, however one defines it, or of "bad" governance. Pessimistic treatments of Internet governance usually address either proprietary models that limit innovation or the use of infrastructure by repressive governments to censor information. An approach looking more at the positive aspects of Internet governance includes questions of fairness, efficiency, or interoperability, such as: How can resources most efficiently and fairly be distributed? How can systems be completely interoperable? How can globally distributed security response teams coordinate efforts to stop the spread of self-propagating worms? How can systems authenticate users conducting online commerce or making financial transactions? How can law enforcement responsibly and legitimately obtain information about an identity theft suspect? How should social media companies respond to cyberbullying problems? In most democratic societies, these Internet governance questions would reasonably be considered part of public policy, whether implemented via private mechanisms or through public–private cooperation.

This book addresses each of these areas with a critical recognition of the conflicting values extant in each area. The protection of one's free speech can mean the destruction of someone else's reputation. The definition of Internet governance in this book encompasses those areas that fall within the bounds of democratic governance as well as repressive and invasive techniques, whether a government is blocking Internet access for political gain or a private company is surreptitiously collecting and retaining a user's private locational or behavioral data. The scope of Internet governance addresses and critiques both democratic and autocratic forms of control of Internet technical architecture.

INTERNET POINTS OF CONTROL

The remainder of the book is divided into nine chapters. Chapter 2 explores the technologically complex and historically contentious area of the control of "critical Internet resources" (CIRs) necessary for the day-to-day operation of the Internet. Critical Internet resources include Internet addresses, Autonomous System Numbers (ASNs), and domain names. Devices are able to send and receive information if they possess a unique binary number (a series of 0s and 1s) known as an Internet Protocol (IP) address, either assigned permanently or temporarily to each device. Domain names are the unique alphanumeric names, such as www.whitehouse.gov, that make web sites easily locatable to humans. The Domain Name System is the distributed set of servers that translates alphanumeric domain names into their associated Internet addresses necessary for routing information to its destination over the Internet. An ASN is a unique binary number assigned to a network operator, usually called an autonomous system. Collectively, these are the primary virtual identifiers that keep the Internet operational. The requirement that each identifier be globally unique has necessitated centralized administration. The global struggle over who controls and possesses these resources has been a long-standing issue of Internet governance.

Chapter 2 explains the underlying technology of critical Internet resources and the distribution of power over these resources. Power struggles, whether rooted in reality or not, have reflected tensions between the United States and United Nations and controversy over ultimate control of the root zone file containing the definitive administrative record of each top-level domain including the mapping between the authoritative name server's name and Internet address(es). The chapter explains the primary governance functions required to administer CIRs and how these functions are distributed among public entities, private companies, and a nongovernmental global institutional structure that includes IANA, various regional Internet registries, domain name registrars and Internet registries, and ICANN. Some of the ongoing and substantive public policy issues around these resources include the privacy implications of unique Internet resources, the ongoing expansion of the Internet's top-level domains (TLDs), and the global impasse over the historic role of the United States in the coordination of critical Internet resources.

Chapter 3 explains the politics of Internet protocols, the standards enabling computing devices made by different manufacturers to exchange information. Routine Internet use requires direct engagement with hundreds of these protocols. Many are household terms such as Wi-Fi, Bluetooth, HTTP, MP3, and Voice over Internet Protocol (VoIP), but there are hundreds upon hundreds of standards necessary for the Internet to work. The development of Internet standards is an important and powerful area of authority over the Internet. Standards serve a critical technical function, but their development and implementation have direct economic and political effects. They are the blueprints providing the technical mediation of the public sphere and determining communicative rights within this public sphere. For example, encryption standards intersect directly with issues of privacy online and must balance conflicting values of individual civil liberties and law enforcement.

Chapter 3 examines the historic role of the IETF in setting fundamental Internet standards such as the TCP/IP suite of protocols and provides a history of the Request for Comments (RFC) series that has served as the Internet's underlying blueprints. It also explains the role of the World Wide Web Consortium and the Internet's broader institutional standards-setting framework. The chapter explores the intersection between standards design and communication rights, including the design of accessibility standards for the disabled, standards that determine individual privacy, and standards addressing broader political and economic questions such as solving Internet address scarcity and promoting innovation and economic competition. Whereas protocol design has economic and political implications, the institutional procedures and degree of transparency by which they are established are a fundamental governance concern related to expertise, public accountability and the legitimacy of private organizations to directly establish public policy.

Chapter 4 explains the public–private distribution of responsibility for securing critical Internet infrastructure. From the 1988 Morris worm to the more recent Stuxnet code targeting Iranian nuclear control systems, Internet security attacks have become increasingly more sophisticated. Internet security is both politically charged and technically complex. This chapter introduces some of the private–public institutional frameworks of Internet security, such as computer emergency response teams (CERTs) and the certificate authorities (CAs) that serve as trusted third parties authenticating Internet transactions via public key cryptography. From a governance standpoint, a combination of private entities, governmental processes, and standards bodies have become involved in certifying these CAs, creating an infinite regress of questions about who vouches for those tasked with vouching for online transactions.

A primary concern of cybersecurity is the challenge of securing the essential infrastructures of Internet governance, including the Internet's routing system, Border Gateway Protocol (BGP) transactions, and the DNS. Beyond explaining these substantive security issues, the chapter also addresses how Internet security attacks have become a proxy for political activity, such as the phenomenon of using denial of service attacks to make a political statement. Chapter 4 concludes with a discussion of the direct political linkages between cybersecurity and national security.

Chapter 5 addresses the geopolitics of the Internet's backbone infrastructure and the system of network interconnection and peering created at Internet exchange points. The Internet obviously has a physical architecture composed of transmission facilities, switches, and routers. This architecture is not a homogenous backbone but an interconnected collectivity of networks, or autonomous systems, that conjoin to form the global Internet. The interconnection of these networks and the technical and financial arrangements through which network operators conjoin is a central area of Internet governance, albeit one not well understood by the general public. These private contractual arrangements have typically existed outside of traditional governance structures of regulation and oversight, although recent global policy controversies have elevated these points of control as a source of international political tension.

This chapter explains the technical and market ecosystem of these interconnection agreements, including an explanation of the role BGP plays in instituting interconnection rules. It also introduces Internet exchange points and the economics of interconnection agreements, ranging from settlement-free peering agreements whereby network operators exchange information without financial obligation, to settlement-based agreements in which one network pays another for interconnection. The market dynamics of who "gets to peer" with whom is an area with high economic stakes and an area based more on market advantage than technical redundancy and efficiency. Interconnection arrangements are intriguing because they are private arrangements of technology based on market factors, but they are also arrangements with public policy implications. This chapter explains several policy concerns surrounding interconnection including the balance between individual market incentives and collective technical efficiency; interconnection challenges in emerging markets; and the question of critical infrastructure protection around interconnection.

Chapter 6 addresses network neutrality, an Internet policy issue that is more prominently situated in policy discussions and media coverage. The basic question of network neutrality is whether Internet service providers should be legally prohibited from discriminating against, meaning blocking or throttling back, specific Internet traffic. This differential treatment of traffic could be based on specific content, applications, protocols, classes of traffic such as video, or some characteristic of the user transmitting or accessing the traffic. Net neutrality, despite the enormous policy attention it garners, applies to a very small swath of Internet architecture, the "last mile" or last segment of user access to a network, whether via wireless or landline broadband.

Unlike most other issues this book addresses, Internet access and net neutrality are geographically bound issues contained within a local or national jurisdiction. It is treated exceptionally as a stand-alone global Internet governance issue in this book because it is a policy consideration addressed in numerous countries, because it is so dominant of an issue in the public consciousness, and because Internet access serves as a choke point determining how individual users access the global Internet.

Net neutrality is not a hypothetical issue. There have been many actual examples of network operators discriminating against certain types of traffic for political or economic reasons. Proponents and opponents of net neutrality sometimes adopt rigid positions either for comprehensive prohibitions on traffic differentiation or for no government regulations over traffic handling whatsoever. This chapter explains how these positions are unreasonable from the standpoint of the technical requirements of infrastructure management. The historical traditions of the Internet's architecture and climate of rapid innovation growth have reflected values preferring a level playing field for competition and freedom of expression. But Internet traditions have also emphasized a sense of minimal government intervention in privately owned infrastructure and a technical understanding that some packet discrimination may be necessary for the routine network management and engineering tasks necessary to keep the Internet reliable and operational.

Chapter 7 addresses the public policy role of private information intermediaries in controlling the global flow of information and determining individual rights online. Private companies that serve as information intermediaries include social media platforms, search engines, reputation engines, commerce platforms, and content aggregation sites. Information intermediaries are typically private companies providing free services to users in exchange for the ability to gather personalized data and serve targeted online advertising to subscribers. These entities rarely generate content but rather aggregate, sort, transact, monetize, or otherwise create economic or social value surrounding existing content. This mediation function bears governance responsibility both over the exchange of products and of social capital.

This chapter explores the ways in which private information intermediaries enact governance over freedom of expression, individual privacy, and reputational issues such as cyberbullying and hate speech. For example, the privacy policies of social media companies establish conditions of what personal information will be collected, aggregated, and shared with third parties. In some cases, individuals agree to privacy policies via end user agreements. In other cases, these policies are not voluntary agreements but are imposed on users, such as the retention of mobile phone locational data or applications such as Google Street View that create a nonvoluntary form of universal surveillance. This chapter provides a framework for understanding the technically mediated governance function of information intermediaries and exposes the challenges private industry faces when asked by governments to carry out law enforcement functions or mediate social controversies such as hate speech within their sites.

Chapter 8 examines the relationship between Internet architecture and intellectual property, including the turn to Internet infrastructure to enforce copyright and trademark protections. The protection of copyrighted movies and music was not a design concern during the original development of the Internet's main technologies and standards. Packets contained information and were routed based on addressing information and engineering optimization rather than based on the nature of the information these packets contained. The introduction of copyrighted multimedia Internet content such as movies, music, and video games, as well as associated advances in processing speeds and bandwidth, changed all this. This chapter explains the transformation in viewing Internet architecture as content agnostic to viewing it as the primary content enforcer for intellectual property rights. It describes the various ways in which Internet infrastructure enacts global governance over intellectual property, including traditional online enforcement via notice and takedown, "three-strikes" laws that cut off individual or household Internet access for multiple counts of infringement, and the turn to the DNS for enforcing copyright and trademark laws. Chapter 8 also explains the intellectual property rights issues embedded within technologies of Internet governance, including domain name trademark disputes, standards-embedded patents, and the role of trade secrecy in information intermediation.

Chapter 9 examines four factious and controversial technological approaches related to Internet governance: deep packet inspection; "killswitch" techniques; delegated censorship; and denial of service attacks. Deep packet inspection (DPI) involves the relatively recent capability of network operators to inspect the actual payload of packets sent over the Internet and throttle back or block these packets based on certain criteria. DPI is used as a network management technique for allocating bandwidth to latency-sensitive traffic or detecting viruses and other destructive code embedded in packets but also provides a powerful tool for content governance such as copyright enforcement, censorship, or highly targeted online ads based on the content a user exchanges. DPI represents an architectural transformation from an environment in which only packet headers, rather than content, were inspected to this routinized inspection technique providing almost any imaginable type of intelligence. This chapter examines the potential effects of DPI on economic competition and communicative freedom.

Chapter 9 also tackles the broader topic of so-called Internet killswitches, explaining the multiple points of concentration enabling content blocking and access termination. A related topic is delegated censorship. Public authorities seeking to censor information or collect personal data about citizens are usually not directly able to do so. Instead, they direct private companies to censor information or disclose personal information about subscribers. This chapter explains these institutional mechanisms of delegated censorship and surveillance and the role of private companies in adjudicating and sometimes pushing back against these requests. Finally, the chapter revisits the everyday occurrence of distributed denial of service, or DDoS (pronounced "Dee-Dos"), attacks in which multiple, unwitting computers collectively flood a targeted computer with so many requests that it becomes inaccessible for use. DDoS attacks create a great deal of collateral damage to human rights and freedom of expression.

The book concludes with Chapter 10, an analysis flagging several unresolved issues and problematic trends in Internet governance. One open issue is the increasing international pressure to change interconnection norms and possibly introduce government regulation at Internet interconnection points. There is a similar tension between multistakeholder governance, in general, and the potential introduction of greater government control such as via the United Nations. The chapter also addresses privacy issues that are emerging in online advertising as Internet business models increasingly trade the provisioning of free information and software for the ability to gather personal and locational data about subscribers. The considerable trend away from online anonymity at the level of technical infrastructure is a similar unresolved issue of Internet governance with implications for the future of free expression. The chapter also raises concerns about the trend away from Internet interoperability in areas such as social media platforms and online voice services and examines what this trend might mean for the future of

Internet innovation and the prospects for retaining a universal Internet. Finally, an open governance concern involves the implications of further shifting the DNS from its traditional technical function of address resolution to becoming the Internet's primary content enforcer, whether for censoring political content or blocking web sites that violate intellectual property rights. The public should be engaged in the resolution of all of these debates, which will directly affect the Internet's stability and universality as well as the freedoms afforded in the digital public sphere.

CHAPTER TWO

Controlling Internet Resources

ONE MEDIA NARRATIVE has warned about a possible Internet governance takeover by the United Nations, particularly its specialized information and communication technology subagency known as the International Telecommunication Union (ITU). The U.S. House of Representatives held a hearing on "International Proposals to Regulate the Internet."[1] The House and Senate passed a resolution articulating that the position of the U.S. government is to support and preserve the fundamental multistakeholder model of Internet governance. One underlying concern involved the prospect of an expansion of ITU oversight of international telecommunications regulations to include the Internet. The ITU's governance structure involves a one-nation, one-vote approach, so some concern centered around the possibly outsized role that countries with repressive online policies would have on Internet freedom. Other apprehension concerned more specific proposals that might add a layer of government regulation and oversight to particular aspects of Internet architecture. Vinton Cerf, TCP/IP inventor and respected "father of the Internet," speaking in his capacity as Google's chief Internet evangelist, warned that "such a move holds profound—and I believe potentially hazardous—implications for the future of the Internet and all its users."[2]

This global power struggle and associated rhetoric actually embodies decades-long international tensions about who should control the

Internet. The international narrative that has long dominated global governance discussions has reflected what is construed to be hegemonic and historic U.S. government control of the Internet. This concern has centered on the role of the U.S. Department of Commerce in overseeing the institutional structure centrally coordinating critical Internet resources. As one example, representatives from India, Brazil, and South Africa unofficially stated that "an appropriate body is urgently required in the United Nations system to coordinate and evolve coherent and integrated global public policies pertaining to the Internet," including oversight of institutions responsible for the Internet's operation.[3]

These concerns about centralized authority would not exist if there were not points of centralized control. Points of concentrated oversight do exist, despite the more general multistakeholder and diffuse nature of institutional oversight. The requirement for some centralized administrative coordination stems from technical design decisions and has been reflected in the evolving construction of coordinating institutions.

The most tangible disagreement over centralized authority, reflecting tensions among the United Nations, the United States, and many other Internet governance stakeholders, has involved the question of who has authority over "critical Internet resources." These finite resources are not physical but virtual, meaning logically defined in software and standards. It is not possible to access the Internet, use the Internet, or become an Internet operator without the unique identifiers known as Internet addresses, domain names, and Autonomous System Numbers (ASNs).

Functioning in the physical world requires the allocation and consumption of scarce natural resources such as water and fossil fuels. Functioning in the online world requires the allocation and consumption of virtual resources. Critical Internet resources—or CIRs—are a technologically and institutionally complex area of Internet administration. This chapter explains the technology and institutional control features of these resources and how CIRs intersect with important economic and individual rights.

Superficially, Internet addresses such as 88.80.13.160 fail to convey an intrinsic politics. But typing this number into the address bar of a web browser such as Firefox or Internet Explorer would have returned the

WikiLeaks web site during the Cablegate controversy when "wikileaks. org" was briefly blocked. Watching racing driver Danica Patrick in a Superbowl ad for domain name registrar Go Daddy obscures the long historical arc of institutional and jurisdictional confrontations over control of domain names or the global trademark regime that has materialized around these names. Many Internet users have probably never heard of ASNs, the central addressing currency of Internet interconnection.

Internet addresses, domain names, and ASNs are the finite virtual resources necessary for the Internet to remain operational. Every device accessing the Internet requires a unique binary number called an Internet Protocol (IP) address. Whereas domain names such as cnn.com are used by humans to locate web sites, computers use binary IP addresses. When someone types a domain name such as www.cnn.com into a browser address bar, the Internet's Domain Name System translates this name into the appropriate, unique binary number that computers use to locate the web site. An ASN is a binary number assigned to a network operator that connects to the global Internet. These network operators are usually described as autonomous systems. ASNs are valuable because receiving a globally unique ASN is a prerequisite for an Internet service provider's network to become part of the global Internet.

To understand these names and numbers by way of analogy, consider how the postal system functions using unique identifiers indicating how a letter should be routed to its destination. Depending on national context, these identifiers include a country name, zip code, state, city, street address, and recipient name. The global uniqueness of each address ensures that a letter can reach its appropriate destination. The Internet, as designed, could not operate without unique identifiers indicating how a packet of information should be routed to its intended destination. These unique identifiers include Internet addresses that computers use to locate a virtual destination online; numbers that uniquely identify network operators; and alphanumeric domain names that humans use to locate specific web sites.

Concern about control of technologically derived resources is not unique to Internet governance. Melees over new scarce resources have always existed in information technology policy, whether electromagnetic spectrum allocation in broadcasting or bandwidth allocation in tele-communications networks. Allocations determine who can use com-munication infrastructures and who can profit economically from these infrastructures.

In Internet vernacular, "critical Internet resources" is fairly bounded, usually describing Internet-unique logical resources rather than physi-cal infrastructural components or virtual resources not unique to the Internet. Underlying physical infrastructure such as the power grid, fi-ber optic cables, and switches are critical Internet infrastructure but not CIRs. By tradition, a common characteristic of CIRs is that they are glob-ally unique identifiers, requiring some central coordination. In contrast, no central coordination requirements limit the implementation of pri-vately owned and operated physical infrastructure. Another part of the distinction is that CIRs are Internet-exclusive and necessary for its op-eration, regardless of physical architecture. Virtual resources that are not Internet-specific, such as electromagnetic spectrum, are not usually ad-dressed in policy discussions about CIRs. Part of the distinction is that issues such as spectrum management can occur in a bounded geograph-ical area whereas Internet resources are inherently global. CIRs are vir-tual, Internet-specific, globally unique resources rather than physical architecture or virtual resources not specific to the Internet.

It is the operational criticality of these resources coupled with the technical requirement of global uniqueness that has necessitated some type of central oversight, a circumstance contributing to debates over who controls these resources and how they are distributed. The distribution of these resources has been not only outside of the direct jurisdiction of most nation states but, particularly in the case of IP addresses and ASNs, also outside of traditional economic markets. Unlike many other types of technologically derived resources, Internet numbers have not histori-cally been exchanged in free markets. Institutions, increasingly multi-stakeholder institutions, have primarily controlled CIRs. Some of these institutions include ICANN, the Internet Assigned Numbers Authority (IANA), various regional Internet registries (RIRs), Domain Name Sys-tem registries, and domain name registrars. There has also been a historic but evolving relationship between some of this institutional structure and the U.S. government.

Control over CIRs has also been controversial because of the substantive policy issues with which they directly intersect. Is the global allocation of these resources equitable? Are there sufficient stores to meet global demand? Do unique numerical addresses obviate the possibility of anonymity online? Who should legally control the domain name united.com—United Airlines, United Van Lines, United Arab Emirates, or the United Nations—and who should decide? How can national trademark laws be enforced in a global naming system? Should the Internet's DNS be used for copyright enforcement? What are the linkages between centralized DNS operations and censorship? How does an organization qualify for an ASN to become an Internet operator? CIRs are a technical area of Internet infrastructure but an area that implicates a host of international political and economic concerns.

This chapter begins with an explanation of the underlying technology of Internet addresses, the DNS (including the root zone file and domain names), and ASNs. It then provides a framework for understanding the complexity of institutions and private companies involved in governing CIRs. Finally, the chapter examines some of the public interest issues and institutional governance controversies that have beset these resources since their inception. Some of these concerns include privacy and the question of identity infrastructures enacted by IP addresses; internationalization and expansion of Internet top-level domains (TLDs); and the international impasse over centralized authority.

DECODING INTERNET NUMBERS AND NAMES

Several technical design characteristics of Internet names and numbers have helped construct a certain form of governance. First, they are a necessary precursor to being on the Internet. Without these identifiers, the Internet as currently designed would not function. Second, because of the technical requirement of global uniqueness for each identifier, they require a certain degree of centralized coordination. The third characteristic is "scarcity"—meaning that they are mathematically or alphanumerically finite resources. To understand the governance structure overseeing CIRs, it is helpful to have some technical background about their design and operation. Anyone not interested in this background or with sufficient technical familiarity is encouraged to skip this section.

The Math of the Internet Address Space Shapes Its Governance

Much policy attention and scholarship about Internet resources have focused on domain names, perhaps because they can "be seen" and directly engaged by Internet users. IP addresses have received less attention but are the most fundamental resource necessary to keep the Internet operational. Each device exchanging information over the Internet possesses a unique binary number identifying its virtual location, either assigned permanently or temporarily for a session. Internet routers use these addresses to determine how to route packets (small segments of information) over the Internet.

Understanding Internet addresses requires familiarity with the binary numbering system. Similar to how the decimal (or Base-10) numbering system consists of ten numbers—0, 1, 2, 3, 4, 5, 6, 7, 8, and 9—the binary (or Base-2) numbering system consists of two numbers—0 and 1. These 0s and 1s are called "binary digits" or "bits" for short. Digital devices contain basic switches that turn on or off to represent 0s or 1s and this binary code can be combined to represent text, audio, video, or any other type of information.

Just to provide a very rudimentary example of how information can be represented in binary, the ASCII standard for representing alphanumeric characters in binary defines a capital "W" as the binary pattern 0101011. So if someone emails a friend using shorthand slang for "whatever," the sender types a "W." But what the computer transmits is the binary number 0101011 along with additional bits that perform administrative functions, such as error detection and correction, security, and addressing. In general, this addressing function appends the source and destination IP addresses to the transmitted information.

Even in 1969 when there were not yet four computer nodes on the pre-Internet ARPANET, Internet engineers created unique identifiers to locate devices. This topic appeared in "RFC 1," the very first "Request for Comments" (RFC) in the system of information publications and standards that collectively provide blueprints for the basic operation of the Internet.[4] RFC 1 provided tentative specifications related to the interconnection of the so-called Interface Message Processors. RFC 1 stated that 5 bits would be allocated as a destination address for each node. Each of the five bits contains two possible values: 0 or 1. Just as flipping a coin (with possible outcomes of heads and tails) five times provides 2^5 or 32 possible outcomes, a 5-bit address theoretically would provide 2^5 or 32 unique destination codes as follows: 00000, 00001, 00010, 00011, 00100, 00101, 00110, 00111, 01000, 01001, 01010, 01011, 01100, 01101, 01110, 01111, 10000, 10001, 10010, 10011, 10100, 10101, 10110, 10111, 11000, 11001, 11010, 11011, 11100, 11101, 11110, 11111.

Increasing the number of available destination codes would require expanding the number of bits in each address, which Internet engineers did as ARPANET grew. Internet researchers expanded the address size in 1972 to 8 bits (providing 2^8 or 256 unique identifiers) and to 32 bits (providing 2^{32} or roughly 4.3 billion identifiers) in 1981. This 32-bit standard, which addressed much more than just address length, was introduced in RFC 791 as the Internet Protocol standard, later called Internet Protocol version 4, or IPv4.[5] This has been the dominant standard for Internet connectivity throughout most of Internet history.

Under the established IPv4 standard, each individual Internet address is a fixed 32 bits in length, such as 01000111001110010011000010100 000. More commonly, this 32-bit address would appear to a user in the following format: 71.60.152.160. This latter number, 71.60.152.160 is actually just shorthand notation—called dotted decimal format—which makes a 32-bit Internet address more compact and readable to humans. Just to take any mystery out of this notation, the following explains the simple mathematical correlation between a 32-bit Internet address and its shorthand dotted decimal equivalent. First, recall how the decimal numbering system works. In a decimal number such as 425, the 5 is in the "ones place," the 2 is in the "tens place," and the 4 is in the "hundreds place." Calculating the value of the number takes place as $4(100) + 2(10) + 5(1) = 425$. It involves multiples of ten. Calculating binary numbers is identical except that binary involves multiples of two rather than multiples of ten. The number places from right to left in a binary number are the "ones place," the "twos place," the "fours place," the "eights place," and so forth.

Dotted decimal format is calculated from a 32-bit address by separating the address into four groups of 8 bits, converting each group of 8 bits into its equivalent decimal number, and separating each of the four resulting decimal numbers with dots. The following shows the step-by-step conversion of the 32-bit address 01000111001110010011000 010100000:

1. Separate the address into four groups of 8 bits:

   01000111 00111100 10011000 10100000

2. Convert each group of bits into its equivalent decimal number:

   $01000111 = 0 + 64 + 0 + 0 + 0 + 4 + 2 + 1 = 71$

   $00111100 = 0 + 0 + 32 + 16 + 8 + 4 + 0 + 0 = 60$

   $10011000 = 128 + 0 + 0 + 16 + 8 + 0 + 0 + 0 = 152$

   $10100000 = 128 + 0 + 32 + 0 + 0 + 0 + 0 + 0 = 160$

3. Obtain final dotted decimal format by separating the decimal values by dots:

   71.60.152.160

Another mathematical prelude to understanding governance questions about IP addresses involves the size of the IP address space, meaning the number of available globally unique addresses. The prevailing Internet address length of 32 bits provides 2^{32}, or roughly 4.3 billion unique addresses. This was an enormously optimistic number in the early, pre-web days of the Internet, but now it is an insufficient number for all the devices requiring connectivity. Around 1990, Internet engineers identified the future depletion of addresses as a crucial design concern and the Internet Engineering Task Force, the organization that sets essential Internet standards, recommended a new protocol, Internet Protocol version 6 (IPv6) to increase the number of available addresses. IPv6 lengthens address size from 32 to 128 bits, providing 2^{128}, or 340 undecillion, addresses. To understand the magnitude of this number, picture 340 followed by 36 zeros. Obviously a shorthand notation is needed for these longer addresses. Rather than writing out 128 os and 1s, IPv6 uses a shorthand notation based on the hexadecimal numbering system (a numbering system using sixteen characters—the numbers 0 through 9 and the letters A through F). The conversion of a 128-bit number is too lengthy of a process to describe in this chapter, but the resulting IPv6 address, when converted to hexadecimal notation, would look something like the following address: FDDC: AC10: 8132: BA32: 4F12: 1070: DD13: 6921. Despite the availability of IPv6 and for a variety of political and technical reasons, the global upgrade to IPv6 has been relatively slow. The depletion of the IPv4 address space and the slow upgrade to IPv6 is a global governance problem discussed in more detail in Chapter 3.

The technical design creates a finite address space and a system of globally unique identifiers, thereby raising specific questions of governance. A unique identifier, combined with other information, can reveal the identity of an individual—or at least a computing device—that has accessed or transmitted some information or performed some activity online. This characteristic places IP addresses at the center of value tensions between law enforcement and intellectual property rights, on one side, and access to knowledge and privacy on the other side. Another governance issue involves the question of who controls the distribution of these scarce resources. If Internet addresses are a critical resource for accessing the Internet, and given that there is a finite reserve of these resources, a significant problem involves who controls and distributes these addresses to Internet users (for example, Internet service providers who in turn assign addresses to individual users and large businesses and institutions requiring large blocks of Internet addresses to operate). From where do these institutions derive the legitimacy to perform such a fundamental task of Internet governance? Another governance problem involves the global depletion of the IPv4 address space and whether there is a need for market or government incentives to extend the life of the Internet address space or encourage deployment of the newer IPv6 standard designed to expand the number of available binary addresses.

The Domain Name System as the Internet's Operational Core
It would be cumbersome to enter a lengthy binary number to reach a web site such as ebay.com. Alphanumeric "domain names" allow individuals to type in or search for an easily understandable virtual location such as twitter.com. Internet users rely on domain names to perform such routine tasks as sending email, accessing social media sites, or surfing the web.

The DNS is a fundamental technology of Internet governance in that it translates between domain names and their associated IP addresses necessary for routing packets of information over the Internet.[6] The DNS is a look-up system that handles billions upon billions of queries per day locating requested Internet resources. It is an enormous database management system (DBMS) distributed internationally across

numerous servers with the purpose of providing the locations of resources such as a web site, email address, or file.

At one time, a single file tracked all domain names and Internet
numbers. The modern DNS system arose in the early 1980s. Before this
time, locating information on the Internet, then known as ARPANET,
was accomplished quite differently. The number of ARPANET hosts and
users measured in the hundreds rather than billions. Users needed to
access resources such as mailboxes and server locations. To do so, there
needed to be a mapping between host or computer, names and Internet
addresses. Despite its small size by contemporary standards, the
network was growing rapidly and the diversity of host environments
made it difficult to institute consistent mechanisms for referencing
each host.

A single global table mapped host names and numbers. The Network Information Center (NIC), a U.S. government–funded function
located at the Stanford Research Institute (SRI) in Menlo Park, California, maintained this table. Each ARPANET host had a unique name
as well as a number assigned originally by Jon Postel, an individual
whose foundational role will be described later in this chapter. To add a
new host computer to the Internet, NIC would manually update the table that mapped each host name with its corresponding numerical Internet address.

This centrally updated table was known as the HOSTS.TXT file, up-
loaded to all networked computers as information changed. This host
file would then actually reside on each computer. As Internet engineer
Paul Mockapetris explained at the time, "The size of this table, and especially the frequency of updates to the table are near the limit of man-
ageability. What is needed is a distributed database that performs the
same function, and hence avoids the problems caused by a centralized
database."[7]

Mockapetris, an engineer at the University of Southern California's
Information Sciences Institute, proposed the basic design of the DNS
architecture in 1983. This design appeared in RFCs 882 and 883 (1983),
was superseded four years later by RFCs 1034 and 1035, and has been
elaborated in various specifications since that time.[8]

The DNS replaced the single centralized file. It retained the same
mission of maintaining a consistent and universal name space and re-

ferring queries for information or resources to their appropriate virtual locations. The most significant architectural change involved the distribution of this referral system across numerous servers. The DNS design also presupposed the existence of a diversity of underlying communication systems and network components. The only requirement for universality was in the consistency of the name space itself.

Another prominent design feature of the DNS was its hierarchical structure, which also affects the types of governance that are possible. Understanding the domain name space begins with the term "domain." In 1984, SRI engineers Jon Postel and Joyce Reynolds authored an official policy statement of the Internet community about domain name requirements. This statement summarized the purpose of domains: "Domains are administrative entities. The purpose and expected use of domains is to divide the name management required of a central administration and assign it to sub-administration."[9]

This hierarchical design stemmed in part from the administrative decision to distribute DNS management into collections of names, or domains, which would enable the address resolution process in each domain to be administered by a single authority. At the heart of this division is the system of "top-level domains." In 1984, the Internet engineering community created a handful of unique administrative categories for top-level domains as well as country codes which would be based, with a few exceptions, on the International Organization for Standardization's two-letter standard codes for countries. No country code TLDs were yet established but eventually there would be scores of country-code TLDs, or ccTLDs, such as .cn for China or .uk for the United Kingdom.

The original top-level domains were .gov for government, .edu for education, .com for commercial, .mil for military, and .org for organization (.arpa was considered a separate administrative category, as was .int). At the time, the Network Information Center at SRI would serve as the coordinator for all domains. By 2010, the number of English-language top-level domains had expanded to twenty-one administrative categories (plus .arpa, which was reserved), and the institutional structure overseeing these categories also had expanded (see Table 2.1). There were also subsequent initiatives to massively expand the number of TLDs, described later in this chapter.

Table 2.1

Historical Snapshot of Generic Top-Level Domains

.aero	.asia	.biz	.cat	.com	.coop	.edu
.gov	.info	.int	.jobs	.mil	.mobi	.museum
.name	.net	.org	.pro	.tel	.travel	.xxx

Each top-level domain space is further segmented into subdomains, represented in the syntax of the uniform resource locator (URL)—such as www.law.yale.edu. In this address, the "edu" is the top-level domain, the "yale" is the second-level domain, and the "law" is the third-level domain. In this sense, the domain name space is organized as a hierarchical tree. Administrative coordination over each domain can be delegated to each subdomain. Each domain has to contain at least one "authoritative" name server that returns official answers to queries locating resources within its sphere of influence. The DNS requires that some entity maintain definitive authority and responsibility for identifying resources in its domain.

A hierarchical structure has an apex. In the DNS, the technical apex consists of the Internet's *root name servers* and a single master file known as the *root zone file*, more accurately known as the *root zone database*. The root zone servers, now mirrored (replicated) around the world for redundancy and efficiency, are the starting point for the resolution of names into IP addresses. They publish the definitive file mapping top-level domains into IP addresses. The root zone file is a relatively small list of names and IP addresses of all the authoritative DNS servers for top-level domains, including country-code TLDs.

Describing how the DNS works is a prelude to explaining what institutions and entities actually operate the DNS. Examining the technology explains why administration of the Internet's domain name space has always been a critical and central task of Internet governance. The Internet would not function without the DNS and it is one of the few areas of Internet technical architecture which, as designed, requires consistency, hierarchy, universality, the use of unique name identifiers, and therefore some degree of centralized coordination. The following lists the main coordinating tasks necessary to sustain reliable operations and ensure the integrity and security of the DNS.

Coordinating Tasks Necessary for the DNS to Operate

- Assigning domain names
- Resolving names into numbers for each domain
- Controlling and making changes to the root zone file
- Authorizing the creation of new TLDs
- Adjudicating domain name trademark disputes
- Operating and housing the root zone servers
- Authorizing the use of new language scripts in the DNS
- Securing the DNS

The next section briefly introduces the technical operation of Autonomous System Numbers and then explains both the institutional governance framework responsible for CIRs and the evolution of policy controversies surrounding these resources.

Autonomous System Numbers as the Internet's Central Currency
High-speed core routers interconnect to form the networks that collectively comprise the Internet. Produced by manufacturers such as Alcatel-Lucent, Cisco, and Huawei Technologies, these devices interoperate because they are built according to common routing protocols. Within an Internet operator's network, routers use interior routing protocols that instruct the router how to exchange information with other routers within the same network. Between networks, routers use what is called an exterior routing protocol known as Border Gateway Protocol (BGP). All interconnections among networks are based on BGP, so it is as important to the operation of the Internet as the Internet Protocol. Routing protocols in turn rely on the virtual resources of ASNs to function.

In Internet governance nomenclature, an "autonomous system" (AS) is, roughly speaking, a network operator such as a telecommunications company, a large content provider, or an Internet service provider. More technically correct, an AS is a collection of routing prefixes (for example, IP addresses within the network's domain or in a domain operated by a network that pays a fee to the system to connect to the Internet). This collection of routing information is used within the network and advertised to neighboring networks using BGP. Autonomous systems exchange this routing policy information with neighboring networks when they connect and regularly send updates when routes change. In combination with each other, this collection of autonomous systems makes up the global Internet.

Each of these autonomous systems must have a globally unique number for use in this exterior network routing. ASNs are a unique binary number assigned to each AS. In this sense, they are similar to IP addresses in creating globally unique identifiers. Also like IP addresses, the size of the unique identifier has had to expand with the growth of the Internet. The original 16-bit ASN format, allowing for 2^{16} unique numbers, has been expanded to 32-bit numbers to provide exponentially more globally unique network identifiers that can be assigned to network operators.[10] This expanded address size allows for 2^{32}, or roughly 4.3 billion, autonomous systems.

The thousands of ASN registrations to date are publicly available and interesting to view to gain a sense of the types of network operators and other entities that serve, or could serve, as autonomous systems. Many of the first ASN registrations went to American universities and research centers involved in early use and development of the Internet. For example, Harvard holds ASN 11; Yale holds ASN 29; Stanford holds ASN 32. Network equipment company Cisco holds ASN 109. Companies formed after the rise of the Internet, including Google and Facebook, have higher ASNs. Google holds ASN 15169, among many others; and Facebook holds ASN 32934.[11]

Many governance concerns about IP addresses and ASNs are similar: Who controls the distribution of these numbers and how are they distributed; who is eligible for these numbers; and what does an ASN assignment cost? The following section explains the global distribution of governance over CIRs.

DISTRIBUTION OF POWER OVER CRITICAL INTERNET RESOURCES

Control over Internet names and numbers is considerable power. CIRs are the necessary precondition for being on the Internet. Their underlying technical requirements of universality, globally unique identification, and hierarchical structure have necessitated forms of governance that are paradoxically both globally distributed and centrally coordinated. Not surprisingly, authority over the administration of the Internet's names and numbers has been a contentious area of global Internet governance. At the technical level, the institutional apparatus keeping the DNS operational, efficient, and secure is a crucial governance function necessary for modern society's basic functioning. Economically, concerns about CIR governance have always involved questions of distributional efficiency and fairness of resource allocations. Politically, concern centers around national sovereignty, social equality, and the question of how new global institutions derive the legitimacy to administer these resources.

Existing governance structures are neither market-based nor legally constructed. The question that has perhaps garnered the most attention winnows down to the issue of sovereignty over the Internet's nucleus. The institutional system coordinating CIRs has changed significantly over the years with the growth and internationalization of the Internet. It involves an acronym-laden array of global institutions, including IANA, ICANN, the RIRs, root zone server operators, domain name registrars, registries, and various other entities. This section describes the modern institutional structure that centrally oversees critical Internet resources, the control of the root zone file, the operation of the DNS servers, the registrar system for assigning domain names, and the distribution of Internet numbers via RIRs.

Origins of Centralized Coordination

Management of names and numbers began with a single person. Based on the technical constraints engineered into the design of the domain name space, the Internet can be a universally interoperable network only if it maintains a globally unique name space.[12] As Internet governance has evolved, these resources have become managed by an institutionally bound hierarchical framework involving scores of private companies and other organizations. But in early Internet history, a single individual provided this central coordinating function. Before ICANN, there was Jon Postel. This was crucial but fairly noncontroversial work during the period when the network was primarily an American phenomenon and there was a large reserve of more than 4 billion numbers from which to allocate to institutions. The function Postel and colleagues performed was called the Internet Assigned Numbers Authority (IANA), under contract with the U.S. Department of Commerce. Vinton Cerf reminisced about Postel's function after his death:

Someone had to keep track of all the protocols, the identifiers, networks and addresses and ultimately the names of all the things in the networked universe. And someone had to keep track of all the information that erupted with volcanic force from the intensity of the debates and discussions and endless invention that has continued unabated for 30 years. That someone was Jonathan B. Postel, our Internet Assigned Numbers Authority, friend, engineer, confidant, leader, icon, and now, first of the giants to depart from our midst. Jon, our beloved IANA, is gone.[13]

IANA eventually became a function under ICANN, formed in 1998 under a contract with the U.S. government as a private, nonprofit corporation (incorporated in the state of California) to administer the Internet's names and numbers. The U.S. government–led formation of ICANN was an attempt to move from American government control to more privatized control. ICANN, consistent with Jon Postel's original responsibilities, would provide the following functions: "1. Set policy for and direct allocation of IP number blocks to regional Internet number registries; 2. Oversee operation of the authoritative Internet root server system; 3. Oversee policy for determining when new TLDs are added to the root system; and 4. Coordinate Internet technical parameter assignment to maintain universal connectivity."[14]

ICANN has fundamental governing authority for both Internet domain names and addresses. This authority, and its contractual linkage with the U.S. Department of Commerce, has been a contentious and central question of Internet governance. The IANA function under ICANN is still responsible for allocating Internet addresses for regional assignment; overseeing the assignment of domain names, although delegated to other organizations; and administering the root server system and maintaining the root zone file.[15]

United States Administration of the Root Zone File
Administrative oversight of the root zone file resides with the U.S. government, and specifically with the National Telecommunications and Information Administration (NTIA) subagency of the Department of Commerce. The agency has delegated operational aspects of executing

root zone operations to a private corporation and to the IANA function under ICANN. The responsibility for the actual updating, publishing, and distribution of the file rests contractually with VeriSign, a publicly traded American corporation headquartered in Reston, Virginia. The cooperative agreement describes the company's operational management of the root zone file as the following: "VeriSign's responsibilities include editing the file to reflect recommended changes, publishing the file, and then distributing the file to the root server operators."[16]

IANA maintains and manages the DNS root. With its direct historical roots in the work of Jon Postel and colleagues in the 1970s, IANA is one of the Internet's most venerable and consistently functioning organizations. As the global coordinator of the topmost hierarchy of the DNS, IANA maintains the root zone file serving as the central and authoritative record tracking TLDs, their operators, and the IP addresses of the authoritative server for each TLD. To understand the administrative function of the U.S. government, note that even ICANN's role in operating the IANA function is contractually provided by the NTIA. For example, the NTIA renewed ICANN's IANA contract for the period of October 1, 2012 until September 30, 2015 with two options for two-year renewals (for a total of seven years until 2019).[17]

There is a considerable degree of international and multistakeholder coordination over and participation in ICANN and IANA. In this respect, they are international institutional forms. Much has been written about the contested nature of this internationalization and the ensuing tensions between various government actors and private entities. But the underlying U.S. administration of the root, though delegated to private industry and to international institutions, has remained a global power struggle that underlies many of the efforts to modify Internet governance arrangements.

A Small Number of Organizations Operate the Root Name Servers
A collection of servers run by a small group of technical operators contains the root zone file and distributes this information to the world. This system of root name servers is not controlled by a single corporation or government but by twelve organizations. Recall that the root zone file is the information itself, maintained by IANA, contractually linked to the U.S. Department of Commerce, and distributed by VeriSign. A

separate function is the dissemination of this information via the root name servers. There is a physical geography of the Internet's architecture as well as a virtual one. To emphasize this in the most obvious way possible, root servers are housed in buildings and run by people. The physical management component requires power supply backups, physical security, the installation of equipment, and climate-controlled rooms to house equipment. Each of the root name servers contains the most current root zone database. Root servers are the gateway to the DNS so operating these servers is a critical task involving great responsibilities in both logical and physical management.

There are thirteen distinct root server implementations operated by twelve different entities, all in close coordination with each other. Although the root servers are actually a distributed physical network of hundreds of servers located across the globe, they are, in the DNS sys-

Table 2.2

Official IANA List of Internet Root Servers

HOSTNAME	IP ADDRESSES	MANAGER
a.root-servers.net	198.41.0.4, 2001:503:BA3E::2:30	VeriSign, Inc.
b.root-servers.net	192.228.79.201	University of Southern California (ISI)
c.root-servers.net	192.33.4.12	Cogent Communications
d.root-servers.net	128.8.10.90, 2001:500:2D::D	University of Maryland
e.root-servers.net	192.203.230.10	NASA (Ames Research Center)
f.root-servers.net	192.5.5.241, 2001:500:2f::f	Internet Systems Consortium, Inc.
g.root-servers.net	192.112.36.4	U.S. Department of Defense (NIC)
h.root-servers.net	128.63.2.53, 2001:500:1::803f:235	U.S. Army (Research Lab)
i.root-servers.net	192.36.148.17, 2001:7fe::53	Netnod
j.root-servers.net	192.58.128.30, 2001:503:c27::2:30	VeriSign, Inc.
k.root-servers.net	193.0.14.129, 2001:7fd::1	RIPE NCC
l.root-servers.net	199.7.83.42, 2001:500:3::42	ICANN
m.root-servers.net	202.12.27.33, 2001:dc3::35	WIDE Project

tem, logically configured as thirteen root servers. Table 2.2 displays the official IANA-published list of these thirteen root servers, along with their Internet addresses and the entities that manage them.[18]

Although many of these server implementations are operated by American institutions (for example, corporations including VeriSign and Cogent; American universities such as the University of Maryland; and U.S. governmental agencies including the National Aeronautics and Space Administration and the Department of Defense), many of the implementations are distributed on servers located around the world.

As the operators themselves describe their relationship, they are "a close-knit technical group" with a "high level of trust among operators."[19] Each root server operator is most concerned with the physical and logical security of its systems, as well as how to overprovision capacity to maintain high levels of performance and reliability. These operators face a significant operational challenge in dealing with distributed denial of service (DDoS) attacks and other security threats. One way they address these threats is through "Anycast" techniques that establish identical copies, or mirrors, of these servers around the world with the same IP address. When a DNS query is initiated, Internet routing techniques detect and use the nearest server with this IP address. Chapter 4 addresses some of the specific security challenges related to the DNS and Internet root servers.

Administrative Responsibility for Top-Level Domains and
  Domain Name Assignment

Just as the root zone file has a distinct owner maintaining a single record of mappings, every subdomain under the root is maintained by a single administrator to create a universally consistent and globally unique name space. Registry operators, historically also called network information centers (NICs), are the institutions responsible for maintaining a database of names and associated IP addresses for every domain name registered within a given TLD. IANA, in its role centrally overseeing the DNS, delegates authority for overseeing each generic top-level domain to these registry operators. There is a registry operator for each country code TLD and all of the generic TLDs. Some of these registry operators are also domain name registrars, meaning that they assign domain names to individuals and institutions requesting these names.

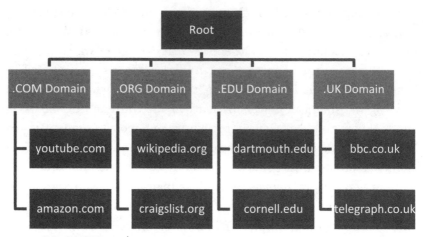

FIGURE 2.1: DNS Hierarchy

A great variety of registry operators oversee the top-level domains. VeriSign, Inc. operates the .com and .net domains, among others. A nonprofit organization called EDUCAUSE has long maintained (most recently under a 2001 Department of Commerce contract) the authoritative mapping information for the .edu domain and also assigns domain names in the .edu space. The only institutions eligible for the .edu domain name are American colleges accredited by agencies recognized by the U.S. Department of Education. The China Network Information Center at the Chinese Academy of Sciences is responsible for the .cn domain. The U.S. Department of Defense Network Information Center is responsible for the .mil name space. The Vatican country code, .va, is overseen by the Holy See Secretariat of State Department of Telecommunications. These are only a few examples of entities responsible for the various domain zones, but they serve to indicate the variety of organizational forms, including private companies, nonprofit organizations, and government agencies serving as registries.

Note that the similar-sounding words "registry" operator and "registrar" imply different administrative functions. (To complicate the terminology even more, "regional Internet registry" suggests a different function discussed in the next section.) Registry operators maintain the database of domain names for particular top-level domains. Registrars are companies that sell web domain name registrations to customers. In some cases, the registry operator is also the registrar, such as in the .edu space. In other cases, top-level domains have hundreds upon hundreds of registrars that can assign domain names in various TLDs.

Controlling Internet Number Distribution
Individual Internet access is not possible without an IP address, usually provided through an Internet service provider. Becoming an ISP is not possible without the allocation of a block of IP addresses. Becoming a network operator further requires an ASN. The organizations that control the allocation and assignment of these numbers serve an essential Internet governance function.[20]

IANA has retained its historic role as the organization centrally responsible for allocating IP addresses and ASNs, albeit now formally under the auspices of ICANN. IANA in turn delegates reserves of addresses and assignment authority to five regional Internet registries, central and influential institutions in the Internet governance landscape. The five RIRs are:

- AfriNIC: African Network Information Centre (Africa)
- APNIC: Asia Pacific Network Information Centre (Asia-Pacific Regions)
- ARIN: American Registry for Internet Numbers (Canada, United States, North Atlantic islands)
- LACNIC: Latin America and Caribbean Network Information Centre (Latin America, Caribbean)
- RIPE NCC: Réseaux IP Européens Network Coordination Centre (Europe, Middle East, parts of central Asia).

These institutions are set up as private, nonprofit entities that have been approved and recognized by ICANN. As Internet governance has been enacted in the early twenty-first century, ICANN has overseen the establishment of new RIRs. From ICANN's perspective, it is not likely that many more (if any) RIRs will become accredited. As ICANN policy states, "in order to ensure globally fair distribution of IP address space, and to minimize address space fragmentation, it is expected that the number of RIRs will remain small."[21] The number of RIRs has slowly increased over time, with ICANN formally recognizing the fourth and fifth RIRs—LACNIC and AfriNIC—in 2002 and 2005, respectively.

These RIRs in turn allocate address space to local Internet registries (LIRs) or selected national Internet registries (NIRs) such as the Chinese state-controlled registry China Internet Network Information Center (CNNIC) for further allocation or assignment to ISPs and end user institutions. RIRs also assign addresses directly to end user institutions and Internet service providers. ISPs further delegate addresses to individual end users exchanging information on the Internet. To summarize, addresses are assigned hierarchically, with IANA serving as the global coordinating body delegating addresses to RIRs for further delegation to these other institutions, ISPs, and end users. In Internet governance terminology, to "allocate" addresses means to delegate a block of addresses to another organization for subsequent distribution; to "assign" address space is to distribute it to a corporation, ISP, or other institution for actual use.

Although the regional Internet registry system internationally distributes control of addresses, IANA still serves as the central coordinating entity over addresses. Therefore, ICANN, via IANA, has formal jurisdiction over the Internet address space. Nevertheless, RIRs have considerable governance authority and administrative flexibility over regional address allocations.

The RIR system is another example of a privatized Internet governance area that is neither market-based nor under government oversight. RIRs are not intergovernmental organizations. They are primarily private, nonprofit institutions responsible for managing the distribution of number identifiers allocated to them by IANA. Each RIR is driven, financially and procedurally, by its extensive collection of mostly private member organizations. Membership is generally open to anyone but is fee-based and typically composed of private operators and other corporations to which RIRs allocate addresses. As a rough example of the fee structure, AfriNIC charges an annual membership fee of $20,000 for LIRs with a relatively large address allocation.[22] RIR membership directly elects the executive boards of these organizations. For example, RIPE NCC members elect the individuals who comprise the organization's executive board. These board members provide guidance to the RIR's senior management team, which has final procedural and operational decision-making power.

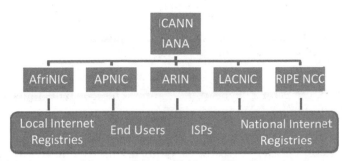

FIGURE 2.2: Institutional System of Internet Address Allocation and Assignment

RIRs have a significant public policy function in determining the allocation and pricing of Internet addresses in their respective regions. Sovereign governments in these regions rarely have formal, special influence over these allocations. The stakeholders with the greatest influence over RIRs are the primarily corporate entities who make up the RIR membership. So the RIRs have some direct accountability to the networks and customers they serve but do not necessarily have direct accountability to broader publics.

The extent to which traditional governments intervene in the Internet address space varies considerably from region to region. There are a limited number of national Internet registries. In addition to China's national registry mentioned earlier, there are also NIRs operating in Argentina, Brazil, Chile, India, Indonesia, Japan, Korea, Mexico, Singapore, Taiwan, and Vietnam. These national registries have some jurisdiction about how addresses are distributed within their own borders but less influence on the overall global allocation of addresses to the regional RIRs from where they obtain nationally allocated addresses.

TECHNICAL RESOURCES AND COMMUNICATION RIGHTS

The most high-profile global debates over CIRs have involved institutional and international struggles over centralized control and corresponding concerns about legitimacy and jurisdiction. Although this jurisdictional concern has dominated Internet governance discourse and scholarship, it is a step removed from the actual substantive policy issues co-produced with the design and operation of the DNS. The governance of Internet names and numbers implicates a host of issues tied to economic and expressive rights.

Throughout most of the Internet's history, domain names had to conform to the Latin alphabet (think "abc"). The root zone, in its design, was limited to characters conforming to the ASCII encoding standard. ASCII provided standardized instructions only for encoding Latin alphabet letters into binary. As the Internet grew, this became an obvious Internet governance-imposed digital divide issue for much of the world. It was not possible to access domain names in native languages that used Chinese characters (中国); Cyrillic script (Россия) used in Russia, Ukraine, and elsewhere; Arabic; or any other non-Roman alphabets and scripts. Native languages in China, Japan, Korea, Eastern Europe, the Middle East, and elsewhere were excluded from the Internet's DNS. The introduction of internationalized domain names in the early twenty-first century enabled multilingual domain names and country-code top-level domains in native language scripts. As with most Internet governance evolutions, the transition required not only technical solutions but also economic and legal solutions related to trademark protection and institutional decisions about who would control various aspects of new domain names, such as registry operation and registrar assignment services.

A separate question of access and equality involves the economic and social effects of the depletion of the IPv4 address space and the slow global deployment of the IPv6 standard designed to expand the number of available addresses. This dilemma is closely tied to the political economy of Internet standards and is therefore addressed in Chapter 3. Another rights-based question about the DNS involves its evolving use as a technologically mediated technique of blocking access to pirated media and for government censorship, also discussed extensively in later chapters.

The following explains three substantive policy issues embedded in CIR design and oversight: the privacy implications of unique technical identifiers; ICANN's significant expansion of top-level domains; and the ongoing international impasse over the United States' historic connection to certain aspects of name and number administration. Another difficult policy issue around domain names, the global system for resolving trademark disputes in domain names, is addressed extensively in Chapter 8.

Privacy and Internet Address Identification

The design decision requiring globally unique Internet addresses brought about a certain governance structure in the institutions of Internet governance. But it also brought about certain possibilities for governing individuals. The use of a globally unique identifier, whether permanently assigned or used for a single Internet session, can directly link material exchanged over the Internet with a general location and with the device or individual sending or receiving this material, especially in combination with other personally identifiable information.

On its surface, the Internet appears to be a public sphere in which anyone can anonymously participate. But entering this sphere usually requires passing through a gatekeeper that possesses personally identifiable information such as name, home address, credit card information, and possibly even social security number. Individuals obligatorily relinquish this information when subscribing to a wireless service plan for a smartphone or a monthly broadband Internet access service from home. Real-name identifiers are also *de rigueur* for using many free social media applications. Hardware devices also contain unique identifiers. Any of these features, in a vacuum, creates a subset of privacy concerns. In combination, a unique ISP-provisioned number identifier appended to information exchanged over the Internet and the real identification data that network service providers collect raise significant privacy considerations.

The use of the Internet Protocol is a necessary precondition for someone being "on the Internet." Indeed, the use of IP arguably can define whether someone is on the Internet. Although this architectural definition could be challenged by application-specific definitions or descriptions that reflect issues of culture or politics, it is a simple and reasonable definition. No matter where someone is on the globe, use of the Internet requires an IP address. This universalization characteristic, coupled with the requirement for each IP address to be globally unique, places IP addresses at the center of debates over privacy and anonymity online. In addition to these technical characteristics of universality and globally unique identification, the Internet's infrastructural and information intermediaries historically log IP addresses. When someone posts a blog, reads an article, views a pornographic video, or searches for a particular term, the IP address associated with these actions can be logged. This information, coupled with personal records maintained by ISPs, can identify the computer and therefore possibly the individual who conducted the online activity.

A device's origination IP address is necessary for a web site to return information to the requesting individual. Without the IP address of the requesting device, the web site would not know where to direct information. However, Internet sites do not use the IP address only to return requested information. They also record, store, and sometimes share this information. As popular Internet company Yahoo! explains in its privacy policy, "Yahoo! automatically receives and records information from your computer and browser, including your IP address, Yahoo! cookie information, software and hardware attributes, and the page you request."[23] This information can be used for a variety of purposes, including the delivery of customized advertising, conducting research, or combining this information with data collected by third parties.

Google's privacy policy also discloses the collection of information when individuals visit a Google site such as YouTube or otherwise interact with content. As Google's privacy policy indicates, these data include the IP address of the device accessing this content. It can also include device-specific information such as hardware model, operating system, and "unique device identifiers"; a history of queries made in Google's search engine; telephone number when applicable; cookies that can uniquely identify the individual's Google account; and location information obtained via a GPS signal from an iPhone or vicinity based on the location of the nearest Wi-Fi antenna or cellular tower.[24]

Like other design features of technologies of Internet governance, the universality and uniqueness of Internet addresses are sites of controversies among various public interest values. On the one hand, the expectation for reasonable online privacy while engaging in news consumption, political speech, or cultural production is the expectation for basic democratic participation. On the other hand, the expectation for national security, law enforcement, the protection of information goods, and consumer protection requires the ability for law enforcement to obtain online identifiers. Identity structures, whether pseudonymous or eponymous, are also the building blocks of the online advertising systems that subsidize free search engines, email, social media products, content aggregation sites, and other applications. Redesigning the technical architecture toward greater anonymity would require a redesign in business model. Wherever one stands philosophically on the balance between these competing values does not change the operational reality. An individual's experiential perception of online privacy also does not change the operational reality. For routine Internet use, the combination of the design of a unique logical identifier, free business models based on data collection and ad serving, and the relinquishment of real identifiers at the point of Internet entry have deeply entrenched personal identity into Internet infrastructure.

.COM Is So Twentieth Century: The Massive Expansion of TLDs
ICANN has gradually introduced additional top-level domains (for example, テスト, .jobs, .travel). Domain name registration represents an enormous economic market so each new TLD expansion has involved some wrangling over institutional ownership and governance of these resources. The addition of new TLDs also complicates the defensive strategies of brand trademark holders and copyright owners in having to address the additional domains in which intellectual property rights infringement can occur.

The introduction of the .xxx TLD was controversial for a different reason. ICANN originally approved .xxx as a top-level domain for the adult entertainment industry. Some advocates for the domain argued that a porn-specific area would make it easier for parents to block children's access to inappropriate content, although there was no basis to believe pornography would not still exist in the .com space and other domains. The U.S. government was among those pushing back against the domain. Michael Gallagher, the Commerce Department's assistant secretary for communications and information under the Bush administration, sent a letter to ICANN requesting a delay in implementing the domain. Gallagher noted that the department had received almost six thousand letters from those concerned about "the impact of pornography on families and children."[25] The Family Research Council and other conservative advocacy groups encouraged constituents to write letters to the Commerce Department and were concerned that the domain would ascribe what it believed to be unwarranted legitimacy to the porn industry.

After delays and much policy deliberation, ICANN approved the .xxx registry, albeit with a number of content and policy constraints placed on the TLD operator. The incident served to emphasize several characteristics of Internet governance, depending on one's perspective: the policy-making and gatekeeping function of ICANN; the connection between the DNS and freedom of expression; and the appropriate role of the DNS. The incident has also been cited repeatedly as an example of the direct influence of the U.S. Commerce Department on the DNS and a justification for a reduction in U.S. government oversight.

In a departure from the measured approach of gradually adding top-level domains, ICANN instituted an enormous expansion by issuing a blanket call for applications for new generic TLDs (gTLDs) between January and April of 2012. Those wishing to pursue a new gTLD would also be responsible for operating the registry, requiring technical knowledge and operational and financial resources. Prior to this expansion, there were 22 gTLDs and 250 ccTLDs.

The announcement was met with mixed reactions. Some viewed the expansion as the natural evolution of the Internet, providing more spaces for speech and innovation as well as more top-level domains in native language scripts. Others emphasized that the expansion of TLDs would bring with it an expansion of media piracy, counterfeit goods, and cybersquatting. Trademark holders, and those who represent them, anticipated having to buy their own names in hundreds or thousands of new domains. Still others viewed the expansion as a revenue-generating opportunity for ICANN, good and bad.

During the application window, ICANN received 1,930 proposals for new TLDs ranging in tone from .sucks to .sex to .republican.[26] The evaluation fee for each application for a new gTLD was $185,000, so the revenue to ICANN from the applications would theoretically have amounted to roughly $357,000,000.[27] Many of the proposed TLDs were in Chinese and Arabic characters. Not surprisingly, many companies applied for TLDs of their trademarked names and products. For example, Microsoft Corporation applied for eleven gTLDs: .xbox, .bing, .docs, .hotmail, .live, .microsoft, .office, .skydrive, .skype, .windows, and .azure. Apple, Inc. applied for .apple. A number of requested TLDs were duplicative in that ICANN received multiple applications for the same word. Not surprisingly, there were multiple applications for TLDs such as .shop (nine applications), .app (thirteen applications), .blog (nine applications), .news (seven applications), and .inc (eleven applications).

The expansion of TLDs helps illustrate some of the conflicts that arise in the domain name space. For example, in cases of duplicative applications, only one applicant would be selected. ICANN's applicant guidebook explains that, in such cases of string contention, ICANN would encourage resolution among applicants or else possibly institute an auction.

The TLD expansion and application process also drew attention to conflicts that can arise between companies' trademarked names and geographical regions. After reviewing new TLD applications, ICANN's Governmental Advisory Committee (GAC) provided advice expressing initial objections to certain TLDs, including .patagonia and .amazon. The GAC is primarily made up of representatives of national governments and its role is to provide ICANN with public policy advice. The companies Patagonia and Amazon applied for the top-level domains associated with their trademarked names, but countries with the Amazon and Patagonia regions within or across their borders expressed objections to these applications. Even though "Amazon" and "Patagonia" are not nation-state circumscribed regions, and do not necessarily meet one of ICANN's definitions of a geographical domain, these TLDs were contested. The domain system is evolving, and will continue to have to balance conflicting values and multistakeholder interests. As the name space expands, so will the oversight and policy-setting role of ICANN expand.

International Impasse over Centralized Authority

This chapter has addressed some of the policy issues surrounding Internet names and numbers. International contention over control of Internet resources does not always focus on these substantive issues. Attention often reduces to a question of power—perceived United States power versus the power of other nation states and of the United Nations. Furthermore, international discussions about CIRs often involve criticisms not about operational Internet governance practices but, on principle, about the points of oversight the U.S. Department of Commerce has through its historic and ongoing contractual relationship with ICANN and IANA.

Tensions over CIR governance have a long history and entire books have been written about this subject (see Recommended Reading at the end of the book). At the time of the 1998 Department of Commerce white paper calling for the establishment of ICANN as a private, non-profit corporation to administer Internet names and numbers, the policy position of the United States held that its role in critical Internet resource management would gradually transition to a more privatized and international framework. Originally, the U.S. government anticipated that this transition would occur in a matter of a few years. The transition would require ICANN to meet certain conditions, which would be reevaluated on a regular basis. For example, the 2003 memorandum of understanding between the Commerce Department and ICANN called for the phasing out of U.S. funding and oversight by 2006.

In the intervening years, a U.N. Working Group on Internet Governance (WGIG) directly called for the U.S. relinquishment of unilateral oversight of Internet names and numbers. The idea behind this recommendation was to replace U.S. oversight with U.N. oversight. Two weeks prior to the release of the 2005 WGIG report, the Commerce Department under the Bush administration released a "Statement of Principles" that appeared to preserve the U.S. oversight role indefinitely: "The United States will continue to provide oversight so that ICANN maintains its focus and meets its core technical mission."[28] Since that time, ICANN has continued, particularly through its Governmental Advisory Committee, to become increasingly multistakeholder and internationalized but the United States has also continued to hold its position of authority in narrow areas (such as the root zone file) and has continued to allude to some degree of indefinite control over the root. It is in this context that there have been sustained international calls for eliminating the relationship between the U.S. Commerce Department and ICANN.

This impasse over the U.S. relationship with ICANN has garnered great policy and media attention and has sometimes erroneously conflated "Internet governance" with "ICANN-related issues." The functions that the institutional structures under ICANN perform are critical but are only part of Internet governance. The remainder of this book addresses Internet governance areas far beyond the borders of ICANN.

CHAPTER THREE

Setting Standards for the Internet

"BITTORRENT" IS A PROTOCOL. Protocols are the standards, or blue-prints, that enable interoperability among Internet devices. From an information engineering standpoint, BitTorrent serves a straightforward purpose of specifying a standard approach for transferring large files over the Internet. Traditional file transfer involves a direct request to a server, which then transmits the entire file to the requesting device. Unlike this hierarchical and direct file-downloading technique, BitTorrent implements peer-to-peer (P2P) file sharing. Rather than being housed wholly on a single server, the file is broken into fragments and stored onto various end user computers that also use BitTorrent. When an individual initiates a P2P download of a large file, a BitTorrent client connects to the computers of other BitTorrent users (called peers), locates the various pieces of the file, downloads these fragments, and reassembles them into a complete file. P2P file sharing achieves bandwidth and resource optimization in apportioning file distribution over multiple peer computers rather than flooding the resources and bandwidth allocated to a single content-hosting server. Since its inception in 2001, the BitTorrent protocol has been adapted into numerous BitTorrent clients, computer programs that manage upload and download of files based on the file-sharing standard.

Despite the simple technical function this standard performs, Bit-Torrent is often viewed as controversial because it is associated with piracy and has been at the center of lawsuits over illegal file sharing. Digital content such as movies and music requires considerable bandwidth for storage and transmission. P2P networks for sharing movies, music, and other large files, whether legally or illegally, have relied heavily on the BitTorrent protocol to expedite the distribution and access to files. Using BitTorrent as an example helps introduce several features of protocols. The first feature is that they can embody values in their very design. BitTorrent reflects certain technical design values of locating intelligence at end points and equally connecting decentralized computing nodes in a peer-to-peer rather than hierarchical manner. This model of directly connecting end users to each other rather than through an intermediary that hosts content is consistent with the original design values of the Internet and its predecessor networks.

Once implemented in products, protocols can also have direct public interest implications and serve as sites of conflict over competing economic and social interests. BitTorrent implementations, on one hand, meet resistance from economic forces with a stake in preserving traditional media distribution models and minimizing illegal file sharing over P2P networks. On the other hand, the BitTorrent approach can be viewed as enhancing democratic access to knowledge through cooperative distribution. Someone wishing to publish a large file (for example, a documentary film or large scientific data set) quickly encounters bandwidth constraints if demand for the file skyrockets. BitTorrent solves this problem because devices that download the file, in turn, use their upload capacity to share the file with others. As Yochai Benkler explains in *The Wealth of Networks*, "the emergence of less capital-dependent forms of productive social organization offers the possibility that the emergence of the networked information economy will open up opportunities for improvement in economic justice, on scales both global and local."[1]

Every protocol also has a historical context. Examining the discarded alternatives to entrenched standards helps uncover the values and interests at stake in their development and selection. Writing about the metric standard, one historian of science explained that beneath the universal standards "commonly taken to be products of objective science lies the historically contingent. . . . These seemingly 'natural' standards express the specific, if paradoxical, agendas of specific social and economic interests."[2] The usage context in which BitTorrent emerged included copyright infringement and ensuing lawsuits. BitTorrent predecessor Napster had incorporated a centralized element in its design: an index of which computers contained which file components. This indexing function was a factor in lawsuits surrounding Napster. The BitTorrent protocol does not provide this indexing function. Protocol design is historically contingent.

Protocols also have a conservative momentum. Once widely implemented, considerable economic or social forces are necessary to displace entrenched standards. The number of active users accessing BitTorrent networks has been reported to exceed the Internet usage experienced by subscription-based video streaming services Hulu and Netflix combined.[3] As social scientists Geoffrey Bowker and Susan Leigh Star have explained, "There is no natural law that the best (technically superior) standard shall win—the QWERTY keyboard, Lotus 123, DOS and VHS are often cited in this context. Standards have significant inertia, and can be very difficult to change."[4]

Like other protocols, the BitTorrent standard is text, not software or hardware. Standards provide written rules that hardware and software developers use to ensure that their products can interoperate with other products. The BitTorrent standard is freely available for software developers to use to create computer code, or BitTorrent clients. Peers are end user computers with an installed BitTorrent client. BitTorrent is only one protocol. It is dependent on countless other standards that enable the secure, reliable, and interoperable exchange of information.

The Internet works because it is based on a universal technical language. Routine Internet use requires hundreds of standards including Bluetooth wireless, Wi-Fi standards, the MP3 format for encoding and compressing audio files, the JPEG standard for image files, various MPEG standards for video file formats, HTTP for information exchange among web browsers and servers, Voice over Internet Protocol (VoIP), and the fundamental TCP/IP protocols. These are only a few examples of the protocols that provide order to binary streams of zeros and ones to represent content in common formats, encrypt or compress data, perform functions such as error detection and correction, and provide standard addressing structures.

Internet standards setting is a powerful seat of authority and influence over the Internet. It is a form of policymaking established by standards-setting institutions rather than traditional public authorities, raising difficult questions about what interests shape these standards; how the public interest is reflected in design decisions; and what sources of institutional legitimacy are necessary for largely private institutions to perform this policymaking function.

This chapter introduces some of the technical protocols that enable the Internet's fundamental interoperability. It explains the institutional framework responsible for these protocols and some of the procedural traditions and organizational challenges that have accompanied the rise of new nongovernmental global institutions. The chapter also addresses how protocols can have significant public policy implications and addresses procedural routes to legitimacy for this privatization of governance.

THE TECHNOLOGY AND GOVERNANCE OF INTERNET PROTOCOLS

The process of developing Internet technical protocols is a venerable task of Internet governance. Internet protocols are the Internet. They are the fundamental rules that enable devices to exchange information. Rules require agreements and the process of agreeing involves people, procedures, norms, time, money, and knowledge. Protocols can initially seem difficult to understand because they are not visible to Internet users in the same way content and applications are visible.

There is nothing predetermined about these protocols. They are constructed, just like the protocols that dictate human interactions and communication across cultures. Different cultures have different languages, rules for driving, and customs for greeting one another, such as shaking hands, kissing on each side of the cheek, or bowing. Visiting different parts of the world helps make visible the socially constructed nature of human interaction and exposes the scaffolding of culture that permeates every aspect of language and communication. Just as these cultural conventions dictate how humans interact with each other, technical protocols dictate how digital devices interoperate.

The majority of technical standards are determined by private actors, the entities whose products implement these standards. Thousands of individuals participate in standards-setting organizations and most of these individuals are funded by their employers to participate. Technol-

ogy companies make considerable investments in standards development, often through a large staff of employees involved in scores of
standards organizations. Others involved in standards development
work for universities or research institutions. This section explains what
is being standardized, who is doing this standardization, and how it is
being done.

The Internet Engineering Task Force and TCP/IP as the
Magnetic Center of the Internet

The TCP/IP protocols are the fundamental networking standards providing universal rules for information exchange among devices connected
to the Internet. The Internet could function without certain protocols,
such as BitTorrent, but it could not work without TCP/IP standards,
which serve as the common denominator of cyberspace. These protocols
dictate how to format, address, and route information over the Internet
in a way that is compatible with other devices adhering to these protocols. The ability for devices to reach each other over an Internet Protocol
network was one of the original definitions of being on the Internet.
Internet engineers considered TCP/IP to be the "magnetic center of Internet evolution."[5]

The development of Internet protocols, beginning in the late 1960s
and 1970s in the United States, coalesced in an environment inhabited
by trusted users and shaped by Department of Defense funding. Historians of technology, including Janet Abbate[6] and Thomas Hughes,[7] emphasize the influence of U.S. government funding in this context. Vinton
Cerf and Robert Kahn, now widely referred to as fathers of the Internet,
were the authors of what would become the universal TCP/IP family of
Internet protocols.[8]

By strict definition, TCP/IP is two protocols—the Transmission
Control Protocol and the Internet Protocol. Illustrating the complexity
of standards, different characteristics of TCP are specified in numerous
documents. In common usage, the nomenclature TCP/IP often encompasses a broader family of protocols beyond TCP and IP. TCP/IP has
historically been interpreted to encompass protocols for electronic mail
such as SMTP (Simple Mail Transfer Protocol), protocols enabling file
sharing such as FTP (File Transfer Protocol), HTTP (Hypertext Transfer
Protocol) for exchanging information between a web browser and web

server, and many others. The IPv4 and IPv6 standards discussed in the previous chapter are the two current IP standards.

If TCP/IP is the magnetic center of the Internet, IP is the epicenter. The Internet Protocol provides a standard approach for two crucial networking functions: formatting and addressing packets for transmission over the Internet. Each small unit—or packet—of information sent over the Internet has a payload containing the actual contents of the transmission and a header, which holds administrative information necessary for transmitting the packet. IP provides a standard format for structuring this packet header. For example, it contains a field (or space) for bits used to help detect transmission errors, bits indicating the payload length, and bits designed to help assemble packets arriving at their destination. The header also contains the source and destination IP addresses and other logistical information. Reading the original 1981 Internet Protocol specification—RFC 791—helps provide a flavor for protocols and emphasizes that they are texts rather than software or material products. Any of the RFCs can be found at the IETF.org web site.

Prior to the widespread adoption of TCP/IP, a computer network based on one computer company's products could not exchange information with a network using devices made by a different manufacturer. Networks were proprietary, based on undisclosed specifications and not interoperable with any other company's products. There were multiprotocol environments even within a single corporation, which simultaneously used different networks that were isolated technical islands. Just to provide a sense of this acronym stew of incompatible products, it was not uncommon even by 1990 for a single corporation to have network computing environments that included IBM's Systems Network Architecture (SNA), DEC's DECnet, AppleTalk protocols to support Apple Macintosh environments, and IPX/SPX protocols associated with Novell NetWare local area networks. The business model for IBM and DEC at the time involved proprietary approaches that impelled customers to buy all DEC or all IBM products. There was very little interoperability but also recognition that greater interoperability was necessary to meet the emerging needs of an economy based on the digital exchange of information among suppliers and customers across the globe.

At the same time, there was almost no home Internet use and those who were online were usually subscribed to closed systems such as

America Online, CompuServe, and Prodigy. These systems were also "walled gardens" based on proprietary protocols that initially would not interoperate with competing online services. There was not yet a World Wide Web, never mind Google, Facebook, or Amazon. There was no online interoperability for consumers and little interoperability for industry.

While businesses were challenged with multiprotocol environments and home users relegated to proprietary online systems, the Internet was rapidly expanding to support millions of users, primarily in universities and military and research environments. This growing network was based on TCP/IP and interoperability afforded by TCP/IP was revolutionary in the age of business models predicated on closed and proprietary technologies rather than openness and interconnectivity.

TCP/IP and other Internet protocols emerged out of an Internet engineering community eventually known as the Internet Engineering Task Force (IETF). The origins of this engineering community trace back to the 1970s when the technical researchers working on the ARPANET project, including Internet pioneers Vinton Cerf and David Clark, founded an informal committee called the Internet Configuration Control Board and later called the Internet Activities Board (IAB—even later called the Internet Architecture Board). The group would ultimately develop the fundamental Internet protocols still used today. The IAB in turn founded the IETF as a subsidiary institution in 1986.

The IETF's primary mission is the development of Internet protocol drafts. The organization has no formal membership. Participation is uncompensated activity and open to anyone. Agreement about standards does not involve formal voting but is based on what has long been termed in the IETF as "rough consensus and working code." Most work is accomplished in working groups organized around key problem areas via electronic mailing lists, although the IETF usually holds three annual plenary meetings. An area director (AD) leads each working group and these ADs, along with the chair of the IETF, comprise a governance body called the Internet Engineering Steering Group (IESG), which presents Internet draft standards to the Internet Architecture Board for consultation as formal Internet standards.

All of these standards-setting activities now loosely reside under a not-for-profit, membership-oriented organization called the Internet

Society (ISOC). The Internet Society was actually created out of the IETF in 1992 but serves as the umbrella organization encompassing the IETF, the IESG, and the IAB. As the organization describes its mission, ISOC is "a global cause-driven organization governed by a diverse Board of Trustees that is dedicated to ensuring that the Internet stays open, transparent and defined by you. We are the world's trusted independent source of leadership for Internet policy, technology standards, and future development."[9] The original impetus for ISOC's establishment in 1992 was twofold. U.S. National Science Foundation (NSF) funding of the IETF Secretariat was ending and ISOC would be a mechanism to raise funds (primarily via membership) for administratively supporting Internet engineering activities. Also, the IETF as an organization was not a formal legal entity and, considering the Internet's commercialization and internationalization, there were emerging concerns about liability and possible lawsuits related to standards.

ISOC is a nonprofit group, but much of the actual work of standards development in the IETF emanates from the private sector. The primarily private industry composition of IETF participants is evident by the institutional affiliations of those in the various working groups, those who serve as ADs, and those who author the specifications that become standards. For example, ADs work for multinational router manufacturers such as Juniper Networks and Cisco Systems, and telecommunications equipment companies such as Ericsson and Qualcomm. Some of the authors of formal Internet standards work for software company Oracle or messaging security firm Cloudmark.

There is sometimes a residual misperception that academic researchers or government experts primarily establish Internet standards, a notion possibly attributable to ARPANET's roots in government and university research centers. The operational reality is that private industry is, and has been, at the center of developing Internet standards. Even TCP/IP developer Vinton Cerf has consistently been affiliated with private companies, most recently Google, while involved in Internet governance activities.

In terms of governance and procedures, the IETF is an open standards-setting organization, with processes that adhere to democratic principles of transparency and participation. Other standards-setting organizations do not necessarily rise to the same level of procedural and informational openness. Anyone may participate in IETF standards development regardless of affiliation or credentials. In practice, there are barriers such as technical knowledge and financial backing to attend events but institutionally the IETF is completely open to those wishing to participate. The organization also demonstrates a great deal of transparency in its development process, with records of mailing list interactions and minute meetings openly published. The organization also has defined appeals and dispute resolution procedures.

Beyond the development process, the IETF community makes the standard itself (that is, the document) freely available. This is important from a governance perspective for two reasons. For standards that have public interest effects, the open publication of the standard provides opportunity for public oversight and accountability. The free publication of these standards promotes innovation and competition in that companies can access the specifications and develop products that are compatible in the Internet marketplace. The IETF also has a strong tradition of advancing standards with minimal underlying intellectual property rights claims in the way of standards-based patents, discussed in Chapter 8. If the standard does have intellectual property rights claims, the preference is for those that provide royalty-free licensing of the standard. In other words, companies wishing to make products for the Internet can base the design of these products on the standard without having to pay royalties to another company. The IETF does not have an official intellectual property requirement, but this consistent preference for open standards has contributed to the rapid pace of innovation in Internet software and hardware.

The RFC Records as the Internet's Blueprints
A collection of documents called the Request for Comments (RFC) series records the IETF's Internet standards. The RFCs are (now) electronic archives that, since 1969, have documented Internet standards, governance procedures and institutional responsibilities, and other information related to interoperability. Anyone developing hardware or software for the Internet can consult these documents to ensure that products are compatible and interoperable with other products. The RFCs provide

a detailed history of proposed and final Internet standards and opinions from Internet pioneers and current leaders. The late Jon Postel edited and archived more than 2,500 RFCs for twenty-eight years beginning in 1969. After Postel's death in 1998, Joyce Reynolds assumed these responsibilities, later expanding to a group funded by the Internet Society.

More than six thousand RFCs historically and technically chronicle the evolution of Internet standards. As described in Chapter 2, the first RFC—RFC 1—was called "Host Software."[10] Authored by Steve Crocker in 1969 in advance of the first four original ARPANET computers becoming operational, RFC 1 lays out technical specifications for networking these first four ARPANET nodes. The entire RFC series is available online at www.rfc-editor.org, although originally the RFCs were literally pieces of paper, or notes, that sketched out and tracked specifications. Cerf described them as having "an almost 19th century character to them—letters exchanged in public debating the merits of various design choices for protocols in the ARPANET."[11]

Not all RFCs are actual Internet standards. Many are informational; others are procedural; others are humorous. Even when a proposed standard is published as an RFC, it might not reach the level of a formal Internet standard. An RFC might be a company's preferred specification that never rises to the level of Internet standard; and many proposed standards in RFCs directly compete or are in contention with other proposed standards. Therefore, when the press cites an RFC as a definitive Internet standard or suggests that "X,Y, and Z is under consideration by the IETF," this is not necessarily the case. Understanding this requires understanding some nomenclature about the RFC process.

"Historic" RFCs document previous standards that have been "deprecated," meaning they have become obsolete or replaced by an updated version. Others are "informational" documents that provide general information for the Internet community. For example, RFC 4677, "The Tao of IETF," is classified as informational because it provides an introductory overview of the IETF. Informational RFCs do not necessarily represent the consensus of the Internet standards community but are usually considered to be helpful information. The RFC series includes several types of documents:

- proposed standards
- draft standards (no longer used)
- Internet standards
- informational documents
- historic documents.

Only the first three of these directly address the standards-development process. Some RFCs are not standards but best current practices serving as guidelines issued by the Internet standards community. The designation "experimental" refers to a protocol specification in the research and development stage but published for the informational and collaborative benefit of the Internet community. Informational and experimental documents are published at the discretion of the office known as the RFC Editor.

RFCs published on April 1 are likely to be April Fool's Day jokes, many of them quite witty, such as David Waitzman's RFC 1149, "A Standard for the Transmission of IP Datagrams on Avian Carriers," explaining an experimental technique for encapsulating data on "a small scroll of paper in hexadecimal . . . wrapped around one leg of the avian carrier." The RFC notes that "Multiple types of service can be provided with a prioritized pecking order. An additional property is built-in worm detection and eradication. . . . While broadcasting is not specified, storms can cause data loss. . . . Audit trails are automatically generated, and can often be found on logs and cable trays."[12]

More seriously, the process of bringing a formal Internet standard to fruition is an arduous one based on peer review, institutional norms, and working technical rigor.[13] Specifications on the standards track have historically progressed, if successful, through three levels: proposed standard, draft standard, and Internet standard. This changed in 2011 from three to two maturity levels of proposed standard and Internet standard.

The first step involves publishing an Internet draft and submitting it for peer-review comments. Individuals can submit Internet drafts at the behest of their companies, but often they emanate from IETF working groups formed to solve a specific problem. The developer of the draft then rewrites the specification to reflect these comments and can actually progress through this comment and revision process several times.

At this point, the working group chair, or appropriate individual if not developed in a working group, submits the Internet draft to an area director and the IESG for consideration.

The document becomes a "proposed standard" if the IESG approves the draft. In practice, many widely implemented Internet standards are still in the category of proposed standard, not because they did not rise to the level of Internet standard but because administratively this process did not formally occur. Rising to the level of Internet standard requires an assessment of the IESG that the standard is "characterized by a high degree of technical maturity and by a generally held belief that the specified protocol or service provides significant benefit to the Internet community."[14] Another criterion requires that two or more independent implementations of the standard are successful and interoperable.

Specifications formally adopted as Internet standards are given an additional label "STD"—short for standard. Some of these most formal core Internet standards (with the STD designation) include STD5, Internet Protocol; STD9, File Transfer Protocol; STD13, Domain Name System; and STD51, the Point-to-Point Protocol. The RFC series documents many Internet standards but, as the following sections explain, many other protocols in other areas necessary to keep the Internet operational have evolved outside of this system.

The W3C and Core Web Standards
The World Wide Web Consortium (W3C) is another central Internet standards-setting body. Because the web is a more recent invention than the broader Internet, web standards setting also has a more recent history. British computer scientist Tim Berners-Lee invented the web while a researcher at CERN (the European Organization for Nuclear Research) in Geneva, Switzerland. At the time, CERN was a large node on the Internet. First proposed in 1989 and brought to fruition in the following years, Berners-Lee combined hypertext computing concepts with Internet protocols to propose the distributed hypertext system that would become known as the World Wide Web.[15]

Berners-Lee founded the W3C at MIT in October 1994 with the mission of developing protocols and growing the web. At the time, companies were developing competing products for the web, such as browsers, and there needed to be a standardization effort to ensure interoperability among these emerging products. Like the government-funded early roots of the IETF standards, the W3C initially had support from the Defense Advanced Research Projects Agency (DARPA) and the European Commission.[16] The W3C later adopted a membership model of funding, based on a sliding scale accounting for factors such as location in the world and type of entity. Whereas the IETF emphasizes individual participation, W3C members can be companies, universities, governmental organizations, nonprofit entities, or even individuals. Similar to the IETF, many of the active members work for companies whose products embed these standards. The W3C explains the fee structure as follows:

> In order to promote a diverse Membership that represents the interests of organizations around the world, W3C fees vary depending on the annual revenues, type, and location of headquarters of an organization. For instance . . . a small company in India would pay $1,905 annually, a non-profit in the United States would pay $6,350, and a very large company in France would pay 65,000 EUR.[17]

W3C standards are called "Recommendations." Like the IETF, the process of W3C standards setting is based loosely on consensus, with an opportunity for all voices to be heard and an emphasis on deliberative processes and working code. The W3C has worked on essential Internet standards such as HyperText Markup Language (HTML) and Extensible Markup Language (XML), among many others. HTML and XML are both "markup languages" that provide common specifications for encoding information in formats that can be interpreted and displayed by a web browser. All W3C standards are freely published.

The W3C has been one of the leading institutions promoting open standards that enable the widest possible implementation of a standard and associated innovation. The W3C's policy governing patents in standards indicates that they must be able to be implemented in products on a royalty-free basis. In other words, those using the standards do not have to pay royalties to patent holders. As its patent policy states, "W3C will not approve a Recommendation if it is aware that essential claims exist which are not available on royalty-free terms."[18]

The W3C and the IETF, despite some procedural and institutional differences, share a very similar governance philosophy of co-producing and sharing the rules of the road for Internet interoperability. They rightly attribute the Internet's growth and innovation, in part, to open standards. This philosophy translates into institutional norms about open participation, transparency of processes, open publication of standards, and a preference for royalty-free standards. This can seem obvious because it embodies the historical traditions of Internet development, but many other organizations that set standards for the Internet have more closed approaches.

The Internet's Broader Institutional Standards Ecosystem
The IETF and the W3C have developed many of the core protocols for the Internet, but these are only part of a vast protocol system required to provide interoperability for voice, video, data, and images over the Internet. Other institutions have considerable Internet governance authority in setting standards for the web, for multimedia Internet applications, and for Internet security. For example, the International Telecommunication Union (ITU) sets telecommunications standards in areas such as Internet telephony. The Institute of Electrical and Electronics Engineers (IEEE) works on vital specifications such as the Ethernet LAN standards and the Wi-Fi family of standards. Countless other entities develop specifications for the technologies that collectively enable the transmission of information over the Internet including national standards bodies such as the Standardization Administration of China (SAC); the Moving Picture Experts Group (MPEG); the Joint Photographic Experts Group (JPEG); and the International Organization for Standardization (ISO). Keep in mind that the seemingly simple act of emailing a picture from a smartphone relies on hundreds of technical standards developed by various organizations with different governing policies about how these standards are developed, and by whom, and how they can be implemented in products.

STANDARDS AS PUBLIC POLICY
Protocol development is one of the more technical areas of Internet governance but also an area with significant economic and social implications. Standards intersect with the public interest both because of the criticality of interoperability in public infrastructures and because they can be enactments of governance in themselves. Technical protocols en-

able government agencies to exchange information with citizens. They provide, or should provide, the necessary interoperability among first responders during emergencies and natural disasters. The modern public sphere and broader conditions of political speech are completely dependent on interoperability standards. As cultural and political expression has moved online, the democratic public sphere has become dependent on the technical specifications that enable interoperable and secure communications. Internet protocols have become a fundamental building block keeping the economic sphere operational and secure.

Apart from the general ways in which Internet standards are necessary for political and economic life to flourish, standards design also more specifically sets policies that shape communication rights. The following sections provide a few examples of this policymaking function: designing web access for the disabled; designing the extent of individual privacy online; addressing Internet resource scarcity; and promoting innovation and economic competition.

Standardizing Accessibility Rights for the Disabled
Internet users obviously have different abilities in regard to movement, vision, hearing, speech, and cognition. A number of governments have specific policies about accessibility requirements for information technologies. The United Nations Convention on the Rights of Persons with Disabilities (CRPD) is an international instrument that, among other things, recognizes the ability for disabled people to have equal accessibility to the Internet as a basic human right.[19] Standards-setting institutions are, in many ways, the international bodies that design these rights into technical specifications, such as closed-captioning in online video.

As an example of work in this area, the W3C has a Web Accessibility Initiative (WAI) designed to make the web accessible to people with various cognitive or physical disabilities. Accessibility is something that has to be designed into standards and implemented in products and web sites. For example, standards developers design the interoperability around the use of assistive devices such as screen readers that speak aloud the contents of a screen or speech recognition software to help those with physical limitations use the web.

The W3C published a formal standards Recommendation called the Web Content Accessibility Guidelines (WCAG 2.0), designed to make web sites more accessible.[20] The W3C also provides instructions for how to meet these guidelines. For example, nontext elements such as an image on a web page should be accompanied by a text alternative so it can be translated into Braille and other formats. Other guidelines address the availability of captions or sign language interpretation for prerecorded audio; the adaptability of web content into different forms of presentation such as a simpler or larger layout; the ability to make all functioning available from a keyboard; and avoiding content design believed to cause seizures (for example, the number of flashes). Internet standards-setting activities are the spaces in which global online accessibility guidelines are agreed on and operationalized, helping to illustrate the public interest function these institutions perform.

Designing Privacy

Standards design can also set policies related to individual privacy online. Routine Internet usage relies on numerous unique identifiers: hardware identifiers in phones and other devices, browser information, cookies, and a variety of protocol parameters. Local area network addressing standards create a globally unique physical identifier tied to an individual piece of equipment. Internet addresses create a unique logical identifier. Although not tied to a physical address, these Internet addresses create a traceable identifier when coupled with other information such as that attainable from an Internet service provider. Cumulatively, these trace identifiers and unique parameters make it difficult to achieve individual privacy without the implementation of specialized anonymization techniques (for example, Tor). An Internet privacy working group of Internet standards engineers and privacy advocates refers to this phenomenon as digital "fingerprinting."[21] This technical reality is quite different from the perception some users have about the extent of their own privacy and anonymity online.

Internet protocols intersect with individual privacy in two ways. Protocols created for a purpose other than privacy sometimes raise privacy concerns. Protocols that create unique identifiers fall into this category. Because of the reliance on these protocols to keep the Internet operational, it would be nearly impossible to undo this identity ecosystem. Many other interoperability standards similarly raise associated privacy considerations, such as electronic health care standards that specify how health care records are digitally stored and shared.

Internet protocols also intersect with individual privacy in more direct ways when they are designed specifically for protecting the identity of individuals or information. Authentication and encryption standards are designed to protect the privacy of individuals and information on the Internet. An example of a specific protocol designing privacy into Internet architecture is the IETF's privacy extension to help protect individual identity when communicating using the IPv6 protocol.[22] Another example is the W3C's effort called Platform for Privacy Preferences Project (P3P), although this protocol is not widely implemented. The idea behind P3P was to provide a standard way for web sites to announce to browsers the types of information it would be collecting about users. In turn, a web browser using P3P could be configured by its users to restrict the information it shared with a web site.[23]

A separate effort called "Do Not Track" was proposed by privacy researchers and published as a draft standard by the W3C. "Do Not Track" is a standard mechanism for individuals to customize and restrict the type of data companies can collect about their online behavior.[24] These few examples illustrate the role of standards organizations in addressing individual privacy rights as well as the unintended effects that interoperability standards can have in creating identity infrastructures that complicate online privacy.

Addressing Internet Resource Scarcity

One of the most interesting public policy issues in the history of Internet standards has involved the depletion of the prevailing Internet address space. The 2009 book *Protocol Politics: The Globalization of Internet Governance* provides a detailed history of the depletion of the IPv4 Internet address space and an examination of the new protocol, IPv6, designed to increase the number of available addresses. The following very briefly explains this policy issue.

Under the Internet's long-prevailing IPv4 address standard, there are approximately 4.3 billion available Internet addresses. Recall that each unique IPv4 address is 32 bits long, providing a total of 2^{32}, or roughly 4.3 billion unique addresses. This standard dates back to 1981 and is still widely used. The success and global growth of the Internet has resulted in the consumption of most of these Internet addresses. All IPv4 addresses have been allocated (delegated to organizations for further assignment) and most of these addresses have been assigned to end users.

On February 3, 2011, ICANN announced in a press release that it had allocated the last of the IPv4 address space. Although ICANN and IANA have completely allocated the IPv4 address space to the five regional Internet registries, these regional institutions still have some reserves for assignment or allocation to corporations, Internet service providers, and regional registries.

Many historical factors have contributed to the depletion of IP addresses, including several administrative and technical decisions about Internet addresses. For reasons of technical efficiency, IPv4 addresses were originally assigned in large, fixed blocks of numbers. For example, a Class A address assignment would distribute more than sixteen million addresses to an end user organization, a Class B assignment would distribute more than sixty-five thousand addresses, and a Class C assignment would distribute 256 addresses. The rationale for this approach was to simplify the routing process. Engineers divided Internet addresses into two parts: a network prefix and a host number. For example, the first 16 bits of an Internet address would designate a specific network and the final 16 bits would represent a specific device (or host) on that network. A unique network number would be assigned to each institution receiving addresses and then that institution would make its own determination about how to allocate the host numbers within its network. Routers would have to read only the network portion of each address to determine where to send packets to reach their destination, saving considerable router processing time and simplifying the router tables tracking the location of IP addresses.

A Class A assignment would reserve the first 8 bits for a network prefix and the remaining 24 bits for individual devices. In other words, a Class A assignment would assign a network number accompanied by a reserve of 2^{24} or 16,777,216 unique addresses. A Class B address block would allow 16 bits for individual devices, allowing for 2^{16} or 65,536 unique addresses. A Class C address block would assign 8 bits for individual devices, allowing for 2^8 or 256 unique addresses.

Large American organizations in the early days of the Internet often requested the largest block of addresses, or more than sixteen million addresses. Publicly available records of these allocations indicate that the following organizations, among many others, received assignments of more than sixteen million addresses: Apple, Digital Equipment Corporation, Dupont, Ford, GE, IBM, Halliburton, Hewlett-Packard, Merk, and Prudential.[25] A number of American universities (for example, MIT, Stanford) also received large assignments. Large American institutions were among the first to receive these blocks because of the Internet's inception and early growth in the United States. This geographical consideration, as well as the technical design choice of routers reading only network prefixes, resulted in the assignment of a relatively sizable portion of the IP address space.

Even prior to the invention of the web, Internet engineers anticipated the eventual depletion of these 4.3 billion Internet addresses. This concern showed great optimism for the Internet's growth and future potential in a pre-web context in which fewer than fifteen million people used the Internet. Engineers, primarily those working in the institutional context of the IETF, developed short-term conservation strategies and also embarked on the design of a new Internet address standard that would significantly expand the number of available Internet addresses.

The new design was for IPv6—Internet Protocol version 6—expanding the size of the Internet address space to an unfathomably large number by extending the length of each Internet address to 128 bits. This address length would provide for 2^{128} unique addresses. The IPv6 standard was completed in the 1990s and has been widely available in products (routers, operating systems, network switches). However, the actual deployment of IPv6 has been relatively slow, primarily because IPv6 is not directly backward compatible with IPv4. In other words, a device using only native IPv6 cannot directly communicate with an IPv4-only device. Although retrospectively this seems like a design problem, at the time IPv6 was selected, the assumption was that Internet users would want to upgrade for the network's overall good.

Operationally, a transition mechanism is necessary to implement IPv6. Usually this transition mechanism involves the implementation of both IPv4 and IPv6, which defeats the purpose of conservation because it still requires IPv4 addresses. Government policies advocating for IPv6, particularly in parts of the world with fewer IPv4 addresses, have failed to incentivize adoption of the new standard to any great extent. Decisions about protocol adoption are decentralized in that they must be implemented by end users and network providers. Most Internet users (with large installed bases of IPv4) have not had the economic incentive to upgrade.

This has become a difficult policy problem. The IPv4 address space has become scarce, a phenomenon with potential implications in parts of the developing world without large existing reserves of IPv4 addresses. Natural market incentives and government policies seeking to encourage IPv6 implementation have not spurred usage. Two policy issues are simultaneously being played out, one in the Internet standards community and one in the global community of regional Internet registries and among private entrepreneurs. The first circumstance involves the IETF's efforts to create new mechanisms for making IPv4 and IPv6 inherently interoperable. The later policy circumstance involves the introduction of Internet address exchange markets to free up IPv4 addresses that are already assigned but unused. This issue, though briefly discussed here, helps illustrate the public policy impacts of standards and the reality that new standards are not necessarily embraced by markets.

Promoting Innovation and Economic Competition
Published Internet standards provide common formats and specifications for developers to use to ensure that their products are interoperable with products made by other manufacturers. As such, standards perform a key economic function of providing a common platform for product innovation and the production of multiple, competing products. The IETF and the W3C have traditionally published their standards freely and have preferred the selection of standards with no (or minimal) intellectual property restrictions on the use of their standards. This open approach is often credited with contributing to an economic climate of rapid innovation and market conditions with competition among Internet companies.[26]

In general, and despite the openness of IETF and W3C standards, other information technology standards have underlying patents that require royalty payments for use. Companies wanting to use these standards have to seek licenses and pay royalties to the patent holder. Even some standards widely used to access the Internet have underlying intellectual property restrictions. For example, Wi-Fi standards have been at the center of long-running patent lawsuits and associated financial settlements.

Standardization is also directly related to global trade conditions. When a country's technology companies have access to global Internet specifications, they have the opportunity to develop and invest in innovative products that will interoperate with products made by their global competitors. The World Trade Organization (WTO) Agreement on Technical Barriers to Trade (TBT) acknowledges the role of international standards in the facilitation of global trade "by improving efficiency of production and facilitating the conduct of international trade" and asserts that WTO members shall "ensure that technical regulations are not prepared, adopted or applied with a view to or with the effect of creating unnecessary obstacles to international trade."[27]

As technology changes rapidly, there is nothing preordained about the Internet's underlying standards remaining open. The tradition of the openness and interoperability afforded by freely published and royalty-free Internet standards is one that has to be preserved to provide ongoing opportunities for rapid product innovations based on these standards.

STANDARD SETTING AS A FORM OF GOVERNANCE

The previous sections have provided a few examples of the policy effects of Internet standards. If Internet standard setting did not establish public policy in these ways but involved questions only of technical efficiency, then the process in which standards were set would not be a public concern. But standards do sometimes establish public policy. Protocol design is an example of nongovernmental rulemaking in areas with possible societal implications and by entities that might have a direct material interest in the outcome. The primarily private industry development of these standards serves a beneficial social function of financing the ongoing development of the protocols that serve as the scaffolding for the political sphere, economic markets, and social life. But it also raises questions about the sources of legitimacy for this privatized governance, how the public interest can be reflected, and what is the responsibility of governments, if any, to encourage the promotion of certain types of standards.

Standards-setting processes are able to derive legitimacy through several routes—technical expertise, a history of working success developing effective standards, and procedures that adhere to democratic principles of openness, accountability, and participation. These principles enter into several aspects of the standards process. The first is the question of participatory openness in standards development, meaning who is permitted to contribute to standards design. Despite barriers to participation that emanate from expertise and other constraints, the possibility for a diversity of input into standards decisions contributes a certain degree of multistakeholder legitimacy. The second issue is informational openness and transparency, a value that is essential for providing accountability in governance processes. If standards establish public policy, then the public should be permitted to access information about the development of a standard and associated deliberations, minutes, and records. More important, the public should be able to view the standard. Standards organizations that do not publish the standards they develop offer no opportunity for public accountability and oversight.

A related question involves the question of when governments should intervene in standards, whether as developers, procurers, or regulators. Some governments have established procurement policies about their information and communication technology expenditures that indicate preferences for implementing open standards.[28] Particularly in the developing world, governments are large parts of information technology markets and can exert considerable market influence in their procurement processes. For example, India instituted a "Policy on Open Standards for e-Governance" serving as a framework for selecting standards for the hardware and software underlying eGovernance systems. India's policy requires that the government of India adopt open standards that have been developed in an open-participation organization, that are available for developers to use and, if they have underlying patent claims, are made available on a royalty-free basis. The Brazilian government also adopted an interoperability framework that enacts a policy of preferring open standards.

The move in the past thirty years from proprietary protocols to open Internet standards that provide interoperability was a major sociotechnical transformation that can be taken for granted. Beginning with U.S. government funding and through the transition to primarily private industry–driven standardization, the digital public sphere has provided ever more interconnectivity, regardless of what device, email system, or operating system an individual uses. Some developments in the consumer Internet market raise the specter of regressing to conditions in which ubiquitous interoperability was not possible. For example, social media platforms and platforms controlled by a single company create a different information environment in which the only applications permitted are those authorized by these respective gatekeepers. Portability of information from one platform to another is not always possible. Universal searchability is not always possible. Just as the shift to open standards had significant economic and social effects on the online public sphere, movements away from open Internet protocols to proprietary specifications controlled by gatekeepers would be a radical shift with repercussions for global interoperability.

CHAPTER FOUR

Cybersecurity Governance

IMAGINE THE AC/DC SONG "Thunderstruck" blaring from computers at an Iranian nuclear facility in the dead of night.[1] An Iranian scientist claimed that a cyberattack shut down selected computers and prompted others to blast this classic rock song, although the Iranian government denied the account. The history of Internet security has always been a political history as much as a technical one. From virulent worms to the decades-long spate of politically motivated distributed denial of service (DDoS) attacks, cybersecurity is an area of Internet governance with immediate and direct impact on the public. Societal concerns involve much more than preserving access to the web and social media. Internet security is at the center of national infrastructure protection and is a crucial governance function concerned with protecting data, transactions, and individual identity. Threats to information infrastructure are threats to the financial and industrial systems on which basic social and economic life depends.

The legendary Stuxnet worm exemplifies the politically and technically intricate nature of modern Internet security. A computer worm is autonomous code that, once unleashed, is self-propagating and self-replicating without any action by humans. Worms exploit security holes in applications, protocols, and operating systems and inflict harm by modifying computer files or launching coordinated attacks that flood a targeted system with such an overwhelming number of requests that it essentially debilitates the system. By worm standards, Stuxnet was extraordinarily sophisticated. It had a highly targeted purpose of infecting and sabotaging industrial control systems supporting nuclear centrifuges in Iran. The worm spread via a Windows vulnerability and targeted the SCADA (Supervisory Control and Data Acquisition) systems of Siemens software.[2] Detected in 2010, Stuxnet disabled some of Iran's nuclear centrifuges, presumably obstructing the country's ability to manufacturer nuclear arms. Media narratives about Stuxnet described the worm as a coordinated American and Israeli effort to sabotage Iranian nuclear weapon aspirations, although neither government has officially acknowledged this.[3]

The political ramifications of Internet security breaches were similarly evident in the 2007 information infrastructure assault against the Eastern European nation of Estonia. Denial of service attacks effectively disabled government and private industry web sites. Estonian officials had recently relocated a statue of a World War II–era Soviet soldier from a park in the city of Tallinn. Many Estonians considered the statue to be an unpleasant reminder of the Soviet occupation of their country. When the statue was removed, some Russian minorities responded with street protests and scattered incidents of looting. This political tension simultaneously manifested itself online when DDoS attacks disabled critical information infrastructures including government servers, private banking systems, and news agencies. Prior to the actual cyberattack, Russian-language online forums were reportedly discussing the expected attack on Estonia's information infrastructure.[4] The scale of the attack was massive and continued over a three-week period.

Critical infrastructure attacks can have catastrophic consequences for a nation's reputation and economy but can also create public safety issues. In 2000, a disgruntled former employee in Queensland, Australia, was convicted to two years in prison for using a laptop and radio transmitter to release millions of liters of untreated sewage into a storm water drain.[5] The sewage flowed into a local river, park, and hotel grounds, causing environmental damage and economic and social disruption, as well as creating a health hazard to the local population. According to court records, the attacker had worked for a contractor that helped develop the sewage control system and was retaliating after being rejected for a permanent position with the public water treatment facility.[6]

Security is one of the most important areas of Internet governance and one that responds to a variety of problems related to authentication of individuals, critical infrastructure protection, cyberterrorism, worms, viruses, spam, espionage, denial of service attacks, identity theft, and data interception and modification. In the twenty-first century, national security and economic security, as well as freedom of expression, are dependent on Internet security. A nation's ability to secure cyberspace is a prerequisite for its ability to conduct global trade and perform basic government functions, including military operations.

This chapter introduces how Internet security governance occurs via national and international policies, the private sector, and new institutions such as certificate authorities and computer emergency response teams. Particular attention is paid to securing some of the central technologies of Internet governance such as the Internet's routing system and the DNS. The chapter also examines the increasing connection between Internet security and politics, including forms of dissent using distributed denial of service attacks and the emergence of Internet security as a proxy for national security.

BLACK THURSDAY AND THE RISE OF CYBERSECURITY

A defining moment in Internet history occurred in the fall of 1988 when a self-propagating computer program spread through the Internet and crashed thousands of computers. Shortly after the attack began, a NASA researcher posted an alarming message on an Internet discussion board: "We are currently under attack from an Internet VIRUS. It has hit UC Berkeley, UC San Diego, Lawrence Livermore, Stanford, and NASA Ames."[7] Internet users at Stanford and MIT reported similar attacks. At the time, approximately 60,000 computers were connected to the Internet, and an estimated 10 percent of these were attacked.[8] The pervasive outages interrupted Internet usage for several days at universities, research institutions, and military facilities.

This first significant Internet security breach was technically a worm, malicious computer code that, once unleashed, can autonomously replicate from computer to computer by exploiting security vulnerabilities in software and protocols. Worms are distinct from viruses, which are malicious code disguised in legitimate programs like email and activated when a user takes some action such as downloading an attachment. Worms can be more insidious because they do not require activation by an end user to spread. Like modern denial of service attacks, this worm was technically "benign" in the sense that it did not steal information or delete files. But, like denial of service attacks, the worm was malicious in effect. By replicating itself onto infected computers, it consumed resources to the point of effectively disabling these devices.

Cornell University graduate student Robert T. Morris was convicted of releasing the worm and violating the United States Computer Fraud and Abuse Act (CFAA).[9] His claimed motivation was to highlight Internet security vulnerabilities but the Cornell Commission investigating the event suggested that the vulnerabilities were well known and required no "act of genius or heroism" to attack.[10] The incident reverberated through the Internet's technical community and brought the Internet into public consciousness during a time when very few had even heard of the network. It also alarmed U.S. officials and served as a harbinger of the types of attacks that would follow.

Threats to commercial and personal Internet use can be carried out using one of several main techniques. A few of these include:

- computer viruses and worms
- unauthorized access to private data and computing resources
- identity theft
- critical infrastructure attacks
- denial of service attacks.

Responsibility for preventing and combating these threats is quite distributed, with private industry taking a central role. Telecommunications companies implement security measures to protect their own infrastructures. Private entities like banks and retail companies enact mechanisms that protect internal networks and secure transactions with consumers. Computer companies issue software upgrades to ameliorate vulnerabilities they discover in their products. The onus is also on private citizens to implement firewalls and virus detection software on personal computers. All of these private security measures, collectively, comprise a great deal of the Internet security ecosystem.

Many other functions of Internet security are overseen by governments, naturally interested in protecting critical information infrastructures, and by relatively new governance institutions that perform particular functions to keep the Internet operational. The following sections describe several of these areas of Internet security governance: the public–private computer emergency response teams that respond to security incidents; the certificate authorities that create systems of trust by vouching for the encryption keys that authenticate web sites; and the system of institutions and technologies faced with the complex challenge of securing core systems of Internet governance such as routing, addressing, and the Domain Name System.

Computer Emergency Response Teams (CERTs)

Long after the 1988 Morris incident, Internet worms and viruses have continued to present inexorable security challenges. They not only compromise data and debilitate networks; they also consume billions of dollars in computing resources and human capital. The potential destructiveness of viruses became evident in 1999 when the Melissa virus spread across the Internet as an infected electronic mail attachment in Microsoft Word.[11] The email subject line read, "Important Message from [name]," but opening the attachment infected an individual's computer and triggered the computer to email a copy of the virus to the first fifty contacts in the individual's address book. The rapidly propagating virus quickly overloaded mail servers and disrupted major computer networks. The virus infected more than a million computers in North America and caused economic damages of more than $80 million. The virus's creator pled guilty and ultimately served twenty months in prison.

Within a year of Melissa, an even more potent and destructive program called the "I Love You" virus spread globally using similar tactics but maliciously overrode files and resulted in substantial financial losses. The virus originated in the Philippines and quickly spread throughout North America, Europe, and Asia. Congressional testimony about the virus in the United States estimated that 65 percent of North American businesses were affected, at a cost in North America alone of $950 million.

Internet worms are even more powerful than viruses because they propagate autonomously. At least one or two major Internet worms appear annually and spread across the Internet in minutes. Some of the most notorious of these over the years have been Code Red, Nimbda, Slammer, Blaster, My Doom, Stuxnet, and Flame. Battling viruses and worms requires constant updates, or "software patches," that software companies develop and release to mitigate known security vulnerabilities in their products.

There are also public–private institutions that coordinate responses to problems, report incidents, and educate the public about Internet security. These institutions are "computer emergency response teams" (CERTs) or "computer security incident response teams" (CSIRTs). The U.S. Department of Defense established the first CERT after the Morris worm incident. This initial CERT was housed at a Carnegie Mellon University research center and tasked with centrally coordinating responses to Internet security problems.

In the years immediately following the September 11th terrorist attacks in the United States, the Homeland Security Department's National Cyber Security Division founded a federally operated US-CERT (in this case short for United States Computer Emergency Readiness Team) focusing on critical infrastructure protection, as well as worms, viruses, and other security threats. The Carnegie Mellon-based CERT would also continue to operate.

The mission of US-CERT is to improve the cybersecurity environment of the country. It operates a 24-7 operations center that accepts reports of incidents, responds to problems, and provides technical assistance. A significant role of the organization is to publicly disseminate information about security attacks, vulnerabilities, and software patches. For example, US-CERT released an alert entitled "'Anonymous' DDoS Activity" when it received information that the loosely affiliated hacker collective "Anonymous" was coordinating DDoS attacks against government servers and entertainment industry web sites in protest of, among other things, the proposed SOPA and PIPA legislation.[12]

US-CERT also serves as a central location for circulating information from vendors about known vulnerabilities and recommended mitigation strategies, such as downloading software updates and patches. So, for example, US-CERT will pass along a Microsoft security bulletin identifying vulnerabilities in Internet Explorer or Windows and issuing an associated software patch. The identification and mitigation of vulnerabilities is a constant reality for any software provider and CERTs serve to aggregate this information for all major software vendors. US-CERT also focuses on industrial system critical infrastructure protection through its Industrial Control Systems Cyber Emergency Response Team (ICS-CERT).

At one point, there was a single response team reacting to Internet security problems. This evolved over time into more than 250 CERTs distributed around the globe. Some are publicly run; some are private; some involve public–private cooperation. Most countries have at least one federal CERT. The following are just a few examples of the hundreds of CERTs:

- Brazil Computer Emergency Response Team (CERT.br)
- Indian Computer Emergency Response Team (CERT-In)
- Iran Computer Emergency Response Team (IrCERT)
- Japan Computer Emergency Response Team/Coordination Center (JPCERT/CC)
- National Computer Network Emergency Response Technical Team/Coordination Center of China (CNCERT/CC)
- New Zealand National Cyber Security Centre (NCSC)
- Thai Computer Emergency Response Team (ThaiCERT).

Although one of the original objectives of the first response team was to centrally coordinate responses to Internet-wide security breaches, what has materialized over time is a mosaic of hundreds of independently operating CERTs across the world. Although some loose coordination takes place within this ecosystem, the prospect of achieving rapid coordination among hundreds of autonomous organizations seems implausible. Most countries have founded a CERT organization and some have multiple CERTs performing similar functions. Hundreds of organizations have been formed to monitor Internet incident activities and respond to threats.

Despite the nationalization and regionalization of the CERT function, much responsibility for Internet security rests with the private sector, including both institutional and individual users of the Internet and also private technology companies that manufacture software and hardware and issue regular advisories and technology updates when their products contain vulnerabilities.

Certificate Authorities as "Trusted" Third Parties

The ability to conduct retail sales and other financial transactions over the Internet is predicated on the ability to authenticate web sites and protect the privacy of personal information including credit card numbers during transactions. Those accessing Amazon or eBay need to have a reasonable assurance that these sites are actually operated by these companies rather than counterfeit sites. Conducting online banking similarly depends on reliable authentication processes that verify online sites.

A security approach known as public key cryptography performs this function by associating a unique encryption code, or certificate, with a web server and making this number available to browsers so that a browser "knows" whether a visited web site is authentic. Entities known as "certificate authorities" are the governing bodies that vouch for sites and that browsers rely on for this authentication process.

Encryption, the mathematical scrambling of information prior to transmission, is at the heart of both authenticating web sites and protecting information privacy during transmission. Encryption begins with a predetermined algorithm, or cipher, that encodes information prior to transmission to make it indecipherable to anyone other than the information's recipient. The information can be decrypted only if the receiving device understands the mathematical algorithm that reordered the data. In addition to understanding the cryptographic algorithm, the receiving device must also have an "encryption key," a binary number necessary to begin decrypting the cipher. The longer the length of this number (that is, the encryption key length), the more secure the encryption. Key lengths of 128 bits and higher are common. A binary key length of 128 produces 2^{128} unique keys, an enormous pool of unique binary numbers.

Cryptography has always been a controversial technology. Pragmatically, it is necessary for securing basic email and web transactions. Politically, the ability for governments to apply encryption, and sometimes break encryption, is necessary for military, intelligence, diplomatic, and law enforcement strategies. Different governments have different regulations restricting the use of encryption. Some ban encryption outright; some restrict the key length and strength of encryption that citizens may use; some require licenses for using encryption; and others restrict the sale and exportation of encryption software to certain countries.

At the most basic level, there are two forms of encryption, private key (symmetric) and public key (asymmetric). Private key encryption requires the sender and receiver to possess the same encryption key. This approach has limitations because it requires all parties to have direct knowledge of this private key in advance of the transaction or else requires transmitting the key in advance, exposing the key itself to possible interception.

Public key encryption, technically called asymmetric cryptography, solves these problems. Rather than each party using the same private encryption key, each party uses two keys, a private encryption key that no one else knows and a public key accessible to anyone. When a device sends an encrypted message, it looks up the recipient's public key and uses this key to encrypt the message. The recipient then uses the public key and the private key that only this recipient knows to decrypt the message. Originally theorized in the late 1970s by Whitfield Diffie and Martin Hellman, public key systems are the basis for modern encryption standards for email (for example, or Secure Multipurpose Internet Mail Extensions, or S/MIME) and web transactions (for example, Transport Layer Security, or TLS).[13]

Public key encryption also responds directly to the need to authenticate Internet sites. Authenticating individuals who access a site is relatively straightforward through the use of password protection and more advanced techniques such as biometric identification (for example, fingerprints, retinal scans) or token-based authentication in which an individual has a physical device that displays a one-time code synchronized with the server. Authenticating an online site often uses "digital signatures" based on public key encryption. Digital signatures are unique digital codes associated with an entity. This system can work only if there is some way to vouch that the digital signature associated with a site is legitimate. Digital certificates linking an entity with its public key have to be vouched for by a trusted third party.

Certificate authorities (CAs), also called trusted third parties (TTPs), perform this digital certificate vouching process. The purpose of certificate authorities is to serve as the trusted third party that certifies to someone relying on the certificate, such as an individual buying something on Amazon via a browser like Firefox or Internet Explorer, that the public key of the site is legitimately associated with that site. Web browsers "trust" CAs (usually dozens of them) and incorporate this trust into basic web functionality for individual users. CAs in turn charge commercial sites for providing this digital certification function.

A basic governance question is what makes these third parties sufficiently trustworthy to vouch for the digital identities of web sites. This is a classic problem of infinite regress in that someone has to instill trust in the entity that certifies trust in another entity that certifies trust in a web site, and so forth. A combination of independent private entities, government processes, and standards bodies have become involved in certifying CAs. For digital certificates associated with legally binding transactions, this oversight is highly balkanized and dependent on local regulations and accreditation mechanisms.

For routine web transactions, the certificate authority market is composed of private companies, such as Symantec, Go Daddy, and Comodo, as well as government entities and nonprofit organizations. Browsers identify a list of CAs they trust to authenticate web sites and will accept the digital signature of any web site trusted by these CAs. These certificate authorities charge web sites for issuing digital certificates so it is in their economic interest to maximize the number of web sites they trust. Individual Internet users can easily examine the list of trusted authorities their browsers incorporate. Many of these trusted parties would be completely unfamiliar organizations to these individuals. A quick examination of the Firefox browser's CAs reveals more than fifty unique certificate authorities the browser trusts. Some of these are corporations, such as Chunghwa Telecom, Wells Fargo, Symantec, and Verizon/Cybertrust. Others are clearly governments, such as "Government of France."

Internet policy scholars have suggested that this approach for certifying and authenticating web sites is "deeply flawed."[14] As one scholar has suggested, just for argument's sake, what if the Chinese government compelled browser-trusted certificate authority CNNIC to certify an imposter Gmail server that the government could use to enact direct surveillance on citizens? In this hypothetical scenario, a browser that trusts CNNIC would falsely authenticate an imposter site. The entire system of authenticating web sites is based on a third-party trust model that spreads trust over dozens of entities that in turn trust web sites. This is the prevailing web authentication system, but a system that is only as secure as the least common denominator.

Securing Core Systems of Internet Governance—Routing,
  Addressing, and the DNS

Another security governance area dependent on trust is the Internet's basic routing system. Until outages occur, it is easy to take for granted the stability of the Internet's underlying routing system and focus instead on end user security issues like viruses and web site authentication. But securing the Internet's routing and addressing system, as well as the DNS, is one of the most vital tasks of Internet governance.

A routing problem occurred in 2008 when YouTube became temporarily unreachable from a substantial portion of the Internet. The Pakistan government had just requested that all ISPs block access to a YouTube URL because of a video that violated the country's blasphemy laws. To be compliant with the government's order, Pakistan Telecom filtered access to YouTube by redirecting the Internet address block associated with the YouTube content into a technical black hole. To block access within the country, this block of Internet addresses should have been diverted only locally to routers within the country. But Pakistan Telecom also advertised these redirected routes, seemingly inadvertently, to networks beyond its borders. These routes became reproduced throughout the global Internet, essentially diverting and blocking requests to reach YouTube. The next chapter explains this process of advertising routes via external routing protocols such as, Border Gateway Protocol in greater detail, but this episode and others like it illustrate how easily security can be compromised in routing infrastructures.

When someone types a YouTube URL into a web browser, the DNS returns a numeric IP address which a router uses to determine how to forward the request. Network operators advertise the range of Internet addresses to which they can provide access. There is no technical mechanism to constrain a network operator from advertising routes not in its control, whether accidentally or intentionally. One factor in the Pakistan incident was that the block of advertised addresses was narrower than the block YouTube itself broadcast. This narrower advertised block took precedence and information immediately became redirected.

The routes reachable within each autonomous network are advertised to neighboring networks, and collectively, these announcements make up Internet router tables, a constantly updated directory for how to reach Internet sites. This whole system depends on trust among network operators. The original design of routing systems predated the global expansion and growth of the Internet and arose in an environment in which there was a certain degree of trust among entities implementing these systems. The modern-day reality is that, as the Internet's routing system is designed, it is possible to hijack Internet addresses and therefore block access, at least temporarily, to the web sites to which these addresses should direct.

The Internet engineering community continually works on efforts to shore up the security of the Internet's routing infrastructure. For example, the Internet Engineering Task Force working group Secure Inter-Domain Routing (SIDR) developed a technique called Resource Public Key Infrastructure (RPKI). This technique, similar to certificate authorities described above for web authentication, applies a trust certification system to the Internet's routing infrastructure. An entity that receives or holds blocks of IP addresses may receive a trust certificate validating its authority to announce a particular collection of IP addresses. Because it would be based on certification and public key encryption, this mechanism would cryptographically secure the routing system.

The implementation of RPKI as a security technology is important because it would authenticate IP address routes. But like all technologies of Internet governance, it co-produces questions about institutional control and authority. Internet governance scholars Kuerbis and Mueller have provided an initial analysis of the potential institutional power effects of introducing RPKI.[15] One governance question is who would issue the resource certificates digitally authenticating address possession and routing announcements? The most obvious institutional framework is for the regional Internet registries under ICANN/IANA to provide this certification. All expansions of Internet governance raise questions. For example, if network operators are required to seek formal certification for the IP addresses they already control, and if they are required to seek this certification from RIRs, one can imagine a scenario in which they would also have to justify retaining the IP addresses under their jurisdiction. If an RIR believed the network entity controlled "too many" addresses, would it be able to withhold the certification? Many open questions exist. As Kuerbis and Mueller note, address allocation governance has always been separate from routing responsibility. RIR involvement in routing security would be a significant expansion of their Internet governance responsibility. The original design of the Internet did not necessarily address these types of security concerns, given that those using and developing it were trusted and familiar insiders.

Like the Internet's routing infrastructure, securing the Domain Name System is critical for keeping the Internet operational. Assaults against the DNS root servers have occurred throughout the years, including one in October of 2002 when a DDoS attack simultaneously targeted all thirteen DNS root name server implementations.[16] Most users did not notice any disruption in Internet functionality during the hour-long attack, but it was alarming in that it simultaneously targeted the root servers. Since this attack, the DNS has become even more distributed and employs greater site mirroring and replication. But because of its significance, the DNS is a regular target for those seeking to disrupt Internet infrastructure.

In addition to denial of service threats to the DNS, Internet engineers have identified other known threats. The details of these are well summarized in RFC 3833, easily accessed online. One type of security breach occurs when a seemingly trustworthy server returns false DNS information. A related problem is known as packet interception, in which a malicious party eavesdrops on a DNS query and returns false information, essentially redirecting the web request to a false site, such as impersonating the valid site for identity theft or censorship. A new standard known as DNSSEC (Domain Name System Security Extensions) is intended to make the DNS impervious to these types of attacks. DNSSEC involves the digital signature of DNS query responses, essentially applying public key cryptography to the Domain Name System. It does not keep information private but addresses authentication, certifying whether the returned information resolving a domain name into an address legitimately originates from the owner of that name.

CYBERSECURITY POLITICS

Thus far this chapter has discussed critical security governance issues such as the role of computer emergency response teams in responding to worms and viruses, the role of certificate authorities in providing digital certificates, and the security of the Internet's routing and addressing infrastructure. All of these issues are political in the sense of involving direct multistakeholder governance of technical infrastructure and having direct social implications. But Internet security is overtly political in another sense. Security attacks are often deployed as a proxy for political activism (or to suppress political activism) and traditional warfare. The following sections briefly discuss two examples of cybersecurity politics: the use of denial of service attacks as a form of political activism and the increasing connection between Internet security and national security.

Denial of Service Attacks as Political Theater

Many Internet security incursions, such as identity theft, seem motivated by economic gain. The impetus for denial of service attacks often seems to be the desire to achieve some political or social objective. One politically motivated attack interrupted global access to social networking site Twitter. Millions of people starting their day by checking social media found an error message in place of their Twitter feed. Shortly after the service disruption began, a Twitter blog posting indicated that the company's social networking site was experiencing a denial of service attack.[17] To incapacitate an online presence like Twitter would likely require a DDoS attack launched simultaneously from tens of thousands of hijacked computers.

As the morning unfolded, it became apparent that other social networking sites were also targets of denial of service attacks. The objective of the attacks was not to disrupt the entire Twitter service but to silence a single voice—an Eastern European (Georgian) blogger named Cyxymu. Activists carried out the attack in the context of mounting national tensions between Georgia and Russia over a territorial dispute.

A DDoS attack is an intentional network disruption in which a targeted computer is flooded with so many requests it becomes incapacitated and unavailable for access by legitimate users. These virtual sit-in techniques are considered "distributed" because the requests emanate not from a single source but from thousands of unwitting computers whose owners are usually unaware of this activity. A telephone analogy would be the effects of thousands of concurrent calls to a 911 dispatcher, flooding the system so that legitimate calls could not connect. A unique characteristic of this attack is that it does not involve unauthorized access to a system nor does it alter data or require any user authentication. It simply overwhelms a system with sufficient requests to effectively disable the system. These types of technologically mediated political dissent create significant collateral damage to free expression. They clog bandwidth, consume processing power, and block access for many people beyond those associated with the targeted site.

Using the term "hacker" to describe those who perpetrate DDoS attacks has many connotations, including the sense that the action requires some degree of technical ability. In the case of denial of service attacks, it takes relatively little effort. DDoS software tools are freely available on the Internet. These tools are essentially software code—including a master program called a "handler" and agent programs called "zombies" or "daemons." Attacks also often use worms to scan prospective computers for vulnerabilities and install agent code on these systems from which to launch attacks against a targeted server (see Figure 4.1). Tracing DDoS methods to the originating handler is difficult because the actual attacks originate from distributed third-party zombies.

A denial of service technique is actually not a single method. There are different types of attacks with different types of implications. To provide a rudimentary flavor of these methods, the following explains two representative approaches: TCP/SYN attacks and ICMP flood attacks.

TCP/SYN attacks are a common DDoS method. Most Internet services, including web applications and email, rely on TCP (Transmission Control Protocol), a transport-layer standard responsible for ensuring that information has successfully moved between two points on a network. Transport-layer protocols perform the important function of detecting and correcting transmission errors. Whenever a computing device (a client) requests a TCP connection to an Internet server (such as a web or email server), the two devices exchange a predetermined sequence of messages as shown in Figure 4.2.

This volley of messages is sometimes called a three-way handshake.[18] The client computer transmits a SYN (synchronization) flag to the server. The SYN flag is just a predetermined sequence of bits. The server acknowledges the SYN flag by sending a SYN-ACK (synchronization acknowledgment) message back to the client, which then completes the handshake by sending a final ACK message to the server. This handshake opens a connection between a client and a server.

A denial of service attack using TCP/SYN flooding occurs in the final leg of this handshake. It creates an only half-open connection by

Simultaneous requests by numerous, often unwitting computers
incapacitate the targeted computer

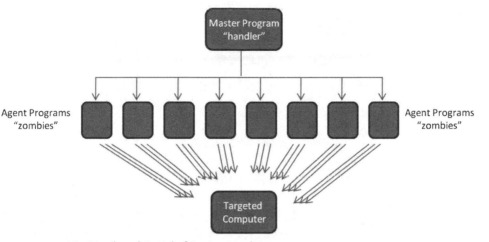

FIGURE 4.1: Distributed Denial of Service Attack

IP spoofing, the act of using a forged source IP address from the client. An attacking client sends a SYN message to a server but the SYN message references an IP address of a system that has not sent the SYN and will therefore not transmit a final ACK message to the server that has sent it the SYN-ACK transmission. The time the server waits for an acknowledgment (that never arrives) consumes server resources. Half-open connections waiting for a final ACK will eventually expire but, in a DDoS attack, attacking clients will issue SYN requests faster than the open connections expire, keeping the server completely overwhelmed with TCP handshakes. This simple method is called TCP/SYN flooding.

ICMP flood attacks are similarly easy to execute. The term "pinging" means to test the reachability of a particular IP address. It is a utility that sends an echo request message, using the Internet Control Message Protocol (ICMP), to an Internet-connected device and then waits for a response. A denial of service attack using this ping utility bombards a system by using "spoofed" broadcast pings. In other words, an attacker sends a ping request containing the targeted computer's spoofed Internet address, to an Internet broadcast IP address. Many computers receiving the ping request will respond with their own echo replies, collectively bombarding the targeted message with echo replies. The targeted computer

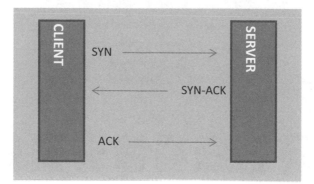

FIGURE 4.2: Three-Way TCP Handshake between a Client and Server

can be flooded to the point that bandwidth is not available and legitimate information requests are blocked. This technique is sometimes called a ping attack or a smurf attack, because the name of one of the older programs used to perpetrate this type of attack was "smurf."[19]

As these types of simple measures indicate, DDoS attacks involve no unauthorized access to a targeted system or modification or lifting of data. Most institutions take numerous measures to reduce vulnerability to DDoS activity: round-the-clock use of traffic monitoring tools to identify changes in traffic patterns; distributing traffic loads across redundant servers so that traffic can be shifted from a targeted computer when necessary; blocking access to TCP/IP ports that are known to be vulnerable; using software tools that scan systems for the presence of agent software; and patch management strategies that routinely upgrade software with known vulnerabilities.

One of the earliest high-profile DDoS attacks occurred in 2000 when several prominent Internet sites were disrupted. The first noticeable outage affected Yahoo!'s web site on February 7, followed by attacks in the subsequent days targeting CNN.com, Amazon, eBay, and eTrade.[20] Some Internet users visiting other sites also perceived degradation in access speeds as a result of the collateral damage of traffic flooding the Internet. "Mafiaboy," a Canadian teenager, pled guilty to the attacks, which he carried out using freely available DDoS tools.[21] Targeted companies can suffer negative publicity from the outages, incur substantial costs in defending against the attacks, and suffer lost advertising and transactional revenue.

The history of denial of service attacks on the Internet is more of a political history than a technical one because high profile incidents have typically made some ideological statement. This is an example of how dissent is expressed not always through content but through technical architecture. Denial of service attacks in Estonia in 2008 and Georgia in 2009 were politically motivated. Cyberattacks as well as street protests erupted in Iran in the wake of perceived electoral fraud in the 2009 election of Mahmoud Ahmadinejad over opposition candidate Mir-Hossein Mousavi. Some bloggers and activists on Twitter called for the use of denial of service techniques to flood Iranian government web sites including Ahmadinejad's blog (ahmadinejad.ir), Iran's official news agency the "Islamic Republic of Iran Broadcasting" (irib.ir), and other official sites. Some of the techniques directed at Iranian servers did not rely on sophisticated botnets or worms to implant zombie programs on computers. Instead, activists directed protesters to sites such as "Page Reboot" (http://www.pagereboot.com/) that automatically refresh any URL every few seconds or more. This type of program is intended for uses such as closely monitoring the changing auction bids for an eBay item or a sports site providing up-to-the-minute news. The efforts to disrupt Iranian servers was more of a collective action approach using crowd-sourcing rather than a typical technique of implanting agent software on computers from where the attacks would launch.

Although many DDoS incidents are directed at political systems and traditional governments, they are also directed at other majoritarian or dominant systems such as religious power structures and cultural institutions. Others specifically target independent media and human rights groups to silence speech.[22] Politically motivated attacks intended to suppress speech often target the platforms on which dissident voices rise up against governments. Similar to the denial of service attack targeting Twitter to silence a single user, other content platforms that serve as part of the digital public sphere have also been targeted.

Still other denial of service efforts target private industry. After WikiLeaks published U.S. diplomatic cables, journalists and political figures debated about the content WikiLeaks published and whether it should have published it. Beneath this discussion of content, DDoS responses simultaneously occurred. MasterCard's main public-facing web site was knocked offline. Visa's web site experienced intermittent outages. Amazon and PayPal were also disrupted.[23] The loosely affiliated group of hacker activists known as Anonymous used DDoS attacks to disrupt these businesses in retaliation for their decisions to terminate technical and financial services to WikiLeaks in the aftermath of the so-called Cablegate incident. The WikiLeaks web site itself had also been hit by a DDoS attack.

Regardless of motivation, DDoS attacks are a common technique for making a political statement or silencing opposition. These attacks, because they can disrupt entire content platforms or flood network segments, instill significant collateral damage to freedom of speech and the ability to communicate or make transactions over the Internet. In most parts of the world, there are statutory prohibitions against DDoS attacks. In the United States, for example, the Computer Fraud and Abuse Act (CFAA) is the primary federal statutory mechanism for prosecuting denial of service attacks and other computer-related crime.[24]

Internet Security as a Proxy for National Security
Cybersecurity governance intersects with national security in several distinct ways. First, the basic functioning of government depends operationally on the use of information and communication technologies and Internet connectivity. Internal government communication, such as file sharing and basic email exchanges among federal agencies, uses TCP/IP-based technologies and transmits over the Internet or networks that connect to the Internet. Government communication with citizens, to an even greater extent, relies on Internet access and technologies, whether citizens are accessing informational web sites about government benefits, downloading administrative forms, or filing electronic taxes from home. Citizens interact directly with government services via social media platforms and email. A Pew Internet survey found that nearly half of all Internet users have turned to an online government portal to find information about a public policy issue or download government forms.[25] All of these routine functions of eGovernment require secure connections and data and in some cases reliable authentication of users.

Points of vulnerability for security breaches are ubiquitous, and disruptions in service can potentially create a national security crisis by obstructing the basic functioning of government or creating a loss of faith in public services. Both United States and South Korean government web sites were the subject of an Internet security attack in July of 2009.[26] The attacks reportedly targeted U.S. federal agencies including the FAA, FTC, and the Department of Homeland Security. The attacks were a DDoS assault, as mentioned, a regular occurrence and problem for prominent online sites including government servers. Most governments have one or more security organizations designed to address and respond to cybersecurity vulnerabilities. After the Estonian DDoS attacks, for example, the North Atlantic Treaty Organization (NATO) announced the opening of a "Cooperative Cyber Defense Centre" in Tallinn, Estonia.[27]

National security is also predicated on securing critical information infrastructures that support water treatment facilities, nuclear plants, transportation systems, networks of hospitals, and the power grid. Internet points of access into this system are pervasive, and the computer systems controlling this infrastructure are always potential targets. The fallout of a security attack that disabled a banking system or water system, for example, would create widespread national hardship and panic that would, in many ways, mirror the effects of traditional warfare.

Finally, conventional warfare occurs both online and offline, inextricably linking Internet security practices to national security practices. This is an area of Internet security governance completely relegated to national governments rather than international cooperation or global institutions. It is also an area marked by rapidly changing technology and receiving a great deal of government attention and funding.[28]

Some countries have official cyberwarfare policies and train military personnel in these techniques. Some of these methods are defensive, geared toward preserving information and communications during warfare or carrying out antiterrorism surveillance and intelligence gathering. Other techniques are much more offensive, such as online cyberwarfare strikes that exploit communication vulnerabilities and unleash destructive code.

The history of the Internet has always also been a history of circulating narratives about the networks' imminent demise to security breaches or architectural failure. Since the early 1990s invention of the web, the topic of Internet governance has been laden with, fortunately, false predictions. Robert Metcalfe, the co-inventor of the core local area network (LAN) Ethernet standards, famously predicted in 1995 in his "From the Ether" InfoWorld column that the Internet "will soon go specta-cularly supernova and in 1996 catastrophically collapse."[29] As the co-inventor of Ethernet and founder of then-prominent networking equipment company 3Com, Metcalfe was a respected technologist and thought leader and his concerns about the Internet's stability were taken seriously by the media and industry. When 1996 came and went without any significant Internet outages, Metcalfe "ate his words" at an industry conference by drinking a glass of water containing a shredded copy of his column.

Internet security governance has arguably been one of the most suc-cessful areas of Internet governance because, despite high-profile secu-rity breaches, the Internet overall has continued to operate. The balance between security protection techniques and destructive code has tipped in favor of security protection. As governments increasingly turn to and invest in tools of cyberwarfare, it remains to be seen whether the suc-cesses of Internet security governance will endure.

CHAPTER FIVE

Governance at the Internet's Core

THE INTERNET has a physical architecture as much as a virtual one. Descriptions of the Internet as a "cloud" do a disservice by portraying an ethereal and virtual void beyond the computer screen. Even when public policy attention is directed at physical network architecture, it has focused primarily on an extremely small swath of infrastructure—access and "last mile" issues of interconnection, meaning the broadband connections that link home networks into the Internet or the wireless links that connect smartphones to telecommunications networks. Chapter 6 will address these local access issues but this chapter examines governance at the Internet's core infrastructure, the series of networks and interconnection points that collectively comprise the Internet's global backbone.

The Internet obviously does not have a single "core" but is a collection of interconnected Internet Protocol networks operated by different companies that conjoin bilaterally or at shared exchange points to form the global Internet. This collection of networks, technically called autonomous systems, has a material architecture but also logically defines the Internet's global routing table listing all Internet address prefixes and the paths available to access these addresses. The technical interconnection and business agreements to exchange Internet packets between autonomous systems are critical areas of Internet governance, albeit quite far removed from public view.

Interconnection agreements are usually private contractual agreements among network providers, large content companies, and content delivery networks. The purpose of this chapter is to explain the architectural and market ecosystem of interconnection among these networks and to present some global policy issues related to interconnection.

The first section explains autonomous systems and Internet exchange points (IXPs). It describes the various types of networks that interconnect to collectively form the global Internet. It also explains how Border Gateway Protocol (BGP) creates the standard technical basis on which interconnection among these operators occurs and introduces Internet exchange points, the shared physical locations at which multiple networks conjoin to exchange packets. The second section examines the economics of interconnection, explaining the various types of interconnection arrangements among companies that operate Internet networks. The concluding section presents several Internet policy circumstances at the Internet's interconnection epicenter: the prioritization of individual market incentives over technical efficiency; the uneven distribution of IXPs and associated interconnection challenges in emerging markets; and interconnection points as sites of control and disruption for government censorship and outages as a result of peering disputes. The chapter also foreshadows global efforts to regulate Internet interconnection, a topic more directly raised as an open issue in the conclusion of this book.

AUTONOMOUS SYSTEMS AND INTERNET EXCHANGE POINTS—THE INTERNET'S BACKBONE

Internet operators face an intrinsic collective action problem to a greater extent than many competitive industries. For any of these companies to succeed, they must publicly compete for customers while privately agreeing to cooperate with each other to interconnect their respective networks and agree to handle traffic originating with their competitors' customers. In the pre-Internet world, each of these networks was an autonomous data network with little or no interconnectivity. The global Internet works because of the agreements among these network operators to connect using standard protocols, to carry each other's traffic, and to do so providing adequate levels of reliability and quality of service. Before addressing interconnection among these networks, this section provides some background on the various types of networks that inter-operate to form the global Internet.

The Evolution of Network Operators

The manner in which Internet providers interconnect depends on several characteristics of each provider's network, including geographical reach, traffic volume, and the nature of the company's existing inter-connection arrangements. The Internet is a collection of independent IP networks owned and operated by private telecommunications companies, content companies, and content distribution networks, also called content delivery networks (CDNs). A few examples of these types of companies include AT&T, British Telecom, Comcast, Korea Telecom, Verizon, hundreds of other Internet providers, large content providers (for example, Facebook and Google), and content delivery networks such as Akamai Technologies. Content companies often run their own enormous networks and connect to other operators at various points around the world. The high-speed networks that content providers and CDNs operate form an important part of the global Internet.

Collectively, these networks operate hundreds of thousands of miles of transmission facilities, including terrestrial fiber optics, microwave systems, submarine cable, satellite links, and traditional twisted pair copper. These backbone facilities aggregate Internet traffic and transmit bits at rates upwards of 40 Gbps (for example, OC-768 fiber optic transmission).

Historically, network operators have been categorized into Tier 1, Tier 2, and Tier 3 classifications. This terminology is useful as a taxonomy and has a basis in history but it overemphasizes hierarchical network relationships when, in practice, Internet interconnection is now much messier, complicated, and flatter than this simple hierarchy would suggest. Nevertheless, the difference between these classifications generally indicates a measure of the reach of these networks and the manner in which these networks connect to other networks.

A "Tier 1" network is the name typically given to network operators that can reach any network on the Internet via mutual peering agreements. In other words, Tier 1 networks generally do not pay to interconnect but mutually agree to exchange customer traffic with other Tier 1 networks at interconnection points. With some exceptions, these companies do not pay other companies to reach any part of the global network. They connect via mutually agreed upon arrangements to peer and to connect directly to customers (including other smaller networks) that pay them for interconnection to the global Internet. Through peering relationships, they have access to the Internet's entire routing table. CDNs, for historical reasons and because of the asymmetrical flow of information between CDNs and Internet operators, have traditionally not been considered Tier 1 networks, even though some connect directly to almost all Tier 1 network operators.

This historical definition of a Tier 1 provider reaching any part of the global Internet solely via mutual peering agreements with other networks and without paying any transit costs to reach the global Internet belies the actual complexity of interconnection. However, an example of a Tier 1 company that principally meets this definition is the large network operator Level 3. This company peers with large companies such as Deutsche Telekom, Sprint, NTT, Tata Communications, Tinet SpA, and many others; does not purchase transit from any providers; and sells Internet transit services to numerous network operators.[1] In practice, any large global company like AT&T, NTT Communications, and Verizon is usually viewed as Tier 1 network.[2]

More general definitions of Tier 1 providers consider additional characteristics outside of the strict economic variable of not paying any fees to interconnect and being capable of reaching the entire Internet routing table. Some of these characteristics include level of traffic volume, worldwide presence, control of international or transoceanic fiber lines, peering arrangements on multiple continents, and control over multiple autonomous systems, which will be described below.

"Tier 2" nomenclature traditionally describes a network operator or content distribution network that engages in some mutual peering agreements but also purchases transit connections from other companies to establish a global Internet reach. Often these network operators are industry giants with far-reaching high-speed networks but purchase transit interconnection to some part of the global Internet. "Tier 3" nomenclature refers to network operators or content networks that are "stubs," meaning they do not sell connections to other networks but just purchase transit from another network operator or operators to reach the

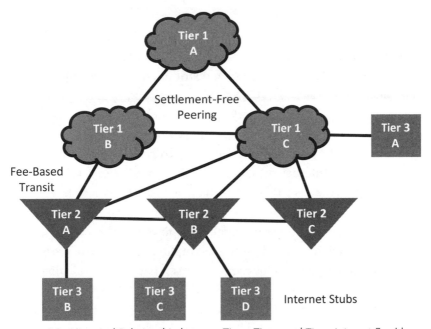

FIGURE 5.1: Historical Relationship between Tier 1, Tier 2, and Tier 3 Internet Providers

global Internet. Examples of Tier 3 Internet companies include small ISPs that resell Internet connectivity via transit connections through a larger Internet operator, or web hosting services (or other content distribution networks) that might access the global Internet by purchasing transit connections through a Tier 2 or Tier 1 provider. Figure 5.1 provides a high-level representation of the general relationship among Tier 1, Tier 2, and Tier 3 Internet companies.

The hierarchical arrangement this terminology conveys is no longer how interconnection works and is based on older traffic engineering assumptions of fairly symmetrical flows of traffic between endpoints and an economic system of access-based business models. The flow and monetization of traffic has shifted to bandwidth-intensive media content downloads and business models based on online advertising. Companies that would once be considered Tier 3 purchasers of transit have more leverage for peering or even paid peering arrangements because of the intrinsic value of their close proximity to end users and their ability to directly connect content companies to consumers.

Content Networks

CDNs are networks designed to replicate and globally distribute content and bring it closer to the users accessing this content. More traditional Internet terminology for this content distribution includes "Internet web replication" and "caching."[3] CDNs are a newer classification of Internet company than traditional network operators such as telecommunications companies, ISPs, wireless services, and cable companies. They operate large IP networks that distribute servers globally and connect these servers to the global Internet, often at Internet exchange points. CDNs monitor traffic patterns over thousands upon thousands of servers and use optimization algorithms to perform load balancing of traffic across these resources. These networks optimize data flows based on a number of variables ranging from bandwidth consumption, utilization of processing power on servers, and storage requirements. They also provide their customers with real-time statistics about global content access patterns.

An entire industry of commercial CDNs arose in the opening decade of commercial and individual Internet use.[4] For example, Akamai is a large CDN whose customers have included NBC, Yahoo!, and a sizable percentage of large content companies. Signifying the enormous scale of leading CDNs, Akamai has nearly 100,000 servers distributed over 1,900 networks in seventy-one distinct countries and serves "all of the top Internet portals" and "all 20 top global eCommerce sites."[5] Large telecommunications companies also provide content delivery services as part of the products they sell to customers.

CDNs are designed to solve several problems. They respond to the colossal increase in the volume of online video, audio, and multimedia content as well as the problem of flash crowd access to information. During "flash" crowd access, large numbers of people simultaneously download the same content. In some cases, this content is just a cultural meme such as a viral Internet video. But in other cases, the content could be an online journalism site reporting on an act of terrorism or natural disaster, a weather site in the wake of an approaching hurricane, or an Internet commerce site selling products or services to consumers. In all of these cases, a sudden escalation in access to online materials can overwhelm a server optimized for more routine or median access. Replicating (also called mirroring) this information on distributed servers located around the globe via a CDN solves this problem by balancing the access load over numerous distributed servers and access links rather than over a link to a centralized information repository.

CDNs also help mitigate the latency, or delay, that users experience if they access distant multimedia information that must traverse many "hops" or routes before arriving at its destination. Bringing widely accessed information closer to users eliminates this network performance problem and makes access to digital content faster and more reliable as well as providing a higher perceived quality of service (QoS) for users.

Some content-oriented companies, such as Google, operate their own enormous private networks that connect directly into the Internet's infrastructure at interconnection points located around the world. For a company with massive amounts of bandwidth-intensive content, such as Google's YouTube site, it is more technically efficient to replicate this information on servers located around the world rather than on servers housed in a single centralized repository. This distribution of content provides higher delivery reliability because of the inherent redundancy of information and provides lower latency because the content is pushed to the edge of the Internet and closer to users.

Autonomous Systems and the Role of Border Gateway Protocol
  in Interconnection

Networks that interconnect to form the global Internet are called autonomous systems. Generally speaking, autonomous systems are telecommunications companies; ISPs; CDNs; content providers, such as Google and Yahoo!, that have enormous amounts of outbound traffic; and large institutions, such as government agencies, that operate networks. More technically precise, autonomous systems are routing domains, collections of routers under the administration of some entity such as a telecommunications company. In other words, each AS manages a collection of IP addresses that either resides in that domain or resides in a domain operated by an entity that pays a transit fee to the AS to connect to the Internet. As discussed in Chapter 2, each of these autonomous systems has a unique Autonomous System Number. By 2012, approximately 58,000 ASNs had been assigned by RIRs, which in turn receive their allocations from the Internet Assigned Numbers Authority (IANA).[6]

Not every network is an autonomous system. The key defining characteristic of an AS is that it presents a consistent routing policy to networks with which it connects. As Internet engineers have historically defined it, "An AS is a connected group of one or more IP prefixes run by one or more network operators which has a single and clearly defined routing policy."[7]

Autonomous systems are central to how routing works over the Internet. Routing protocols are standard specifications that instruct routers how to interact with each other and exchange information. Each AS uses an interior routing protocol, also called an interior gateway protocol, which communicates routing information to all networks within the AS. Each router within the AS uses this interior protocol to calculate how to route packets to the next best router (sometimes called a "hop") to forward packets to their destination within the autonomous system.

An exterior routing protocol dictates how routing occurs between autonomous systems. All Internet interconnections among autonomous systems occur via a standard called Border Gateway Protocol (BGP). In this sense, BGP, like the Internet Protocol, is one of the core technologies keeping the Internet operational. BGP is the de facto standard for routing information between autonomous systems. BGP is not as well known a protocol as IP and HTTP, probably because it is not directly used by end users but is used by the networks that interconnect to form the global Internet. The important function BGP performs is sometimes referred to as inter-AS routing. Neighboring autonomous systems typically exchange a complete accounting of routing information under their respective control when first connected. After that, updates are usually sent only when a route has changed.

BGP's basic function is to allow networks to exchange information about "reachability"—meaning which systems each autonomous system (or network of routers under common administration) can reach. In this sense, BGP is an inter-AS routing standard. The current version, called BGP-4, has been in effect since 2006 and is well documented in RFC 4271, titled "A Border Gateway Protocol 4 (BGP-4)."

The Evolution of Internet Exchange Points
Interconnected networks physically conjoin at bilateral connection points housed in a network operator's facility or, increasingly, at shared Internet exchange points. IXPs are the physical junctures where different companies' backbone trunks interconnect, exchange packets, and route them

toward their appropriate destinations. Thinking about the Internet as a cloud sometimes obfuscates the reality that Internet switches are housed in buildings with air conditioning, raised flooring, and a soda machine. IXPs are physical and virtual infrastructure housed in buildings.

Historically, IXPs were called either Network Access Points (NAP), Commercial Internet eXchanges (CIXs), or Metropolitan Area Exchanges (MAE). This original terminology explains why some IXPs still use these acronyms, such as MAE-EAST and MAE-WEST in the United States and NAP.cl in Chile. The Internet's original NAPs were all located in the United States.

The first commercial IXPs were established in 1993 when the National Science Foundation began transitioning the NSFNET infrastructure to private coordination and established the original four exchange points operated by four companies: Ameritech, MFS, Pacific Bell, and Sprint.[8] The London Internet Exchange (LINX) was founded shortly thereafter in 1994 and its original switch has actually become an exhibit in the London Science Museum. Over a twenty-year period, the number of these exchange points grew from four in the United States and in a few scattered locations to more than a hundred located around the globe.

Many of the organizations that run IXPs are nonprofit organizations with the basic mission of enabling unlimited information exchange. One of the largest IXPs in the world, at least based on throughput of peak traffic, is the Deutscher Commercial Internet Exchange (DE-CIX) in Frankfurt, Germany. DE-CIX was founded in 1995 and is owned by the nonprofit eco Internet Industry Association.[9] This IXP connects hundreds of Internet providers, including content delivery networks and web hosting services as well as Internet service providers. To provide some scale, DE-CIX Frankfurt interconnects 450 Internet providers. For example, Google, Sprint, Level 3, Ustream, and Yahoo! all connect through DE-CIX. An IXP is not always in a single building but can locate high-speed switches in various data centers in a city or a region and then interconnect these switches on a very high-speed fiber optic ring. A single logical IXP can actually be physically distributed. As an example, the peering interconnection service DE-CIX provides in Frankfurt is available at more than ten data centers throughout the city. Similarly, the Amsterdam IXP (AMS-IX), as of this writing, operates eight interconnected data centers in Amsterdam.

To provide a clearer picture of the types of organizations that connect through a large IXP, the following lists a small sampling of the companies that are full members connecting into the London Internet Exchange:[10]

- Facebook
- Google
- AboveNet
- AT&T Global Network Services
- BBC
- British Telecommunications
- Telecity Group UK
- UPC Broadband
- Clara Net
- Telstra International
- France Telecom
- Global Crossing
- Packet Clearing House
- Renesys
- RIPE NCC
- Akamai
- Cable & Wireless
- XO Communications
- Limelight Networks
- China Telecom
- Turk Telecom
- Tata Communications.

The diverse categories of companies that connect at IXPs help illustrate the flattening of interconnection, with content companies and "eyeball companies" that connect directly to end users no longer at the bottom of the interconnection hierarchy but interconnecting directly to providers in local economies at exchange points. For a service with an enormous amount of bandwidth-intensive content, it is much more efficient to replicate this information on servers around the world than to operate fairly centralized repositories.

To become a member of an IXP, a company pays a membership fee and must meet certain technical, administrative, and legal requirements.

For example, the London Internet Exchange requires that a company requesting membership be a legally recognized or incorporated entity; hold an assigned ASN (assigned by an RIR); present (make visible) an autonomous system to a LINX transit router; and use BGP-4 for peering.[11] IXPs receive several types of fees including membership into the IXP association (for example, approximately EUR 2500 annually for a large corporate member of DE-CIX) plus recurring monthly charges for private interconnection and public peering services.

Any network connected at an IXP is technically able to exchange packets with any other network connected at the IXP although they have no obligation to do so. In addition to the agreement to connect with the IXP, each independent network can choose to peer with other companies with no exchange of money (typically between networks of a similar size) or may negotiate other financial arrangements, such as charging a network for exchanging traffic.

THE ECONOMICS OF GLOBAL INTERNET INTERCONNECTION

The agreements among network operators to interconnect are private contractual arrangements. Global proposals to regulate interconnection have been controversial because this part of Internet infrastructure has been market-driven and privately negotiated. Once these contractual arrangements are made, information flows seamlessly between service providers' networks through high-speed fiber optic cable connected to shared or privately owned switching equipment. Interconnection arrangements have historically bifurcated into two broad categories of private contracts—peering and transit. By the early twenty-first century, these agreements became much more complicated and hybridized.[12] The following sections describe the various types of interconnection arrangements, including peering arrangements in which no financial settlements are required and other arrangements in which one company compensates another for connectivity.

Settlement-Free Interconnection

Full peering agreements, usually called "settlement-free interconnection" refer to mutually beneficial arrangements whereby network operators interconnect their networks with no exchange of money. Peering, in the purest sense, involves the exchange of information originating on one network and terminating on the peer network. Voluntary private peering agreements allow network providers to share the costs of exchange points and sometimes commit to service-level agreements (SLAs) for characteristics such as reliability and latency. In addition to the physical interconnection necessary to exchange information from one backbone provider's network to another, the exchange requires use of common protocols such as BGP-4.

So-called Tier 1 network operators peer with other Tier 1 operators, collectively reaching any segment of the Internet and therefore cumulatively containing, in theory, the entire Internet routing table. Large global operators are not the only types of networks that can peer. Any two ISPs can enter into private contractual agreements to interconnect and directly exchange information originating and terminating on their respective networks.

There is no standard approach for the actual agreement to peer, with some interconnections involving formal contracts and others just verbal agreements between companies' technical personnel.[13] Formal contracts can establish conditions under which packets are exchanged and conditions under which the peering agreement could be terminated.

The motivation for peering agreements has an obvious economic as well as technical basis. Service providers normally require a number of interconnection points to the global Internet to provide adequate service to their customers and to engineer sufficient redundancy, network capacity, and performance. But once these requirements are met, it is economically in a large company's interest to minimize the number of settlement-free peering agreements to leave more room for paid transit interconnection agreements.

AT&T is an example of a large network provider that engages in settlement-free peering agreements with other large network operators. The company stipulates a specific set of requirements that should be met before voluntarily consenting to a settlement-free peering agreement. Commensurate with other network operators, the AT&T network encompasses much more than a single autonomous system. Part of this is explainable by the sheer size and geographical expanse of its network, some achieved through mergers and acquisitions. For example, AT&T's AS7132 number was formerly associated with the SBC Internet backbone.[14] AT&T is not accepting new peers for that system but has the following autonomous systems potentially available for peering:[15]

- AS7018: Available for private peering in the United States
- AS2685: Available for in-region peering in Canada
- AS2686: Available for in-region peering in Europe, the Middle East, and Africa
- AS2687: Available for in-region peering in Asia-Pacific
- AS2688: Available for in-region peering in Latin America.

A network provider interested in peering with one of AT&T's networks has to submit its request in writing with supporting details including a list of the ASNs and IP address prefixes the network serves; whether the network is national or regional; if regional, which countries are supported by the network; a list of IXPs to which the network connects; and information about the type of traffic the network carries.

For connectivity to its U.S. network AS7018, for example, AT&T delineates very specific peering requirements related to technical specifications, geographical expansiveness, global connectivity, and institutional relationships to other network operators. Table 5.1 summarizes some of these requirements.

Many network operator peering requirements are not publicly available and revealed only under nondisclosure agreements (NDAs). Among those companies who choose to disclose these requirements, some aspects are quite similar to AT&T's peering criteria and sometimes use very similar language. Each set of network operator peering agreements also has differences.

Comcast's settlement-free interconnection requirements call for conjoining at a minimum of four mutually agreeable U.S. interconnection points. Comcast also requires prospective peers to sign a nondisclosure agreement prior to commencing negotiations on further particulars of the peering agreement. Comcast also requires a ninety-day interconnection trial before it formally accepts a peering agreement.[16]

Verizon operates multiple autonomous systems including AS701 (Verizon Business—U.S.), AS702 (Verizon Business—Europe), and AS703 (Verizon Business—Asia Pacific). To engage in settlement-free

Table 5.1

Peering Requirements for Interconnection with AS7018

Technical Requirements for IP Backbone
- Transmission backbone speeds primarily OC192 (10 Gbps) or higher
- Backbone must also interconnect to two non-U.S. peering locations on distinct continents
- Network must agree to interconnect to AT&T at three distributed U.S. points
- Interconnection point bandwidth must be at least 10 Gbps

Operational and Business Requirements
- Peer must maintain 24-7 network operation center
- Peer must agree to cooperate to resolve security attacks and operational problems
- Customers of AS7018 may not simultaneously be settlement-free peers
- Peer must demonstrate financial stability

Traffic Requirements
- Average U.S. traffic to/from AS7018 must be at least 7 Gbps during peak monthly hour
- The traffic ratio between peer network and AT&T must be balanced
- Peer traffic should have a low peak-to-average ratio and a ratio of no more than 2.00:1 between networks

Routing Requirements
- Peer must announce a consistent set of routes at each interconnection point
- Peer may not announce third-party routes, only those of peer and peer's customers
- Peer must not engage in abusive behavior, such as forwarding traffic for destinations not advertised

Source: "AT&T Global IP Network Settlement-Free Peering Policy," last updated May 2011. Accessed at http://www.corp.att.com/peering/.

peering with Verizon, the network operator must "have a backbone node in each of the following eight geographic regions: Northeast; Mid-Atlantic; Southeast; North Central; Southwest Central; Northwest; Mid-Pacific; and Southwest."[17] Verizon further requires that a network operator requesting settlement-free peering agree to a mutual NDA.

Examinations of numerous publicly available peering agreement policies help demonstrate some general features of global peering agreements. There is no guarantee that any peering request will be accepted, regardless of whether the potential peer is eligible for settlement-free interconnection under the criteria required by the requested peer. As the AT&T Settlement-Free Peering Policy specifies, "Meeting the peering guidelines set forth herein is not a guarantee that a peering relationship with AT&T will be established. AT&T shall evaluate a number of business factors and reserves the right not to enter into a peering agreement with an otherwise qualified applicant."[18]

Indeed, it may be in a large network operator's financial interest not to engage in settlement-free peering with an additional network because each of these potential peering partners is also a potential customer (or possibly an existing customer) of the network operator's transit service in which dedicated Internet access services are provisioned for a fee. As Comcast's settlement-free interconnection policy states, "A network (ASN) that is a customer of a Comcast network for any dedicated IP services may not simultaneously be a settlement-free network peer."[19] Another observation is that there is no timeframe guarantee in which a network operator must respond to a request for peering. Network operators agreeing to peering arrangements also reserve the right to terminate these agreements at any time in the future if agreed upon criteria (for example, traffic, quality of service) are not met.

Content distribution networks and large content companies are also major players in the Internet peering landscape. Large content companies operate their own autonomous systems and engage in peering agreements. For example, Google manages a number of ASNs including the following: AS36040, AS43515, and AS3656. Content distribution networks peering with traditional network operators normally have more complicated peering agreements and sometimes settlement-based peering because of the asymmetrical nature of information flows coming from CDNs.

Settlement-Based Interconnection

Interconnection often requires payments from one network operator to another. When the flow of traffic between networks is asymmetrical, reciprocal peering is not economically optimal because it disproportionately burdens one network over the other. This circumstance usually warrants paid peering agreements whereby the two networks bilaterally agree to exchange traffic but whereby one network operator pays the other for interconnection. Whether the network originating the heavier traffic flows pays the lighter traffic network or vice versa is not consistent in practice but context dependent. For example, mobile and home broadband networks that "touch" consumers may try to require networks that originate the content consumers download (presumably ad-supported content that benefits from reaching these consumers) to pay transit to the lower traffic network. Regardless of how private arrangements are negotiated, these agreements to peer for a fee are usually called "settlement-based peering."

Whereas peering agreements involve the exchange of information originating on one network and terminating on the peer network, transit agreements involve one network paying another network with interconnection, or reachability, to the entire Internet or to a subset of the entire Internet. Transit agreements inherently are paid financial arrangements. A network provider paid by another network via a full transit agreement performs two functions. The network provider agrees to announce to the Internet all of the routing prefixes the paying network controls. In other words, it tells the global Internet where to locate all of these routing prefixes. The transit provider also agrees to exchange all the information coming to and from the paying transit customer. It essentially provides a gateway to the rest of the Internet. While there is nothing fixed about this distinction, the term "full transit" refers to the ability of the paid network to reach the entire Internet, either inherently or by purchasing transit from other providers. The term "partial transit" refers to the ability to reach part of the Internet. Transit arrangements help optimize the topography and capacity of the Internet because they provide market inducements for large providers to add capacity when demand increases.

PUBLIC POLICY CONCERNS AT THE INTERNET'S INTERCONNECTION EPICENTER

Interconnection agreements are an unseen area of privatized Internet governance. There are few directly relevant statutes, minimal regulatory oversight, and little transparency in private contractual agreements. Unlike the traditional telecommunications system, whose interconnectivity evolution was tightly controlled by various state regulatory functions, Internet inter-connection evolved over time with little government oversight.

Interconnection at the Internet's core, whether via private bilateral agreements or exchange points, serves a critical technical function of transforming individual, privately operated networks into the global Internet. As this chapter has explained thus far, this interconnection is made possible by virtual and physical infrastructures and by market arrangements among network operators, ISPs, cable companies, large content providers, and CDNs. The technological enablers of interconnection include switching and routing equipment, the allocation of unique virtual resources of ASNs, and the core exterior routing standard BGP-4. The market agreements include bilateral peering, settlement-based peering, and full and partial transit.

Interconnection choices are not only technical and market arrangements but arrangements with a variety of public interest implications. This section describes several public interest concerns at the Internet's epicenter, including the prioritization of individual market incentives over technical efficiency; the uneven distribution of IXPs and associated interconnection challenges in emerging markets; and interconnection points as sites of disruption or control due to either peering disputes or government censorship.

Market Incentives versus Technical Efficiency
Interconnection presents an enigma. Individual market decisions of companies, which naturally seek to optimize individual profit and ensure technical redundancy for their customers, do not necessarily translate into a collective picture of a technically optimized network when these individually optimized networks connect.

The overall landscape of global interconnection is not based on a top-down view of how to optimize the distribution of interconnection points using global traffic engineering techniques. Individual network operators and content distribution companies make business decisions designed to meet certain technical requirements for their customers while minimizing their own interconnection costs and, when possible, optimizing profit from transit interconnection fees.

Incumbent network operators, once they establish adequate peering agreements for their customers to be able to reach anywhere on the

Internet with acceptable latency, redundancy, and low enough packet loss, are incentivized to not establish additional peering agreements. They are economically motivated to have restrictive peering policies and to pursue interconnection strategies with additional networks based on transit agreements in which these other companies pay for interconnection.

The financial disincentive for first mover global incumbents to peer with newer networks can have pronounced implications in developing markets, where newer network entrants are viewed as potential customers. The business model of large network operators is dependent on their ability to charge transit fees for other networks to interconnect to them. This interconnection "scarcity" not only affects economic competition and network pricing but also means that the Internet's interconnection architecture can be based on incumbent pricing strategies rather than on overall market efficiency or technical expediency. This can also provide a disincentive for large content distribution networks to locate regionally based servers in certain areas.

This incentive structure provides motivation for large, incumbent operators to connect to as many smaller and newer operators as possible, but as transit customers rather than settlement-free peers. This phenomenon, on its surface, would inherently provide a great deal of network redundancy and technically diverse routes. But this is not necessarily the case in practice. Although large, incumbent providers are economically motivated to make as many transit agreements as possible with smaller and newer providers, these smaller providers have an adversative incentive structure to connect to the lowest number of settlement-seeking providers that would enable adequate reach and redundancy.

The historical model of hierarchical Internet interconnection with Tier 1 networks at the top does not always match interconnection in practice. Content providers and lower tier network operators sometimes use peer circumvention techniques in which they peer to each other as much as possible (to incur no settlement fees) but connect to the fewest number of so-called Tier 1 networks possible to minimize transit fees they incur. The Internet industry sometimes refers to this as the "donut Internet" or "donut peering."[20] Recall that the historical definition of a Tier 2 network is one that purchases IP transit to access some portion of the global Internet but peers with other Tier 2 providers. Many of these networks, such as cable companies and midsized or small ISPs, are geo-graphically near the edge—meaning close to customers. These networks support a large number of Internet users. They also have a market incentive to minimize the amount of traffic they must send via a transit connection through a Tier 1 provider.

Traffic optimization would suggest that Tier 2 providers connect to multiple Tier 1 operators. But Tier 2 companies make interconnection decisions not based exclusively on traffic engineering and hop minimization but based on cost minimization. For example, they may route traffic around Tier 1 interconnectivity and instead transmit packets through peer connections with other smaller networks. Depending on the destination of the packet, it is possible that routing through a Tier 2 network is actually the shortest path to a destination.

The topology of Internet interconnection is influenced by transit cost minimization incentives whereby so-called Tier 2 networks maximize settlement-free peering arrangements with other Tier 2 companies but minimize the transit connections through the Tier 1 core of the Internet. In practice, the network design of the Internet's core infrastructure is based on individual business model optimization rather than collective technical values of overall global redundancy, efficiency, and reliability.

Interconnection Challenges in Emerging Markets

This chapter has explained what Internet exchange points are but has not addressed where they are. Although the worldwide establishment of IXPs has grown rapidly since all network access points were originally located in the United States, as many countries still do not have IXPs within their borders as countries that have them. Many of the hundreds of IXPs are concentrated in specific regions, such as Europe and North America. In countries without IXPs, there can still be (but there are not necessarily any) bilateral connections among network operators but there are no IXPs.

IXPs serve as critical Internet infrastructure within nations because they connect network operators within countries and also serve as information gateways to the rest of the world. The lack of policy attention to this phenomenon is an example of how "bridging the digital divide" efforts focus on last-mile access or undersea cables without attention to the geopolitics at the Internet's core.

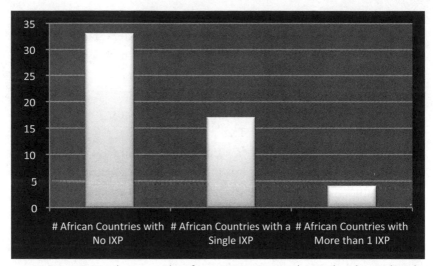

FIGURE 5.2: IXP Distribution on the African Continent. Based on author data gathered prior to January 1, 2012.

Half of the world's countries do not even operate a single IXP. Figure 5.2 uses the African continent as an example, illustrating that, of the African states that are members of the United Nations, 61 percent do not have an IXP within their borders, and 31 percent have only a single IXP. Only four African countries have more than one IXP. In total, Africa has fewer than forty exchange points. To put this in perspective, the following countries each have ten or more IXPs: Australia, Brazil, France, Germany, Russia, the United Kingdom, and the United States.

Significant progress in Africa has included the installation of additional undersea cables to and from the continent and significant increases in national fiber backbones. However, the Internet Society's director of regional development has noted that much of this infrastructural improvement has been within but not between African countries: "despite an increasing amount of infrastructure within individual African countries, much data traffic destined for networks in the same country and neighboring nations is often sent to Europe to be exchanged and then returned to Africa."[21] This paucity of IXPs is not a problem unique to the African continent given that approximately half of the world's countries do not have an IXP. Countries without one or more IXPs face political, technical, and economic consequences. IXPs allow local or national networks to efficiently connect and exchange Internet traffic originating and terminating locally. This domestic and regional connectivity is not a given and, in some cases, information originating and terminating does not pass from one network to the other within the nation's border. Instead, it can be routed to an IXP in a neighboring country and then routed back to the originating country. When local information has to be exchanged far beyond a nation's border and then routed back to the region, this creates technical inefficiency and adds unnecessary transmission delay.

Routing local traffic through a foreign IXP also has economic consequences. The Internet Society estimates that the presence of a local IXP can amount to cost savings of 20 percent or more as well as a tenfold increase in local access speeds.[22] One benefit of a nationally located IXP is that it creates market efficiencies that save money for that country's Internet users. Some of this cost savings accrues because IXPs enable local networks to exchange traffic locally rather than having to exchange traffic via a remote IXP in a neighboring country. Local traffic comprises a significant percentage of all Internet traffic. It is not technically or financially efficient to route this local traffic through an IXP located in another country.

One caveat is that the presence of an IXP does not necessarily translate into local, settlement-free peering. Even in places with multiple IXP options, peering can be difficult because the dominant network operator can charge other providers significant transit sums for interconnection. In some cases, smaller companies choose to pay for interconnection in Europe, rather than in their native country.

From a political perspective, there are national infrastructure protection implications for countries without at least one IXP because of exposure to Internet outages in the event of an international Internet cable cut or a disruption in connection to a foreign IXP. International cable outages can occur for a simple physical reason, such as a ship anchor severing an undersea cable; a virtual reason such as a switch outage at a foreign IXP; or because of an institutional-level outage such as a political sanction imposed against the IXP-dependent country by the nation state that houses the foreign IXP.

Any of these outages for a country without an IXP cannot only cut off the nation's connectivity to the outside world, but also stop the flow of Internet traffic among network companies operating in that country.

If network operators are not connected within the country, and if they do not have bilateral interconnection agreements with all other network operators in the country, this type of outage can essentially disrupt all Internet traffic even within the country's borders. The exception to this exists in countries with only a single network operator, whether because of market conditions, size, or the context of a single state-controlled network infrastructure. In these exceptional cases, lack of interconnection would have no bearing on national intraborder communications in the event of an international outage.

Interconnection Points as Sites of Control and Disruption
Interconnection points are Internet points of control. Although an outage at an Internet exchange point would have serious consequences for national economic security, government Internet security policies sometimes overlook the possibility of terrorism or Internet security attacks at these concentration points. Because they concentrate the flow of traffic between network operators, these points are also sites of potential government filtering and censorship.

Interconnection outages have caused significant disruptions to customers. Outages are not necessarily caused by problems with physical architecture or coordinated attacks on IXPs but by problems with peering and transit agreements. A 2008 Internet outage stemmed from an interconnection dispute between Cogent and Sprint, for example.[23] At the time, these companies were two of the largest Internet operators in the United States. Before they directly interconnected their networks, traffic originating from one network and destined for the other was carried via a path through a third party.[24] Sprint and Cogent decided to sign a private contract in September 2006 agreeing to the terms of how it would interconnect. In the ensuing months, the companies connected their networks in ten cities around the globe.

Each company provides a slightly different perspective on the details that transpired after this point. Generally, after the interconnection trial period ended, Sprint notified Cogent that the company had failed to meet the trial test requirements. The problem reportedly was that the links failed to carry an adequate volume of traffic.[25] Normally problems occur when too much traffic is transferred, particularly in an asymmetrical manner that overburdens one of the two connecting agreements. In this case, Sprint wanted Cogent to pay for connectivity as a transit customer rather than as a peering partner. At this point of the disagreement, the companies remained connected but Sprint began submitting transit bills to Cogent, which Cogent refused to pay because it believed Sprint's actions violated the terms of their private contract. Sprint eventually cut all ten connections with Cogent.

Severing these interconnection points between the two companies affected customers. An outage originating in a peering dispute had the same effect as any disruption to critical Internet infrastructure. As a media account about the outage summarized, "In an instant, customers who relied solely on Sprint (like the US federal court system) for web access could no longer communicate with customers who relied solely on Cogent for their web connections (like many large law firms), and vice versa."[26]

Both companies involved presumably could have, prior to the interconnection delinking, modified their routing tables so that users on each network could have reached each other through an alternative third-party route. After a great deal of public concern and media coverage and after three days of the outage, the companies reconnected. The story was much more involved than recounted here but it helps suggest how peering disputes can have direct implications for the digital public sphere.

Sizable segments of the digital public sphere can be (and have been) disrupted with no warning by de-peering situations. De-peering, the decision to terminate settlement-free interconnection between two private network operators, can occur for a number of reasons: if one company engages in abusive behavior such as unduly using the peer company for transit to another network; if the traffic exchange ratio between the two networks becomes unbalanced because of changing business requirements or traffic engineering circumstances; or if one of the peering companies decides to peer with the other company's transit customers, essentially reducing the other company's own transit revenues.

Having greater transparency and insight into the arrangements and configurations at these sites of potential government intervention is important and is an area in need of additional Internet governance inquiry.

Unlike traditional telecommunications services, there has been very little market-specific regulation of interconnection points, either at the national or international level. Market forces, coupled with antitrust oversight, have historically been considered sufficient to discourage anticompetitive behavior in backbone peering and transit agreements.[27] Conversely, some have cited concerns about lack of competition in Internet backbones, dominance by a small number of companies, and peering agreements among large providers that are detrimental to potential competitors.[28]

Questions about introducing regulatory oversight of Internet interconnection have always been present, whether to incentivize interconnection or mediate equitable payment structures for the exchange of traffic between network operators. As a study convened for the European Commission summarized, "A recurrent theme in the discussion of IP interconnection is whether network operators will be motivated to interconnect (on reasonable terms) in the absence of a regulatory obligation."[29] Chapter 10 discusses some open issues and concerns surrounding contemporary discussions about the prospect of introducing a regulatory overlay onto private interconnection markets.

CHAPTER SIX

Internet Access and Network Neutrality

"NETWORK NEUTRALITY" is an Internet policy concern situated prominently in the public consciousness, particularly in the United States but also in many other countries. Even the late-night comedy show *The Daily Show with Jon Stewart* tackled the subject with correspondent John Hodgman's hilarious sketch explaining the "Net Neutrality Act" by distinguishing between the Internet as a dump truck and a series of tubes. His distinction satirized the description of the Internet as "a series of tubes" by Senator Ted Stevens, then chairman of the U.S. Senate Commerce Committee, in the context of his opposition to network neutrality legislation. The comedians explained net neutrality as follows:

JOHN HODGMAN: With net neutrality, all of these packets, whether they come from a big company or just a single citizen, are treated in the exact same way.

JON STEWART: So what's the debate? That actually seems quite fair.

JOHN HODGMAN: Yes, almost *too fair*. It's as though the richer companies get no advantage at all.

Technologically, the network neutrality question addresses a very small swath of Internet infrastructure—last-mile Internet access. "Last mile" is shorthand for the ways in which end users directly access the Internet through a network operator. It is the last segment, or last leg, of a network connecting an end user to the global Internet or other communication system. Network neutrality, as a principle, also focuses primarily on individual citizen access to the Internet rather than how businesses access the Internet.

The central question of network neutrality addresses whether a network operator should be legally prohibited from prioritizing or blocking the delivery of certain types of traffic relative to other traffic on its network. Practically speaking, the various things that could be blocked, prioritized, or delayed include specific content such as pirated movies, indecent material, controversial speech, or speech critical of government; specific classes of traffic, for example, prioritizing voice or video over text-based information or premium subscriber traffic over lower priced service; specific protocols such as P2P file-sharing protocols or VoIP; specific web sites such as YouTube, Netflix, or Hulu; or specific applications such as Skype or BitTorrent clients.

The local, geography-bound aspect of net neutrality distinguishes this issue from other network governance topics that transcend jurisdictional boundaries and are more global than local and more virtual than physical. In this regard, net neutrality is a national or even regional policy issue rather than a clear issue of global Internet governance. Last-mile access is only one component of an immense ecosystem of Internet infrastructure. But because this is the network segment mediating between individuals and the global Internet, it is a de facto choke point determining the nature of one's access to information. It is also an area that, in some subscriber markets, often does not provide significant user choice. Some areas lack even one option for broadband Internet access and, in others, there may be only one or two alternatives such as an incumbent monopoly cable service provider and an incumbent monopoly telecommunications carrier. Because access technologies are a choke point through which individuals access the global Internet and because net neutrality has emerged in policy debates as a central topic of Internet governance, the subject is included as a stand-alone chapter in this book.

Last-mile access includes cellular, stationary wireless, or fixed broadband. "Last mile" is only an expression because this last leg of connectivity can obviously be much longer or much shorter than a mile. One of the most common ways to access the Internet is via mobile wireless, meaning access allowing subscribers to use the Internet while in transit via cellular service provided by network operators such as AT&T and Verizon. The frequency spectrum associated with cellular telephony is allocated by a government authority such as, in the United States, the Federal Communications Commission (FCC). The range of frequencies allocated for this purpose is roughly in the 800 MHz to 2 GHz range. Cellular companies must license frequencies within this radio spectrum range to provide cellular services to customers. Because a finite amount of radio frequency spectrum is available for cellular services, conserving frequency is a system design requirement. This conservation occurs through the basic design of cell phone systems, which split geographic areas into smaller regions called "cells." Each cell is served by an individual antenna, usually called a base station, transmitting at a low enough power to only serve the antenna's immediate cell. When a mobile subscriber passes out of that cell area, the wireless device is "handed off" to an adjacent cell, which uses a different frequency. The purpose of this multicell configuration is frequency conservation. The same frequency can be used concurrently in nonadjacent cells as long as the antennas are far enough apart to not experience signal interference. This frequency reuse approach enables service providers to handle a large number of subscribers with a relatively small number of channels.

Another dominant form of wireless Internet access is through a static (stationary) wireless technology such as satellite antenna, WiMAX, or Wi-Fi. Wi-Fi, or Wireless Fidelity, is a general name designating products that conform to the IEEE 802.11 wireless standards using radio frequencies in the range of roughly 2.4 GHz to 5 GHz. Unlike the frequencies used in cellular telephony, Wi-Fi frequencies fall legally, at least in the United States, into the unlicensed category, meaning that using these frequencies does not require formal licensing. Although Wi-Fi is wireless, it is not necessarily mobile, meaning that a device used by someone moving in a car would not automatically hand off from one Wi-Fi router to the next without intervention by the user.

For fixed access from a home, the most popular type of connectivity is broadband "landline" access, such as a coaxial cable connection provided by a traditional cable company or a telecommunications provider service, either over copper twisted pair cable (for example, Digital Subscriber Line or DSL) or fiber-to-the-premises. This type of access is often accompanied by a local Wi-Fi router providing fixed wireless access.

Businesses and other entities that require higher bandwidth connections to the Internet can also lease a high-speed dedicated private line from a telecommunications company. For example, a dedicated fiber optic link to the Internet, such as an OC-48 link, can provide dedicated bandwidth of 2.488 Gbps (2.488 billion bits per second). Each of these access technologies provides different opportunities for carriers wishing to differentiate traffic delivery based on content or some other characteristic of the transmitted information.

Those advocating for net neutrality regulation seek to legally prohibit Internet service providers from discriminating among different content, protocols, web sites, or applications. This chapter provides some examples of network discrimination that have occurred in the twenty-first century, explains the arguments for and against net neutrality regulation, and describes the history and status of this contentious Internet policy topic in global context.

FOUR CASES OF INTERNET ACCESS DISCRIMINATION
The net neutrality issue is not a theoretical concern. Throughout recent history, there have been some instances of network operators providing differential treatment to network traffic for a variety of reasons. This section provides examples of how Internet access discrimination actually occurs in practice, with "discriminate" broadly defined as blocking or throttling back (slowing) some traffic over other traffic.

The Technology of Throttling, Blocking, and Prioritization
One basic technical question is whether network operators have the ability to discriminate among different types of traffic. The answer is an easy yes. Information sent over the Internet is segmented into small units called packets and transmitted by routers via the most expeditious route to the packets' destinations. Each packet can take its own individual path and be reassembled at the endpoint. All that is required is for routers to read the "header" of each packet, meaning the administrative information such as the destination and origination Internet address appended to the actual content. For routing purposes, it has not historically been necessary for intermediate nodes to view the "payload" (that is, content) of each packet. Not only was it not necessary, it was not easily possible

because of the processing power that would be required to view the payload content as well as the header information. Rapid advances in network computing power have removed this constraint and have enabled new technological approaches such as deep packet inspection (DPI) which network operators can use to inspect the contents of packets for a variety of network management or security reasons, or potentially to discriminate against certain types of traffic, applications, protocols, users, or content. It is technically quite feasible to block or throttle back (slow) traffic based on content detected in the payload.

Payload content is not the only characteristic network operators could technically use as the basis for traffic discrimination. Other possible variables include protocols, IP addresses, port numbers, and application type. For example, a network operator could slow down traffic that uses a protocol such as BitTorrent. It could also block traffic originating from certain IP addresses or destined for certain IP addresses. It could also make discrimination decisions based on port number. Transport-layer protocols, such as Transmission Control Protocol (part of TCP/IP), add a 16-bit source and destination "port number" to Internet packet headers. This number associates with both the type of protocol used and the IP address. By convention, and as suggested by the Internet Assigned Numbers Authority (IANA), common port numbers include port 25 for email, port 53 for DNS services, port 80 for HTTP web traffic, and ports 20 or 21 for FTP traffic. Network operators can use this unencrypted information contained in a packet header to decide how it will deliver traffic. Carriers also have the technical ability to block traffic based on a specific application. For example, mobile providers can prohibit users from transmitting traffic (over its mobile network) that originates from a voice application such as Skype.

Through an economic lens, one could envision a company's incentive to preserve its business model by blocking traffic that competes directly with its services, such as a telecommunications provider blocking or slowing the use of free voice applications like Skype over its network or a cable company slowing down the delivery of online video sites that compete directly with its core cable programming services. From the standpoint of concern over free expression, one could envision the potential for a company to block content that is critical of the company or block political content that is harmful to forces whose policies favor the company's business model. The following sections provide a few specific examples of network traffic differentiation that have occurred in practice.

Blocking Controversial Speech over Wireless Networks
One way advocacy organizations can reach large numbers of supporters in real time is via text messaging. Any supporter with a cell phone can subscribe to this type of service. Organizations usually provide a "short code" number to which subscribers may send a text to opt in or out of the messaging announcement system. Text messaging is especially favored by advocacy organizations wishing to implore supporters to take some immediate political action such as contacting Congress. In September 2007, abortion rights advocacy group NARAL Pro-Choice America applied for a text messaging short code from Verizon Wireless so that supporters could subscribe to NARAL's text messaging program and receive notifications. Verizon initially rejected this request from the abortion rights organization and suggested that the company was within its right to block "controversial or unsavory" text messages.[1]

After a front-page *New York Times* story about Verizon's refusal of service to NARAL Pro-Choice America, as well as 20,000 email messages to Verizon from NARAL supporters, the company reversed its decision. This reversal happened within twenty-four hours of the incident. A Verizon spokesperson suggested that the company's decision to refuse to transmit the abortion rights group's messages had been incorrect.[2]

Although Verizon's refusal to carry these text messages runs contrary to norms of freedom of expression, it was not clear that this action was illegal. Under U.S. law, telecommunications companies such as Verizon are categorized as "Common Carriers" in the Communications Act and are prohibited from discriminating on the basis of the person speaking or what is being spoken. However, this provision applied to traditional voice service, not to digital data. Without net neutrality rules, most information transmitted over the Internet or cell phone data networks could legally be discriminated against by private entities. As constitutional law scholar Jack Balkin has suggested, "The Verizon/NARAL story and the larger discussion about network neutrality are part of the modern-day debate about private power in telecommunications."[3]

Throttling Back File Sharing Protocols

In the same year as the NARAL controversy, it became public that Comcast, the second largest cable provider in the United States, seemed to be blocking specific Internet protocols.[4] This blocking appeared geared toward peer-to-peer file sharing sites using BitTorrent and Gnutella protocols and also reportedly involved discrimination against Lotus Notes Enterprise Collaboration Software.[5] Recall that P2P protocols enable users to expeditiously and directly exchange very large bandwidth-intensive files. These P2P file sharing protocols are often viewed as synonymous with illegal downloading of copyrighted music and movies but are also used for the lawful sharing of large media files.

Advocacy groups Free Press and Public Knowledge filed a complaint with the FCC and, along with other interest groups, filed petitions for a declaratory ruling from the FCC. In 2005 the FCC had adopted a policy statement on broadband Internet access stating that "consumers are entitled to access the lawful Internet content of their choice" and "to run applications and use services of their choice."[6] The petitions argued that Comcast's interventions in traffic flows over its network violated this policy. Comcast defended its actions by arguing that it had to throttle back P2P traffic to provide necessary management of scarce bandwidth. In response to the petition, the FCC issued an order concluding that Comcast's practices do not constitute reasonable network management and requiring both cessation of these practices and disclosure to the public of any network management practices it does intend to execute.[7] Comcast complied with the order but appealed, contending, among other things, that the FCC did not have jurisdiction over the company's network management practices. In 2010 a federal court ruled that the FCC did not have this jurisdiction.

Throttling Bandwidth for High-Usage Subscribers with
  Unlimited Service Plans

In some cases, network operators have slowed access speeds for customers who consume unusually high levels of bandwidth. For example, AT&T announced that it would reduce the usage speeds it provided to some of its customers with unlimited data plans.[8] The policy was geared toward the 5 percent of AT&T customers with heaviest data usage rates. The company indicated that these subscribers, many of them iPhone users, transmitted on average twelve times more data than an average smart-phone user. At the time, the company had fifteen million subscribers on a tiered subscription plan that contractually specified the amount of data that could be consumed during a billing cycle. These customers would be unaffected by the AT&T announcement. The policy would affect those with unlimited data plans, often contracted with AT&T years earlier.

As AT&T announced, "smartphone customers with unlimited data plans may experience reduced speeds once their usage in a billing cycle reaches the level that puts them among the top 5 percent of heaviest data users."[9] The company suggested it would provide multiple notices before throttling back available bandwidth to these customers, who were described as using an "extraordinary amount of data." The types of con-sumers affected would be ones who streamed large amounts of high bandwidth-consuming video or spent hours a day using bandwidth-intensive multimedia games. The AT&T announcement was designed, in part, to encourage subscribers to use Wi-Fi connections when pos-sible rather than AT&T cellular connectivity. If the usage patterns of customers with unlimited data plans placed them in the top 5 percent of cellular subscriber bandwidth consumption, the company suggested it would limit their bandwidth.

Affected customers reported experiencing network speeds that seemed like dial-up rates. They complained that downloading a web page would take more than a minute rather than a second and that their smartphones would essentially be relegated to voice, text messaging, and email. As one subscriber claimed, "Four years ago when you were advertising the unlimited data plan it was never stated that if you took advantage of the plan at some point AT&T would slow down your ac-cess."[10] AT&T responded that subscriber terms of service provided the company with the right to throttle back usage in certain circumstances. The following section of an AT&T wireless customer agreement pro-vides an example of the contractual language applicable at the time.

6.2 What Are the Intended Purposes Of the Wireless Data Service?

Accordingly, AT&T reserves the right to:

Deny, disconnect, modify and/or terminate Service, without notice, to anyone it believes is using the Service in any manner

prohibited or whose usage adversely impacts its wireless network
or service levels or hinders access to its wireless network, including without limitation, after a significant period of inactivity
or after sessions of excessive usage.

Otherwise, protect its wireless network from harm,
compromised capacity or degradation in performance, which
may impact legitimate data flows.[11]

Those wanting to legally challenge AT&T over these practices were not
able to pursue a class-action lawsuit because of a clause in the subscribers' contracts agreeing to an individual arbitration process and prohibiting class actions. The United States Supreme Court, in *AT&T Mobility v.
Concepcion,* upheld the subscriber contract clause prohibiting class-
action lawsuits. Nevertheless, one customer took AT&T to small claims
court and won $850.[12] AT&T had argued that it had the contractual right
to modify customers' network performance but the judge ruled that it
was unfair to sell a subscriber an unlimited data plan and then intentionally decelerate that same customer's service.

After some public backlash and confusion surrounding AT&T's policy about throttling back traffic for smartphone customers with unlimited data plans, AT&T publicly offered some clarifying parameters about
its practices. The company indicated that an unlimited data customer's
bandwidth would be slowed whenever that customer reached 3 GB of usage in a billing cycle and after a text message alerting the customer that
the limit was approaching. After that billing cycle, speeds would return
to normal.

Blocking Applications That Compete with Carrier Business Models
Voice calls are just like any other Internet application. Audio signals are
digitized, broken into packets, and sent over the same transmission
lines and technical infrastructure as video or data. The transmission of
voice over an IP network relies on a family of technical standards known
as Voice over Internet Protocol (VoIP). VoIP converts an analog wave-
form into a digital format, breaks the digital signal into packets, and
transmits these packets using the packet switching approach underlying
the Internet. VoIP standards include signaling protocols such as Session
Initiation Protocol (SIP) for determining user availability and establishing

and terminating a call, and transport protocols, such as Real-time Transport Protocol (RTP) for transmitting packets between endpoints. The transmission of audio over a packet switching network is a considerable technical departure from the traditional circuit-switched approach of the public-switched telephone system, which establishes a dedicated end-to-end path between a transmitter and receiver and maintains this fixed transmission path for the duration of a call.

Voice services over the Internet are often provided by cable companies as a separate billed service from a high speed Internet connection and a subscription to cable television programming. Calls transmitted over any fixed Internet connection can also be made through a computing device with the necessary VoIP software installed or through an application on a smartphone. This type of mobile call bypasses the billing arrangement of the cellular service provider and is just part of information traffic similar to sending email or accessing a web site. Even though these voice services use many of the VoIP protocols, it is also pertinent to note that some of their protocols are proprietary. For example, a Skype application is not necessarily interoperable and compatible with other voice over Internet Services without the user having to pay an extra billing arrangement for this interconnectivity.

From the standpoint of a business user or individual citizen, voice applications over the Internet are appealing because they save money. Business information technology users choosing to integrate previously distinct voice and data services onto a single Internet Protocol network reduce costs both for services and for operational expenses associated with managing these systems. Particularly for those using voice apps such as Skype, users save considerable monthly fees by bypassing the public-switched telephone network entirely. Even those opting for monthly VoIP services from network operators achieve considerable cost savings over subscribing to a traditional circuit-switched voice service. Obviously, this transition of voice off the public-switched telephone network and onto the Internet has created business model challenges for traditional voice operators.

Therefore, network operators have an economic incentive to block voice over the Internet and preserve their long-standing business models that rely on lucrative voice charging arrangements. For example, network operators such as cable companies that sell voice over Internet services to residential and business customers might have the incentive to block computer applications enabling users to make free Internet calls over their broadband Internet connection without having to additionally subscribe to a separate voice service. Traditional landline phone service providers such as telecommunications companies might have the incentive to block their Internet access subscribers from using Internet voice apps enabling them to cancel traditional voice services. Similarly, mobile phone companies lose revenue when their smartphone subscribers use voice apps like Skype, essentially routing around the billing arrangements these companies have historically relied on for cellular profitability.

Since the introduction of Internet telephony applications, there have been scattered global cases of cellular and telecommunications operators blocking VoIP application access. For example, Deutsche Telekom subsidiary T-Mobile announced it would block Skype calls from iPhones in Germany.[13] The blockage would not affect Skype usage via a Wi-Fi connection from the smartphone but would block Skype usage while the phone transmitted over the T-Mobile carrier service. The obvious incentive for this blockage is revenue preservation but carriers have also argued that this blocking mitigates the network congestion and performance degradation potentially caused by additional audio traffic.

INTERNET GOVERNANCE ENTANGLEMENTS WITH NET NEUTRALITY

Net neutrality, as a principle, suggests that Internet providers should not give preferential treatment to the transmission of certain Internet traffic over other traffic. Net neutrality, if enacted by law, would legally prohibit service providers from executing differential treatment of some traffic over other traffic. Although Internet access traditions have customarily resulted in equal treatment of traffic, the previous examples establish that discrimination can occur. Although net neutrality is often naturalized as a homogenous and self-evident principle by legal scholars, these examples raise much more granular questions about technical governance in practice. Should a cellular provider be allowed to prioritize the delivery of certain apps over others, either to protect its business model or to manage bandwidth allocation over its own network? Should a cable company be permitted to decelerate the transmission speed of content originating from a competitor's site? Should a service provider be able to charge different rates to customers for different tiers of Internet access service? A broader governance matter is whether governments have the obligation or authority to enforce net neutrality principles by restricting the operational and business choices of network operators.

Private companies have a great deal at stake in the outcome of net neutrality debates. Popular Internet sites and portals such as Amazon, eBay, Google, and Yahoo! endorse net neutrality because they would be adversely affected if network operators attempted to charge these content companies premiums for adequate user access to their content sites. In an interview with *Businessweek,* a CEO of a large American telecommunications company famously expressed his inclination to charge content companies for the portion of bandwidth users are consuming to access these content sites, stating "Why should they be allowed to use my pipes?"[14]

Other types of companies that favor net neutrality are those whose services directly compete with Internet provider services. For example, Skype owner Microsoft has advocated for net neutrality, as have Vonage and any companies that offer alternative VoIP services. Similarly, companies such as Netflix and Hulu that offer video services in competition with traditional cable television have an obvious incentive to support non-discrimination principles that would prevent blocking or throttling back of their content by companies whose business models they threaten.

Some prominent Internet engineers, such as web inventor Sir Tim Berners-Lee and TCP/IP creator Vinton Cerf, have been proponents of variations of net neutrality rules, as have a number of Internet advocacy groups such as the Electronic Frontier Foundation and Public Knowledge. The organizations opposing net neutrality regulation are the network operators on which these restrictions would fall. These operators include cellular providers, telecommunications companies, and cable companies. Advocates of free market technological and economic approaches, such as the Cato Institute, also generally oppose net neutrality regulation as part of advocating for market-based approaches and minimal government regulations they believe would diminish economic efficiency and innovation.

*Tensions between Network Management Requirements
and Net Neutrality*

Net neutrality arguments fought by attorneys and politicians sometimes fail to consider the requirements of traffic engineering. Instead, they politicize and envelop this issue within prevailing political framings deployed by either conservative or liberal ideologies. While advocating for net neutrality from the floor of the United States Senate, Democratic senators linked those who oppose net neutrality rules with those who liked the government bailout of large banks and other financial institutions. Republican senators framed the issue as one of bureaucratic overreach and part of a trend of cumbersome government regulations, including new environmental standards. Engineering constraints and requirements are not addressed in these contexts.

One Internet governance and engineering argument against a broad net neutrality regulation is that some traffic discrimination is necessary as a routine part of network management. Achieving an acceptable level of quality of service (QoS) and reliability is an engineering requirement for any communication system. A traditional telecommunications industry metric has always been "five nines" of reliability, meaning that a telephone system should be available to a user 99.999 percent of the time. This translates into only a five-minute outage per year. Contrast this to a system with a 99 percent availability level, which sounds adequate but translates into roughly four days of outages per year, which is completely unacceptable to most subscribers. Well-engineered and managed networks exhibit high reliability, meaning that a system is available when someone needs it, and high performance, meaning that information is transmitted in a timely manner to its destination with minimal signal degradation or information loss. Streaming video and voice over the Internet requires two QoS features that distinguish these applications from lower bandwidth services such as email and routine web browsing. Video streaming and voice calls require high bandwidth and minimal transmission delays.

Every communication technology produces an inherent time delay in the transmission of information. A slight delay in delivering an email to someone's inbox would be imperceptible. Even a one-second delay in receiving a text message or email would probably not be noticeable. In contrast, a one-second delay in a voice conversation would be excruciating.

Those who have experienced the inherent delay of an international satellite call understand this limitation. Voice conversations over the traditional circuit-switched telephone network, as with all communication transmissions, produce a very slight delay. But this delay is imperceptible to the two parties participating in the conversation. Transmitting voice conversations or streaming video over the Internet's underlying packet switching method raises specific engineering challenges.

Applications such as email and voice calls have different transmission characteristics. A continuous voice conversation is considered "synchronous," meaning literally "with time." The traditional telephone system design responds to the synchronous, continuous nature of voice communications. Recall that this "circuit switching" architecture establishes a dedicated end-to-end network path between the two callers and that this path remains open, or dedicated, for the duration of the call. In contrast to synchronous traffic, communication activities such as sending an email or downloading a file are "asynchronous," meaning literally "without time." A dedicated path throughout a network does not need to be held open while someone is composing an email, for example. Only when the email is transmitted does it occupy network resources. Even then, a dedicated path is not established. Rather, it is broken up into smaller pieces called packets, which are transmitted along different paths and reassembled at their destination.

This packet switching approach introduces certain QoS challenges.[15] First, a small percentage of packets are "dropped" along the way, either when a segment of a network becomes overwhelmed with volume or when a signal degrades to the point where the packet is lost. When this occurs, the network tells the originating device to retransmit the affected packets. This retransmission introduces two features that do not adversely affect asynchronous information such as email but that affect real-time, synchronous traffic such as voice. These characteristics are "clipping," meaning a small but noticeable loss of parts of a voice conversation and "jitter," meaning degradation in the quality of a call produced by timing variations in the arrival of packets. Retransmission of packets can also introduce delays when audio information is digitally encoded or decoded as well as during each "hop," meaning when packets traverse a router.

The delay between the time when one person speaks and the other person hears this speech is called latency. One argument against the net neutrality principle is that voice calls, because they are more adversely affected by network latency, should be assigned transmission priority relative to applications not sensitive to this delay.

Another engineering question related to network discrimination is how to handle applications that require enormous amounts of bandwidth. Just to provide a "back of the envelope" description of how much bandwidth an application such as a movie requires when streamed, consider the following example. Each frame (single image) of a movie can use 512 by 512 pixels, with each pixel assigned a 9-bit binary code. The number of bits (os and 1s) representing just a single frame is therefore $512 \times 512 \times 9$, or 2,359,296, bits. If, in a movie, there are twenty-four frames shown per second so that the user perceives perpetual moving video, then each second of the movie contains $24 \times 2,359,296$, or 56,623,104, bits. This is an enormous amount of information to stream per second. Compression techniques reduce the amount of information to transmit or store. Networks also attempt to handle this by buffering information during streaming, meaning introducing a slight delay in viewing a video so that any latency introduced during the transmission of packets is not detected by users.

Bandwidth-intensive applications and time-sensitive applications create net neutrality dilemmas. If a user is streaming an enormous amount of bandwidth consuming information such as video, to the point that this bandwidth consumption affects the quality experience of other users, should this consumptive usage be throttled back to ensure higher performance for other users? Similarly, when time-sensitive information such as a voice call is sent over the Internet, should this latency-dependent traffic be prioritized over other traffic types not as susceptible to latency, jitter, and other QoS features? These traffic engineering questions raise reasonable cases for discrimination based on uniformly prioritizing time-sensitive information or ensuring equitable bandwidth for those paying the same amount for network access.

As the examples of discriminatory practices above indicate, controversial cases of discrimination have more routinely occurred not based on "type" of traffic as described here, but based on either the origination of that traffic, the content of that traffic, or the degree to which information competes with a prevailing business model. Nevertheless, this section has explained why routine network management practices could necessitate, from a traffic engineering perspective, certain forms of consistently applied packet discrimination.

Freedom of Expression, Innovation, and the Role of Government
First Amendment attorney Marvin Ammori has described net neutrality as "one of the most pressing First Amendment questions of our time."[16] Net neutrality is related to First Amendment values because of its fundamental idea of freedom of speech for anyone transmitting lawful material over the Internet. The idea is to prevent censorship of online material by the network operators—such as cable and telecommunications companies—that serve as citizens' access gateways into the global Internet. Freedom of expression advocates would argue that criticizing China for censoring Internet transmissions abroad would be an anemic argument for those who in turn argue for the ability of companies to block Internet speech at home in the absence of net neutrality regulation. Common carriage rules were enacted, in part, so that a telecommunications operator could not exploit its control over the lawful information flowing over its network. Net neutrality advocates consider this principle an issue of free speech. The digital sphere is the public sphere and the highest ideal of net neutrality is to ensure that a private company mediating a user's access to this public sphere cannot control the information the user chooses to transmit. Conversely, some opponents of the net neutrality principle have argued that imposing nondiscrimination rules could violate freedom of speech rights of network operators to be able to act as editors over what material is carried over their network.

In practice and implementation, the net neutrality question is not only about principles of Internet freedom but about the debate, as Barbara van Schewick describes it, "over *whether governments should establish rules* limiting the extent to which network providers can interfere with the applications and content on their networks."[17] Does net neutrality amount to governments "regulating the Internet?" Those concerned about government regulations constraining the actions of Internet access providers are often concerned about the government tampering with the success and trajectory of the Internet. In contrast, net neutrality advocates describe these rules as preventing a considerable change to how the Internet already works with consumers traditionally able to access whatever information they want over their Internet connection. There has been a strong history of cyberlibertarianism advocating for keeping the Internet free from government regulation and this strain has entered into global debates about net neutrality rules. The basic argument is that market choice is preferable to government regulation.

Net neutrality advocates argue that the Internet's historical tradition of access neutrality has actually created a level playing field for innovation and competition. One can only speculate about whether there would be the enormous choices in Internet applications and content sites if telecommunications providers routinely handled the traffic from these sites in a nonneutral manner. Conversely, there is an innovation argument against net neutrality, including concerns that government regulations and restrictions would prevent network operators from differentiating their services. Some types of applications require higher quality of service. Limiting how network operators can achieve the necessary level of performance could potentially stifle innovations geared toward high performance for new bandwidth-intensive applications. This is an argument often cited among those who believe wireless services should be immune from network neutrality legislation. Wireless services, especially for smartphones, are a rapidly evolving area of innovation and also an area with natural radiofrequency constraints.

THE NONNEUTRALITY OF NET NEUTRALITY

Net neutrality is one of the few Internet policy areas with clear jurisdictional boundaries. Whereas many Internet governance questions are fraught with transnational legitimacy complexities because the technologies in question cross national boundaries, net neutrality is a local issue. Therefore, different nations have taken different approaches to net neutrality. Net neutrality debates are playing out in venues around the world but, in the United States, specific issues have included the First Amendment implications of net neutrality, the issue of reclassifying Internet broadband as "transport," controversies over the appropriate role of the FCC, and debates about whether wireless and wired broadband should be treated differently. This has been one of the more hotly contested Internet policy issues in the United States, with too long a history to describe fully here. Back in 2005, the FCC adopted four open Internet principles designed to promote open and accessible broadband Internet access in the United States. The principles were designed to accomplish the following (verbatim from an FCC policy statement):

- To encourage broadband deployment and preserve and promote the open and interconnected nature of the public Internet, consumers are entitled to access the lawful Internet content of their choice.
- To encourage broadband deployment and preserve and promote the open and interconnected nature of the public Internet, consumers are entitled to run applications and use services of their choice, subject to the needs of law enforcement.
- To encourage broadband deployment and preserve and promote the open and interconnected nature of the public Internet, consumers are entitled to connect their choice of legal devices that do not harm the network.
- To encourage broadband deployment and preserve and promote the open and interconnected nature of the public Internet, consumers are entitled to competition among network providers, application and service providers, and content providers.[18]

The FCC later adopted Open Internet Rules more formally prohibiting blocking and unreasonable discrimination, though immediately challenged in ongoing court cases. In the United States and other parts of the world, the issue of net neutrality is somewhat unresolved.

Deliberations about Internet governance controversies are often exercises in framing the construction of language to achieve certain interpretive effects in media discourses and public opinion. So it is with network neutrality. Although the goals of network neutrality are important for the future of the Internet, its rhetorical framing and the rigidity of arguments on both sides create unconstructive positions that weaken the efficacy of the net neutrality discourse as currently formulated.

First, the language of "neutrality" is itself problematic. The term implies a state of being in which an entity or artifact does not take sides. It also implies a degree of inaction. From a governance perspective, net neutrality requires an act of policymakers establishing rules that restrict, to various degrees, the ability of network operators to intervene in the flow of packets over their own networks. In this sense, net neutrality does not imply governmental neutrality in not taking sides between interests for and against net neutrality policies. Rather, the term "neutrality" refers to the expectation that network operators will not be permitted to take action in prioritizing certain packets over others.

The expectation embedded in policy is that technology remains neutral. The scholarly field of science and technology studies has challenged such conceptions of "neutral technologies and neutral science," demonstrating the values that construct the design of technologies or even choices about what scientific knowledge is pursued. Neutrality is itself a value judgment. Philosophers of science and technology examine the relationship between objectivity, neutrality, and normalization in information production. Philosopher of science Sandra Harding explains: "The neutrality ideal functions more through what its normalizing procedures and concepts implicitly prioritize than through explicit directives."[19] Value neutrality is not possible because neutrality embeds prevailing normative values. As Harding's work summarizes, "The point is that maximizing cultural neutrality, not to mention claiming it, is itself a culturally specific value."[20]

It would be helpful to have a reformulation of the net neutrality debate that acknowledges the nonneutrality of technology, that incorporates a more credible understanding of network management and engineering, and that applies a logically consistent approach to both wired and wireless technologies. Examining these values requires a rejection of the possibility of neutrality and rather a making visible of cultural constructs already reflected in these norms. As this chapter has suggested, net neutrality is not neutral but represents a set of values. Many of these are historical values embedded in the design of the Internet's architecture, such as engineering user choice about what information to access and creating a level playing field for the introduction of new information products. These design values of individual freedom and economic competition are emphasized throughout this book, but not under the guise of neutrality.

The economic and political stakes of net neutrality policies are reflected in the titanic battles among content providers versus network operators and free expression versus free market advocates. The stakes are equally high for cable and telecommunications companies seeking to preserve their traditional business models and content providers wanting consumers to be able to download their content without access provider-introduced latencies or blockages.

One unresolved question about the net neutrality principle is the arbitrary distinction that has sometimes been made regarding the applicability of discrimination rules to information accessed via a wired connection (for example, cable, fiber, twisted pair) versus wireless (cellular). There has traditionally been one universal Internet with the goal of making all Internet content accessible from any device. However, the FCC's open Internet rules chose to suggest that the same openness requirements for wired, landline access are not required for wireless. By wireless, proponents of differential treatment for wired versus wireless mean only cellular tower-based wireless rather than Wi-Fi access, which is provisioned from a wired access subscription. In other words, the FCC means mobile wireless rather than fixed wireless. As the FCC has asserted, "mobile broadband presents special considerations that suggest differences in how and when open Internet protections should apply."[21]

The FCC suggests several rationales for treating mobile broadband differently from fixed wired broadband. First, mobile broadband is in an early state of development relative to traditional fixed broadband, which originated with dial-up before progressing to Digital Subscriber Line (xDSL), cable, and fiber access. In contrast, mobile broadband access until years into the twenty-first century was primarily relegated to voice calls and text messaging or stripped-down web access. In this regard, mobile broadband is in a much earlier and rapidly evolving and growing cycle of broadband access innovation. Moreover, in some areas there are more mobile choices than fixed wireline broadband, although this varies considerably throughout the world. As a rough generality, and in average metropolitan areas, citizens sometimes have two broadband fixed-subscription options from homes: cable and telecom companies. In contrast, metropolitan areas can have three or four wireless providers from which users can select services. Finally, broadband mobile speeds tend to be lower than fixed wireline access, introducing the possible requirement for more extensive network management and possible QoS prioritization.

Because of the distinguishing characteristics of wireless, the FCC open Internet rules on mobile broadband openness included only the requirement of disclosure of network management practices and a no-blocking requirement prohibiting broadband wireless providers from blocking voice, video, and other applications that compete with the providers' primary service offerings.

Prior to the release of these open Internet rules, Google and Verizon teamed up to issue a similar policy recommendation advocating different net neutrality treatment for wireless and wired access. The companies' policy recommendations, which they dubbed "Verizon-Google Legislative Framework Proposal," laid out requirements for broadband Internet access providers related to nondiscrimination requirements, transparency, network management, and prohibitions on blocking user access to lawful content. Although the Verizon-Google proposal seems like a strong statement about net neutrality, one salient feature of their recommendation is that the principles for which they advocate should not apply to wireless broadband. The proposal states:

> Because of the unique technical and operational characteristics
> of wireless networks, and the competitive and still-developing
> nature of wireless broadband services, only the transparency
> principle would apply to wireless broadband at this time.
> The US Government Accountability Office would report to
> Congress annually on the continued development and robust-
> ness of wireless broadband Internet access services.[22]

From a governance standpoint, the production of legislative recommendations by private industry fits into a larger political narrative about the role of various industries, for example the banking industry, and private entities, generally, in setting government policy. What should the role of private actors be in setting information policy? In the information policy space, private industry establishes policies in the design of technical architecture, in contracts and terms of service with subscribers, and in influence over government policy. From the specific standpoint of net neutrality policy, the obvious question is whether these exemptions for wireless would lead to exactly the phenomenon net neutrality rules seek to prohibit—access providers charging content providers for prioritized delivery to customers rather than customers choosing which lawful information to access and expecting that broadband subscriptions enable this access without content-based discrimination. The businesses of new entrepreneurs could potentially succeed or fail depending on the priority access providers would afford to these start-ups. The effects of any wireless broadband exemption from net neutrality will yet be seen.

On either side of the debate, very few are satisfied with the current state of open Internet rules. Harvard Law School professor Larry Lessig has commented that "policymakers, using an economics framework set in the 1980s, convinced of its truth and too arrogant to even recognize its ignorance, will allow the owners of the 'tubes' to continue to unmake the Internet—precisely the effect of Google and Verizon's 'policy framework.' "[23]

Cato Institute director of information policy studies Jim Harper described the Verizon-Google legislative statement as " 'regulatory capture' in which a government agency falls under the control of the business sector it is supposed to regulate" and suggested that "the FCC should just go away."[24]

Some have criticized net neutrality policy as not going far enough to preserve the traditional openness of the Internet; others view it as an overreach of government into regulating the Internet industry and addressing a problem that does not yet exist. Given that most sides are unhappy with the state of net neutrality, it is possible that the current state provides an adequate state of equilibrium to balance out these forces. Routine network management practices require some prioritization of traffic in order to provide adequate performance and reliability. This type of prioritization is not content-specific. It may be traffic-specific, meaning prioritizing voice or video over text, for example. But it does not prioritize the contents of one voice call over another, for example. Current net neutrality discussions also call for transparency of these practices, a significant step forward in terms of customers making informed market choices. The battles that are likely to continue, however, relate to three areas: debates over the prospect of content-specific discrimination; the appropriateness of differential treatment of mobile wireless versus wired broadband access; and the role of specific government agencies in overseeing broadband Internet access. However one defines it, neutrality is not neutral.

CHAPTER SEVEN

The Public Policy Role of Private Information Intermediaries

DURING THE 2012 Olympic Games in London, Twitter suspended the personal account of British journalist Guy Adams. The reporter was a Los Angeles–based correspondent for the British newspaper *The Independent* and was using his personal Twitter account to post tweets criticizing NBC's coverage of the games. Adams disliked the time delay before the U.S. public could view major Olympic events as well as the editing that he believed NBC carried out to add suspense to gymnastics and other popular events. Adams also tweeted the email address of an NBC executive so that the public could send complaints about the broadcast delays. Twitter claimed that it suspended the reporter's account at the request of NBC after the tweet that publicized this executive's company email address, claiming that this act was a violation of Twitter rules.

Twitter's suspension of the journalist's account sparked an incendiary public response both on Twitter and in other social media and journalistic outlets. Part of the public frustration stemmed from concern that Twitter's actions were influenced by its cross-promotional business partnership with NBC during the Olympics.[1] After a matter of only days, Twitter restored the journalist's account. Twitter's general counsel acknowledged that it was actually a Twitter employee who proactively identified the offending tweet and encouraged NBC to file a support ticket.

The general counsel clarified that "this behavior is not acceptable and undermines the trust our users have in us. We should not and cannot be in the business of proactively monitoring and flagging content, no matter who the user is—whether a business partner, celebrity or friend."[2]

The private companies that serve as content intermediaries, such as social media platforms and search engines, have a great deal of power over the global flow of information. They have the ability to terminate an individual's account or take down specific content. The end user agreements they contractually enact with subscribers establish policies in areas as diverse as individual privacy, freedom of expression, and cyberbullying.

The challenges of these privatized forms of governance over individual civil liberties are escalating. In the opening decades of the Internet, there were few intermediaries such as search engines or social media platforms and the traditional end-to-end architectural principle of Internet design specified that intelligence should be located at network endpoints rather than at intermediary points.[3] As recently as 1990, digital platforms Google, Facebook, Amazon, eBay, YouTube, and Twitter did not yet exist. More significantly, the web did not yet exist. The Internet's primary uses in this context were text-based email, file sharing, and discussion boards. The advent of the web and home Internet access in the early 1990s brought with it a wave of Internet users and online content, which ushered in an opportunity for third parties to index and organize this content in a variety of ways.

Internet intermediaries are third-party platforms that mediate between digital content and the humans who contribute and access this content. These intermediaries are usually private for-profit companies that do not provision actual content but rather facilitate information or financial transactions among those who provide and access content. They also are not, in their primary function, concerned with the infrastructural transport of this content. Infrastructure intermediaries handle the transmission of information from point A to point B. Traditional network operators are infrastructure intermediaries but are not included in this discussion because they have been addressed elsewhere in this book. Although there is nothing fixed about this distinction, information intermediaries directly manipulate or distribute content or facilitate transactions among users and content. Examples of information intermediaries include:

- search engines
- social media platforms
- blogging platforms
- content aggregation sites
- reputation engines
- financial intermediaries
- transactional intermediaries
- trust intermediaries
- application intermediaries
- locational intermediaries
- advertising intermediaries.

These types of services are primarily manipulating content—sorting, ranking, aggregating, sharing—or facilitating transactions. Communication scholar Tarleton Gillespie notes that these companies often refer to themselves as "platforms," a discursive term "specific enough to mean something and vague enough to work across multiple venues for multiple audiences."[4] Some companies perform a single function, such as a news aggregation site like Drudge Report. Many companies, and particularly Google, simultaneously traverse many of these functions, such as content aggregation (YouTube, Google News, Google Books), social media (Google+, Orkut), blogging platforms (Blogger), and the Google search engine.

To contemplate the types of information intermediaries that are possible in the future, it is helpful to recall the accelerated rise of this class of Internet company. Google has stated that its mission is to "organize the world's information and make it universally accessible and useful."[5] Google is obviously much more than a search engine but search was its original mission when it incorporated in 1998. Initially, there was no need for web search engines such as Google, Yahoo!, Baidu, and Bing because of the manageable number of web sites. In 1989 at the CERN high-energy physics laboratory in Geneva, British computer scientist Tim Berners-Lee had introduced a system of hyperlinked information sharing intended to enable the exchange of research information among servers at research facilities around the world. This system, based on standard protocols and hypertext-based information retrieval, became what was later called the World Wide Web. There are screenshots online of the small but growing list of web servers that Tim Berners-Lee tracked in 1992. As this list rapidly grew, there needed to be some way to sort, index, and locate these sites. Eventually, search engines were able to access pages written in web markup languages like HTML using automated web crawlers that browse the content of pages, extract words, titles, multimedia, and meta tags and store this information in massive indices.

Content aggregation sites have evolved just as quickly. These intermediaries serve as repositories that collect and present information, especially user-generated content like YouTube videos or Flickr images. This information aggregation can also include corporate media content such as news aggregation sites or commercial video distribution sites such as Hulu. These intermediaries do not produce content. They either provide a platform for others to post content or aggregate content from other online (or sometimes offline) spaces and present this material in an organized and searchable format. They provide value in several ways: either by offering an easy-to-use platform for Internet users to upload and share their own content in a way that is searchable and universally accessible; by providing a sorting and indexing service that weeds through large volumes of information, such as news, and presents a smaller amount of relevant information to its target audience; or by connecting suppliers and consumers of commercial media with a platform for the consumption of these media in real time.

Content intermediaries have become the front lines of challenging governance issues in cyberspace. These companies, through their terms of service agreements with users and through the daily decisions they have to make about objectionable or possibly illegal content, are determining some of the most complicated policy questions of the modern era. They navigate difficult social problems related to cyberbullying and online harassment and determine whether to block content that has incited violence and religious hatred. They respond (or do not respond) to law enforcement requests from around the world asking them to divulge information about subscribers.

In addition to this inherent content mediation and policing function, these companies rely on business models in which they collect and aggregate information about users and often share this information with third-party advertising companies. The privacy and data-gathering practices of content intermediaries are themselves a form of policymaking. They are subject to the rules of the jurisdictions in which they operate, but privacy laws often fail to keep up with or understand new forms of technologically mediated data collection.

Although information intermediaries hold a great deal of power in controlling the flow of content online and the extent of user rights to access this content, at the same time, they often have immunity from liability for the content that flows through their platforms. The extent of immunity from legal liability varies by jurisdiction and is subject to constraints and conditions. However, in many democratic societies, the normative societal stance on the legal responsibility of content intermediaries for the content flowing through their sites leans toward immunity. This model of not holding intermediaries accountable for the content that is hosted, sorted, or indexed by the intermediary is an important incentive for innovation and for access to knowledge more generally. Very little of the web would be searchable if search engine companies could be readily sued for information contained on the pages linked from search engine results. There would be very few information aggregation sites if information repositories could be sued for copyright infringement or defamation based on hosted content. There are, however, specific quid pro quo conditions for immunity. For example, immunity in the area of intellectual property rights violations is usually contingent on the implementation of a notice and takedown procedure, discussed in the next chapter.

The following sections discuss how information intermediaries perform several regulatory functions including: the privatization of the conditions of freedom of expression; the establishment of individual privacy rights; and the mediation of cyberbullying and other forms of reputational harm.

THE PRIVATIZATION OF FREEDOM OF EXPRESSION

Private intermediaries have increasingly become the arbiters of online expressive liberty. This arbitration of freedom of expression occurs in several ways. Information aggregators and other platforms receive a constant barrage of government requests to censor content, whether for political gain, law enforcement, or other reason. The phenomenon of a company removing user content at the behest of a government is known as delegated censorship, a subject treated in detail in Chapter 9. Companies also choose to take down or block specific content for other reasons including concerns about reputational harm to the institution or values and norms embedded in end user agreements. Private adjudication of expression can also be enacted through gatekeeping of the apps and software the user is permitted to access via platform-specific repositories (for example, Apple's App Store) operated by the private intermediary. Finally, transactional and financial intermediaries have the autonomy to cease providing these services to customers or sites they find objectionable or which violate the terms of their end user licensing agreements. The following explains these distinct contexts in which private ordering, rather than (or in addition to) laws, norms, or governments, determines the conditions of freedom of expression in the public sphere.

Discretionary Censorship

A terrorist assault on the U.S. diplomatic mission in Benghazi, Libya resulted in the killing of United States ambassador Chris Stevens and three other Americans.[6] The attack occurred contemporaneous with widespread protests in Muslim countries over an amateurish video posted on YouTube. The independently produced video, "The Innocence of Muslims," was a short, low-budget film that incensed communities of Muslims and resulted in widespread rioting. In the wake of this violence and rioting and according to Google's Transparency Report, the company received inquiries about the video from twenty countries, seventeen of which requested that the company remove the associated videos. The company declined to do so. The United States government asked Google to review the relevant YouTube clips to assess whether they violated the company's Community Guidelines. Google determined that the video clips did not constitute a violation of guidelines and therefore did not remove the film, although it did temporarily restrict access to the video in Egypt and Libya.[7] Back in 2007, Google had published an official company blog posting on the question of freedom of expression and controversial content. The following is an excerpt:

At Google we have a bias in favor of people's right to free expression in everything we do. We are driven by a belief that more information generally means more choice, more freedom and ultimately more power for the individual. But we also recognize that freedom of expression can't be—and shouldn't be—without some limits. The difficulty is in deciding where those boundaries are drawn. For a company like Google with services in more than 100 countries—all with different national laws and cultural norms—it's a challenge we face many times every day.[8]

In some cases, information intermediaries comply with the unique laws of each country, such as blocking access to Nazi content in Germany. In other cases, as Google's policy indicates, companies "face questions about whether a country's laws and lack of democratic processes are so antithetical to our principles that we simply can't comply or can't operate there in a way that benefits users."[9]

Although companies are subject to the laws in the various jurisdictions in which they operate, there is a significant discrepancy between the number of requests they receive from governments and the number of requests they actually carry out. This differential illustrates the discretionary policy role private companies assume. The "Innocence of Muslims" video case highlights the intractable challenges that companies face in trying to strike a balance between the often conflicting variables of their own content guidelines, government requests, public perception, and concern about both freedom of expression and public safety.

Private intermediaries perform a governance function when they enact censorship (either requested by a government or of their own volition) or carry out a law enforcement function. Even more so, they wield significant governance power when they use their discretionary authority to *not* carry out censorship requests.

App Censorship
Discretionary censorship is not always directed at specific content but at the applications that serve as gatekeepers to controversial or objectionable material. In the personal computer world, individuals generally select the types of applications to install on their computers and the content

they wish to download. In the era of smartphones and tablets, this is not always the case. As Jonathan Zittrain explains in *The Future of the Internet and How to Stop It*, "These technologies can let geeky outsiders build upon them just as they could with PCs, but in a highly controlled and contingent way. This is iPhone 2.0: an iPod on steroids with a thriving market for software written by outsiders that must be funneled through Apple."[10] Apple has a great deal of discretionary control over the third-party developed apps that appear in its App Store. The same is true with applications developed for other platforms, such as the Android platform or Facebook. The private companies controlling the online application stores for their products filter which apps to include or not to include. When a company decides to block or remove an app from its store, the effect is not only to block the application but to block the content to which the application connects. One can easily envision rationales for a company to block an app: anticompetitive motivations to suppress the popularity of a rival company's service; technical concerns about apps that create security or performance problems; or social concerns about apps that promote violence or bigotry.

Apple reviews every app before approving it for its online store. It also provides "App Store Review Guidelines" containing specific technical constraints such as maximum size and interface design features, as well as social policy constraints related to everything from defamation and offensive material to privacy. Some of the guidelines are interpretatively subjective enough to provide the company with broad discretion to reject apps it deems inappropriate.

Some of this mediation occurs after an app has already been included in an app store, either because of user complaints, government requests, or in response to some controversy. For example, Apple decided to remove a Hezbollah-related application from its online store. The Anti-Defamation League praised the company for this action, stating, "We commend Apple for removing the app from the iTunes store and appreciate their vigilance in ensuring that terrorist-affiliated organizations will not have access to Apple's customers."[11]

Companies filtering the apps available on their platforms exercise considerable discretion about what applications to allow in the first instance, as well as determining when to remove an app that it has already approved. Whereas governments, in many jurisdictions, are subject to legal restraints on what speech they can prohibit (such as the First Amendment to the Constitution in the United States), private companies are not subject to the same constraints.

Transactional and Financial Blocking of Sites

A number of information mediation controversies arose out of the release of U.S. diplomatic cables by WikiLeaks, an online repository for the publication of news and information, often anonymously sourced. During this so-called Cablegate incident, a great deal of attention centered around the content and data WikiLeaks published. Content-focused concerns centered on national security, the protection of diplomats, and the question of how to define a free press in the digital age. For example, the media debated whether what Wikileaks did was comparable to what the *New York Times* does and what press freedoms, if any, should apply.

Although these content questions are critical, a different set of controversies and battles occurred at the level of infrastructure governance and intermediation. EveryDNS, the institution providing WikiLeaks with free DNS resolution services, decided to terminate these services, essentially disrupting WikiLeaks's online presence. The WikiLeaks site had been the target of extensive denial of service attacks and EveryDNS claimed that it terminated service to WikiLeaks in accordance with its acceptable use policy so that the DDoS attacks would not affect services to other customers. Amazon similarly cited its terms of service as a justification to discontinue hosting the WikiLeaks web site on its servers because of the publishing of materials that could endanger individuals.[12] The company specifically explained that it had made its decision independently of any perceived government pressure to block WikiLeaks: "There have been reports that a government inquiry prompted us not to serve WikiLeaks any longer. That is inaccurate."[13] WikiLeaks was able to quickly establish an online presence at wikileaks.ch, but this example serves as a reminder of the concentrated power of private ordering, rather than governmental forces, in determining who is allowed an online presence.

Financial intermediaries also privately made decisions to interrupt the flow of funding to WikiLeaks because of the controversy.[14] As an example, PayPal stated that it was permanently restricting the account used by WikiLeaks because of a violation of the PayPal Acceptable Use

Policy prohibiting use of its payment service for any sites that encourage illegal activity. PayPal's general counsel suggested that the company made this decision after the U.S. Department of State released a statement that WikiLeaks possessed documents provided in violation of U.S. law.[15] The general counsel also stated that PayPal was not contacted by any government organization but rather restricted the account based on its Acceptable Use Policy review.

In an information society, the ability to delete an online presence or stop the flow of money to a site is significant power. There are concentrated control points online and these points of control are in the hands of private industry.

INTERMEDIARY PRIVACY GOVERNANCE

Buying a diamond ring as a Christmas present was once a straightforward affair. After a Massachusetts resident purchased a diamond ring for his wife on the online shopping site Overstock.com, a headline spontaneously appeared on his Facebook page announcing that he had purchased a "14k White Gold 1/5ct Diamond Eternity Flower Ring from Overstock.com."[16] His purchase was publicly broadcast to his Facebook friends, including his wife, ruining the surprise and otherwise creating an awkward situation. Other Facebook account holders discovered that their purchases, including simple activities like buying a movie ticket or viewing a video, also appeared on their account pages.

Social networking companies provide free services to users and thus depend on online advertising revenues for profitability. The success of online advertising depends on the ability to target ads to potential customers based on individual demographics, spending power, and consumer preferences. Systems of online advertising are predicated on the ability to understand consumer data gathered by information intermediaries, such as search engines and social media platforms.

The Christmas present saga arose from an online advertising initiative called Beacon that Facebook had implemented with forty-four partner organizations. Beacon sought to profit from "social advertising," the notion that someone's actions and purchases can exert influence on those connected to them via social networking platforms. Facebook's Beacon partners represented some of the leading online transactional or informational sites of their time including Blockbuster, CBS Interactive, eBay, Fandango, NYTimes.com, Yelp, and the Wedding Channel.[17] When a Facebook member made a transaction on one of these partner sites, that action would trigger a Beacon script (basically a list of computing commands) that resulted in certain actions such as notifying Facebook of the transaction. Examples of transactions that might trigger such a script included posting a comment, submitting a review, placing an order, or viewing a page. The presence of "cookies" in the individual's computer would identify the individual as a Facebook member. Cookies are small amounts of data transmitted between a web server and browser when someone visits a site. For example, visiting Facebook could trigger the transmission of a unique number to the member's computer. This number would identify the computing device as being associated with a Facebook member. If the user making a transaction on one of the partner sites is determined to be a Facebook member, Facebook could trigger a pop-up screen on the user's computer, presumably alerting the user that information about his or her action would be sent to the user's Facebook page. One of the distinguishing features of this approach was that Facebook would be able to engage with its members through a third-party site even if the members did not have Facebook open at the time.

Issues of trust, sociability, and reputation are motivationally at the heart of consumer purchasing decisions. The idea behind social advertising is to persuade a consumer to make purchasing decisions via the influence of the purchases made by those in the consumer's social network. Facebook had provided a privacy control setting for users to disable the new feature but this protection mechanism was "opt out" rather than "opt in." Beacon features would remain activated unless a Facebook user took action so the default was publicity rather than privacy. Furthermore, there did not appear to be a universal opt out. Facebook users would have to opt out on every partner site they visited. The problem with this approach was that a consumer making a transaction might forget to opt out in every instance or might not even see the opt-out pop-up, possibly due to technical parameters such as a slow screen load.

After roughly a month of initial controversy over Beacon, Facebook founder Mark Zuckerberg issued an apology conceding that Facebook "simply did a bad job with the release" and announcing that the company had changed Beacon to an opt-in system and offered a privacy control whereby people could disable Beacon entirely.[18] A number of Facebook members who claimed to have been adversely affected by Beacon subsequently filed a class-action lawsuit against both Facebook and its partner organizations.[19] The Beacon lawsuit was settled in September 2009, with Facebook agreeing to pay $9.5 million to fund a trust geared toward online privacy issues, as well as terminating the overall Beacon system.

This is a particular case of more general questions about the role of information intermediaries in setting privacy policy: What are the tensions between the right of publicity versus the right of privacy; what consumer data are collected by companies and how are these shared; is there adequate transparency; what laws, across national jurisdictions, apply at the intersection of online transactions and individual privacy; what are the necessary business models for free platforms to be profitable; what power do citizens and advocacy groups have to resist possibly objectionable platform design choices?

While using some content intermediaries, there can be the perception of personal privacy while behind the scenes, various types of data are collected and shared. In other environments, individuals voluntarily contribute personal information about themselves and others with the expectation that it will be seen, even if only within the individual's network of friends. Many of these platforms, including Facebook, also have real identification requirements in which anonymous communication or the use of a pseudonym is not permissible.

Social media products like Foursquare are designed to provide information about an individual's location as well as what the individual is doing. There are almost no technical limitations on determining someone's location, whether via a GPS, Wi-Fi location, or cellular triangulation and this locational capability is increasingly becoming integrated with other features. Some of these applications have seemed overly invasive of individual privacy, such as "Girls around Me," an application considered "creepy" because it used locational information and social media data to identify nearby women.

The ways in which information is presented or shared within a site and changes to this presentation also affect the conditions of privacy. Facebook's Beacon episode falls into this category of a platform-initiated change to the conditions of privacy within the social media platform. These changes in architecture create changes in personal publicity and identity. Another example was Facebook's shift to a Timeline layout depicting activity in reverse chronological order. The information itself had not changed, but the layout modification exposed information about people and their pasts in a way that altered conditions of publicity. Part of the relevant privacy policy enactment involves the decision about whether changes to privacy conditions should be opt in or opt out by a user and which should be the default setting.

Disclosing Personal Information

Another mode of intermediary privacy governance involves the gatekeeping role companies assume in responding, or not responding, to government requests for information about individual subscribers. Posting personal information to one's social media space carries an assumption that only those invited into one's network will view the information. Viewing a YouTube video seems like a private action. Searching for medical information about a recently diagnosed condition in the privacy of one's living room seems like a private action. Behind the scenes, companies operating intermediating platforms receive requests from governments and law enforcement for personal information about individuals or their online activities.

In 2002 and 2004, Yahoo! received negative publicity for relinquishing personal information to Chinese authorities about two of its users who were pro-democracy Chinese dissidents. The Chinese government sentenced the men to ten years in prison. Yahoo! apologized for the disclosure and settled a lawsuit the families of the dissidents filed in the U.S. District Court for the Northern District of California. Since that time, information intermediaries have received ever-increasing requests to divulge information about subscribers and have had to make case-by-case determinations about what information to relinquish.

The Fourth Amendment to the United States Constitution states that "The Right of the people to be secure in their persons, houses, papers, and effects, against unreasonable searches and seizures, shall not be violated, and no Warrants shall issue, but upon probable cause." In the global quagmire of Internet governance, circumscribing such rights is more complicated than in offline worlds. The determination of what constitutes a valid or legal request often rests with the private companies confronted with these requests. As economic and social life continues to move online, the number of demands these private companies receive for information about their subscribers is steadily increasing.

Google's Transparency Report discloses information about user data requests the company receives from governments. Over a six-month period, Google received U.S. law enforcement demands for information related to 12,243 users or accounts and complied with 93 percent of these; it received requests from Russian government authorities for sixty-five users or accounts and complied with none of these; it received from German officials requests for user data on 2,027 users or accounts and complied with 45 percent of these.[20] Like other information intermediaries, Google is in the position of having to field these ever increasing inquiries and determine the extent of its compliance with each request. As the company summarizes, "The number of requests we receive for user account information as part of criminal investigations has increased year after year."[21]

Divulging Subscriber Information for Online Advertising
Almost all information intermediaries rely on online advertising as part (or all) of their business model. Online advertising is not a monolithic practice. Some ads are classified properties such as Craigslist or "advertainment" videos on YouTube that seem like entertainment but are advertisements. Four general types of online advertising approaches require the capture of data about either an individual or the content being exchanged—contextual, behavioral, locational, and social advertising. Each approach requires different levels of data retention and aggregation and the gathering of distinct types of data about individuals.

Contextual advertising delivers promotional materials customized to the content gathered around the ad delivery screen. For example, a contextually targeted ad for "used textbooks" might appear alongside an email discussing an undergraduate's upcoming class schedule. Ads for swimwear might materialize on a social media page that announces a family vacation to Hawaii. The ad is delivered based on the context-specific acquisition of data.

Behavioral advertising delivers ads based on user activity and behavior over time, such as web sites visited, ad conversions, and click-throughs or types of recent online purchases. This type of customized online advertising is routine practice, relying on the collection, aggregation, and retention of personal data about an individual over time and across platforms as a way to determine personal consumer preferences.

Locational advertising involves the delivery of advertising, whether to a mobile device or fixed Internet connection, based on the geographical location of the individual. Location-specific information is readily available. The network portion of an individual's IP address provides some general information about the individual's location. A mobile phone with a GPS can pinpoint exact location data. A Wi-Fi connection paints a fairly bounded picture of someone's location, as does triangulation based on proximity to cellular antennas. With this prolifically available locational data about individuals, delivering a targeted ad for a nearby restaurant is technically trivial.

Finally, *social advertising* involves the delivery of ads based on who an individual is voluntarily linked to via social networking platforms or the utilization of these connections to deliver stealth ads that are not actually ads but are publicized information about an individual's preferences or purchases, such as the Facebook Beacon example already described.

Whether or not Internet users are aware of the level of behind-the-scenes data analysis and tracking that occurs, the reality is that almost everyone is tracked in a number of ways. Some of the collected information, based on what intermediaries themselves disclose, includes telephone numbers, IP addresses, tracking cookies, third-party cookies, and unique hardware device numbers. Because of the hidden complexity and ubiquity of data tracking, it has also become quite difficult for consumers to opt out of this tracking. As a team of privacy researchers summarized, "advertisers are making it impossible to avoid online tracking. Advertisers are so invested in the idea of a personalized web that they do not think consumers are competent to decide to reject it."[22]

Personal data retention and aggregation practices essentially create a file of preferences and characteristics of individual users. This is an evolving area of business practices that raises many Internet governance questions related to the obligations of corporations, the choices of individuals, and the role of government in protecting individual civil liberties while promoting conditions that foster profitable business models.

GOVERNING REPUTATION

Intermediaries are similarly on the front lines of problems related to cyberbullying, harassment, and reputational harm online. In countries such as Brazil, there are strong legal prohibitions on hate speech. These restrictions are sometimes constitutionally guaranteed protections. Conversely, countries such as the United States have strong protections of freedom of expression and provide fewer safeguards, outside of defamation law, related to online harassment, cyberbullying, and hate speech. In the online world, information intermediaries are stuck in the middle, faced with daily requests to take down content or close user accounts because of reputationally harmful or harassing information.

There are distinct spheres of governance related to the topic of online reputation. One sphere involves the question of how to deal with online material that can damage the reputation and sometimes create dangerous conditions for individuals. The second governance area involves the policy role of online reputational intermediaries like Yelp and Angie's List. These intermediaries make technical design choices and enact user policies that can have economic implications for businesses or social implications for individuals. They also have to provide arbitration when there is a conflict or controversy on their platform. The following explains some of the governance responsibilities of private companies in the realm of both protecting individual reputation in social media spaces and operating reputation systems.

The Social Currency of Economic Reputation Systems

Online reputation systems offer a crowd-sourced approach to rating products and services. Professional critics once had a near monopoly as powerful arbiters of quality products and the arts. These professionals were intermediaries between markets and products. A single negative review of a product or restaurant had significant influence over market consumption. Online reputation systems, even though they can sometimes be gamed, are a more democratically distributed and public approach for rating products and services. Many of these information intermediaries have the sole objective of providing rating evaluations. For example, Yelp was founded in 2004 to provide local, first-person reviews and ratings of businesses such as restaurants, automobile mechanics, and hair stylists. Other reputation systems are integrated within online sites that have a primary purpose other than ratings and evaluations. For example, Amazon.com allows for public ratings of books and merchandise and provides a space for public comments. Anyone shopping for a book title on Amazon will notice a star rating (from 1 to 5) for each book. eBay similarly integrates a reputation system into its site whereby each party to a transaction can rate their experience with the seller or purchaser involved in that transaction.

Reputation platforms assume regulatory responsibilities that are logically similar to any form of administration. How do they set up the necessary procedural conditions for fair and democratic evaluations, such as minimizing self-evaluations and other ways of gaming systems? For example, some provide technical mechanisms to block multiple evaluations from a single device; some require real-name identifiers; and some require formal memberships, either with or without a small fee to deter "trolls" that indiscriminately disparage products and services or add irrelevant content. Another administrative concern involves the question of corruption or bias within the system. What are the algorithms that reputation sites use to calculate ratings and what is the relationship, if any, between paid advertisements and how ratings or rankings are returned or displayed on these sites?

Reputation platforms sometimes assume an arbitration role when disputes arise over a negative evaluation or when a social controversy overruns the site with commentary or flaming. A lesbian who had been shopping for a wedding dress with her family posted a message on Yelp stating that a New Jersey bridal shop had refused to sell her a dress. The dress shop's online Yelp presence subsequently became inundanted with negative commentaries about its refusal to sell a dress to this woman. In the many cases like this that regularly occur in reputation systems, the intermediary has to make a decision about whether and how to intervene, presumably in accordance with its terms of service. In this particular case, Yelp deleted the evaluations that were external commentaries rather than evaluations of direct experiences dealing with the store.

Online Harassment and Cyberbullying

An American teenager tried to sue Facebook for $3 million in damages after four of her classmates formed a Facebook group with the sole purpose of ridiculing her. Social media platforms have become new spaces for bullying. These platforms escalate the nature of harassment because, unlike something shouted outside of a high school, digital words can be read by a wider social audience and remain visible unless the social media company deletes these words. Despite the increasing number of statutes against cyberbullying across the world, laws often fail to protect young people from online harassment.

Intermediaries have different legal obligations to intervene in circumstances related to harassment depending on jurisdiction. In the United States, Internet providers, including social media companies like Facebook, have almost complete immunity from liability in cases of cyberbullying and harassment. This immunity is a right provided by the Communications Decency Act (CDA). The CDA, passed in 1996 as an amendment to the Telecommunications Act of 1996, was designed to regulate Internet obscenity on the Internet. The United States Supreme Court struck down some of the so-called indecency provisions of the CDA in *Reno v. ACLU*, which upheld a ruling deeming the indecency provisions of the CDA unconstitutional abridgements of free speech. But one of the most influential provisions of the CDA—section 230—is notable because it protects intermediaries from liability for the online actions of its users. Under this provision, information intermediaries cannot be legally treated as the "publisher or speaker" of information appearing on or over its network. Section 230 of the CDA also protects these providers from so-called good Samaritan liability if they choose to restrict access to content or provide a mechanism for others to restrict this access:

> No provider or users of an interactive computer service shall
> be treated as the publisher or speaker of any information
> provided by another information content provider. . . . No
> provider or users of an interactive computer service shall be
> held liable on account of . . . any action voluntarily taken in
> good faith to restrict access to or availability of material that the
> provider or user considers to be obscene, lewd, lascivious,
> filthy, excessively violent, harassing, or otherwise objectionable,
> whether or not such material is constitutionally protected.[23]

Social media companies are in the position of having to set policies and user terms of service related to hate speech, cyberbullying, and online harassment. For example, Facebook's Statement of Rights and Responsibilities includes the provisions that "You will not post content that: is hate speech, threatening, or pornographic; incites violence; or contains nudity or graphic or gratuitous violence."[24] How companies receive complaints and carry out requests to take down hateful or harassing language is complicated by varying cultural norms and laws and challenging because it requires walking a thin line between protecting freedom of expression and promoting safe conditions for subscribers.

CORPORATE SOCIAL RESPONSIBILITY AS PRIVATIZED GOVERNANCE

Information intermediaries occupy a middle position that inherently negotiates transactions among various market and social forces. They provide significant network externalities and create cultural or economic value by increasing the efficiency of information exchange and providing social capital through connecting human transactions. They negotiate market exchanges between supply and demand for goods and information and monetize the transactions of information exchange. This mediation function bears regulatory responsibility both over the exchange of material products and social capital. This obligation also includes the determination of the conditions of civil liberties like privacy, reputation, and expression.

Companies face unprecedented challenges in carrying out their roles in intermediating free expression and decency online. The *prima facie* complexity of corporate decisions is the reality that different societies have differing, and sometimes incommensurable, laws about speech restrictions. Although there are some types of content that are reprehensible in nearly all societies, such as child pornography, in other cases types of speech perfectly legal in one society are prohibited in another. Navigating between a company's values and national laws or norms is particularly challenging for information intermediaries because they are not publishing their own content but providing a venue for content as information repositories and administrators.

From a technical standpoint, information intermediaries such as search engines (for example, Google, Baidu, Yahoo!, and Bing), social networking sites (for example, Twitter, Facebook, Orkut, LinkedIn), and content aggregation sites (for example, YouTube, Wikipedia, Flickr) have the direct ability to delete information, individuals, or social network connections. From a policy standpoint, though, this type of intervention is highly controversial, contextually dependent, and, simply put, evolving. Whether mediating freedom of expression or determining the conditions of privacy and reputation, private intermediaries are enacting transnational governance in spaces that previously were resolved by the state.

CHAPTER EIGHT

Internet Architecture and
Intellectual Property

AN ABC TELEVISION STATION broadcast a news story about the Recording Industry Association of America (RIAA) lawsuit against a teenager suffering from pancreatitis.[1] The antipiracy suit alleged that the teenager illegally shared ten songs online. Under such a lawsuit, the charged individual has only days to respond before a court issues a default judgment. While the teenager was in and out of the hospital, a federal judge ruled against the teenager, who would then owe up to $8,000 in fines. In the news interview, the distraught girl and her mother claimed that she had never illegally shared music and that the Internet account in question was registered to her father, who had since moved out of their home. The teenager was unable to work and her mother earned a modest income. Even if the teenager had been able to respond to the lawsuit, she and her mother would likely not have had the financial resources for legal assistance.

The public relations damage from suing a sick teenager is an example of the challenges of enforcing copyright by targeting individuals. Attempting to take down specific online content has produced its own public relations dilemmas, perhaps most notoriously when Universal Music issued a takedown request of a short YouTube video a mother had posted of her baby dancing to the Prince song "Let's Go Crazy."

Not surprisingly, content industries have somewhat shifted copyright enforcement attention from prosecuting individuals and requesting content takedowns to Internet infrastructure and technologies of intermediation. So-called three-strikes laws (also called graduated response) are an example of this turn to infrastructure. In emerging three-strikes approaches, service providers and information intermediaries commit to disconnecting infringing users from the Internet or implementing various measures such as blocking access to certain sites, portals, or protocols if the individual has repeatedly violated copyright laws. Separately, search engines sometimes factor copyright violations into the algorithms that determine how a web site is ranked in search results.

The Internet's Domain Name System has similarly become an infrastructural tool for intellectual property rights (IPR) enforcement. The DNS has always served a quite circumscribed technical function of translating between the alphanumeric domain names that humans use to request a web site and the numerical IP addresses that computing devices use to locate the requested site. Its use has evolved over time into IPR enforcement in that modifying how the DNS resolves a name into a number can block access to a web site deemed to be illegally selling or sharing intellectual property.

Copyright is probably the most visible of online intellectual property rights issues because of the controversy surrounding the illegal sharing of music and movies online. Copyright is a set of rights granted to the creator of an original work such as a song, photograph, book, film, or computer program. The owner of a copyrighted work is granted the right to control the use and distribution of the work for a fixed amount of time, such as (generally in the United States) the life of the author plus seventy years after the author's death. After this period, the work enters the public domain. The purpose of copyright and other forms of intellectual property rights is to ensure that creators and innovators receive compensation for their original works and to create incentives for the development of new creative works and knowledge.

DNS blocking often involves the seizure of web sites that illegally distribute copyrighted digital content but the technique is also applicable to sites that violate trademark and patents. The online sale of counterfeit luxury products or sports jerseys is an enormous challenge for trademark holders. Other web sites enable patent infringement, such as the sale of unlicensed or counterfeit pharmaceutical products. Although illegal luxury knockoffs or pirated movie sites are the targets of these approaches, one concern is the collateral damage to freedom of expression if the blocked sites include other content such as discussion forums, Internet indices, or search tools. In the United States, domain name seizures have been carried out by U.S. Immigration and Customs Enforcement (ICE), an investigative law enforcement agency of the Department of Homeland Security. There have also been legislative efforts to extend the ability of governments and private content producers to use the Internet's DNS for more extensive intellectual property enforcement.

This chapter examines the mechanics and governance implications of this intersection between Internet infrastructure and intellectual property rights enforcement. It also explores a separate intersection of intellectual property and Internet governance, the intellectual property embedded *within* Internet governance technologies rather than mediated *by* these technologies. Some of these embedded issues include trademark disputes over domain names; Internet standards-based patents; and trade secrecy in technologies of information intermediation.

THE TECHNOLOGICAL SHAPING OF PIRACY AND ENFORCEMENT

For almost a century, music was recorded by converting mechanical sound waves—the physical disturbances of air molecules that propagate from the source of a sound—into analog electrical waveforms that vary in a continuous manner proportional to the physical waveforms. Protection of copyrighted media content was relatively uncomplicated in this analog environment. Storage required a physical medium (for example, a record album) and there was no trivial way to copy and distribute these media. The Internet evolved as a completely separate system, focusing primarily on the digital exchange of alphanumeric text. The system of music and video production and distribution was completely disconnected from primarily alphanumeric Internet applications.

The digitization of multimedia content and the evolution of the Internet to be able to easily disseminate this content have obviously changed the intellectual property rights equation. Increases in digital processing power and Internet bandwidth have radically transformed how audio and video are captured and distributed. In 1965, Intel founder Gordon

Moore made a buoyant prediction about the potential increase in processing power of chips as measured by the number of transistors that could be integrated on a single chip. This prediction became known as Moore's Law, which in its current form predicts that the number of transistors that can be integrated on a circuit will double every eighteen months. This prediction has held true over the years.

The technical processes necessary to record and distribute an MP3 song is not visible to most music consumers. Analog audio waves are first converted into digital streams of os and 1s through a three-step process called "pulse code modulation." Audio signals are sampled at discrete periods of time; each sample is rounded off (that is, quantized) into a voltage value; and then each value is encoded into a binary number that represents that value. In this way, any sample of music can be converted into a stream of os and 1s. This representation of media content in digital formats has made it trivial to regenerate a signal representing the content. As an analog signal moves over a copper wire, it degrades (the wave changes form) over time. Each time an analog signal is reproduced or copied, this wave distortion is amplified, introducing errors and degrading quality. The replication of digital signals produces a near perfect copy of the original because a threshold detector simply needs to ascertain the presence of a pulse (1) or no pulse (0) and then regenerate the signal accordingly.

Multimedia digitization has made it straightforward to perfectly duplicate this content. Increases in processing power have facilitated seemingly infinite storage and manipulation of this content. Increases in bandwidth have enabled the transmission of this content, and standard encoding formats for video (MPEG), audio (MP3), and images (JPEG) have allowed interoperability of this content among devices. P2P file sharing applications have created efficient distribution models for exchanging large media files. From a technological standpoint, it is an uncomplicated matter to access, replicate, store, distribute, and mash up digital content. This is the story from the standpoint of technology. The story from the standpoint of content industry business models is quite different.

The low cost and easy distribution of digital content has destabilized media distribution models of journalistic enterprises, publishing industries, and cultural sectors including music and film production. Regardless of how one frames the issue—as piracy, as cultural mashing up, as the evolution of media models—loss of control over digital content is a primary economic concern of mainstream media industries.

The Recording Industry Association of America has indicated that music sales in the United States alone declined roughly 50 percent—from $14.6 billion to $7.7 billion—in the decade after file sharing site Napster emerged.[2] The Office of the United States Trade Representative (USTR) publishes an annual review of global conditions related to intellectual property rights protection. This publication is called the "Special 301" report. The number 301 refers to Section 301 of the Trade Act of 1974, which requires the USTR to identify countries that fail to provide adequate protections of intellectual property rights. The Special 301 report creates a "watchlist" of countries that the USTR deems deficient in terms of intellectual property rights protection and enforcement and can enable the United States to initiate retaliatory actions such as trade sanctions. For example, one Special 301 Report stated that "piracy over the Internet is a significant concern with respect to a number of trading partners, including Brazil, Canada, China, India, Italy, Russia, Spain, and Ukraine."[3]

In response, laws and international treaties designed to protect intellectual property have ratcheted up the stakes of piracy and illegal file sharing. Some legal scholars have described this reaction as a "second enclosure movement," a comparison of the movement to expand intellectual property protections with the so-called first enclosure movement in England when common public land was fenced off and turned into private property.[4]

From another perspective, some describe digital piracy as a global pricing problem. The Social Science Research Council's report "Media Privacy in Emerging Economies" notes that "relative to local incomes in Brazil, Russia, or South Africa, the price of a CD, DVD, or copy of Microsoft Office is five to ten times higher than in the United States or Europe."[5] From one perspective—the production side—piracy is an economic crisis that reduces revenues and diminishes incentives for the production of cultural arts production and innovation. From another perspective—consumption, particularly in the developing world—piracy provides an entrée for millions of people in emerging markets to access media goods from movies to software.

Strong legal protections of copyrighted and other protected material have not constrained the illegal use of copyrighted material by people in everyday life, whether posting images online, sharing music, or posting a copyrighted video clip to YouTube without securing permissions. The default cultural norm of significant percentages of the younger generation is the expectation that news, videos, and music are instantaneously and freely accessible.

Enforcing copyright laws on an individual basis has not had a significant effect on this evolving norm. If anything, enforcement efforts targeting individuals have been labor intensive and the harbinger of new public relations challenges for media industries. No matter how many lawsuits effectively stop illegal file sharing practices, it takes only a few highly publicized instances of lawsuits against grandmothers, deceased people, and twelve-year-olds to create a public relations problem.

Instead, taking down specific infringing content online is common practice and is carried out by information intermediaries such as social media platforms and content hosting sites. In the United States, under Section 512(d) of the Digital Millennium Copyright Act (DMCA) signed into law in 1998, these information intermediaries are afforded a safe harbor provision that grants them immunity from copyright infringement under certain conditions. One condition involves the provisioning of a "notice and takedown system" in which the company receives notice of an infringement from a copyright holder and expeditiously removes allegedly infringing content. The private companies serving as the information intermediaries are also expected to cancel the accounts of its users who are considered repeat offenders. As Google's terms of service have stated, "Once you accumulate 3 strikes on your account, YouTube will cancel all of your YouTube accounts, taking down all of your videos and refusing to allow you back as a YouTube account holder."[6]

Information intermediaries have a prominent role in carrying out the removal of infringing content online. This role is required, in many countries, by law; codified in their terms of services agreements with users; and borne out by the data these companies publish about the extent of content they remove for violating intellectual property rights. As Twitter's terms of service have stated,

We reserve the right to remove Content alleged to be infringing without prior notice, at our sole discretion, and without liability to you. In appropriate circumstances, Twitter will also terminate a user's account if the user is determined to be a repeat infringer.[7]

The right under the terms of service to terminate an account extends enforcement beyond targeting specific content and back into the more ad hominem approach of punishing a user for repeated copyright violations. It is usually not the information intermediary that proactively detects and takes down content. A copyright holder who believes infringement has occurred contacts Twitter. Table 8.1, with data directly from Twitter's Transparency Report, indicates the number of copyright takedown requests the company received over a six-month period. Note that during this period Twitter complied with copyright takedown requests 38 percent of the time, suggesting that the company assumes some governance role in determining which content it should and should not take down.

Google's terms of service related to copyright have a similar basis in the DMCA and a quid pro quo interest in expeditiously carrying out requests to take down infringing content in exchange for the safe harbor

Table 8.1

Twitter Copyright Takedown Notices and Responses over a Six-Month Period (From Twitter Transparency Report)

MONTH	COPYRIGHT TAKEDOWN NOTICES	PERCENTAGE WHERE MATERIAL REMOVED	USERS/ ACCOUNTS AFFECTED	TWEETS REMOVED
January	437	57	788	782
February	414	42	723	649
March	382	53	1307	1139
April	700	30	1056	994
May	970	26	1129	1016
June	475	47	871	695
Total	3378	38	5874	5275

provisions that provide legal immunity to companies that host content and that abrogate these companies from having to proactively monitor the content they host for possible copyright violations. As Google's terms of service have stated, "We respond to notices of alleged copyright infringement and terminate accounts of repeat infringers according to the process set out in the US Digital Millennium Copyright Act."[8]

Google's Transparency Report provides a great deal of information about the requests it receives to take down information believed to violate copyright. The number of requests it receives per month has risen exponentially over time. In a one-month period ending in September 2012, Google received 6,514,751 copyright removal requests.[9] Only a year earlier, Google received fewer than 100,000 copyright takedown requests. Of the more than six million requests to remove content in a one-month period, these came from slightly more than two thousand copyright owners, including prominent companies such as NBC Universal, Microsoft, and the RIAA. Many of these requests target links to web sites geared exclusively to the peer-to-peer sharing or downloading of media files. For example, Google's Transparency report indicated that it received 28,421 requests in one month to remove links to the web site TorrentHound.

Other requests are geared toward taking down specific copyrighted material from content hosting sites (for example, YouTube). Notice and takedown of content works as follows: When a content hosting company receives a request from a copyright holder to remove content (for example, a video), it removes the file. The person who posted the video has the option of submitting a counternotice, serving as a statement under penalty of perjury that the removal of the material was unwarranted. This counternotice can serve as an invitation for a lawsuit, which the copyright holder can file within two weeks of the counternotice. If a lawsuit is not filed, the video becomes reinstated.

A more technically mechanized form of copyright enforcement involves automatic matching of digital content with a database of copyrighted material provided by content owners. Google platforms can proactively remove videos if they match binary combinations stored in its Content ID program. Content companies have the option of providing a digital clip of their copyrighted material. Google can automatically detect clips on YouTube, for example, that match this stored binary representation and then automatically take down the material. This mecha-nized approach requires no human intervention, oversight, or monitoring so does not account for content that falls legally under fair use, such as a parody or educational video. Despite any problems, par-ticularly related to fair use, this approach to intellectual property rights enforcement at least narrowly applies to specific content. The following sections will discuss the much broader turn to infrastructure for content enforcement, which could potentially shut off an entire household's In-ternet link (rather than something specific such as a YouTube account) and an entire web site (rather than specific content on that web site) for vio-lating intellectual property laws.

INFRASTRUCTURE AS A PROXY FOR INTELLECTUAL PROPERTY ENFORCEMENT

Digital content industries and law enforcement have turned attention from enforcement at the individual or content level to enforcement via intermediary infrastructures. The following sections introduce three infrastructure-based approaches to copyright enforcement: search engine rankings that penalize infringing sites; three-strikes approaches that terminate the Internet access of repeat copyright violators; and domain name seizures that enforce intellectual property rights online using the Domain Name System.

Search Engine Algorithms and Copyright Enforcement

Search engines sometimes factor copyright infringement variables into the algorithms that determine how to rank and return search results. For example, Google factors in the number of legitimate copyright removal notices it receives for a web site URL into its algorithmic calculation for how to rank that site in search results: "sites with high numbers of re-moval notices may appear lower in our results."[10] Whether a site has repeatedly violated copyright laws is one of more than two hundred "sig-nals" the company uses in its algorithms to calculate how to rank the site relative to other sites.

Google receives enormous amounts of data that can feed directly into this algorithmic calculation. As Google senior vice president of en-gineering Amit Singhal explained in 2012: "we're now receiving and processing more copyright removal notices every day than we did in all of 2009—more than 4.3 million URLs in the last 30 days alone."[11] One thing that seems unresolved across search engine brands is the basis on which search companies remove a link in its search returns versus reducing the ranking of the link based on repeated violations. Regardless, search engines serve as an information chokepoint and will remain a focus for those wishing to delegate intellectual property rights enforcement or any other type of content filtering.

Three-Strikes Laws That Cut Off or Throttle Back
Individual Internet Access

Graduated response approaches are designed to address illegal file sharing by disconnecting an infringing user's Internet access or enacting other mitigation measures such as throttling back access speeds or blocking access to certain services. Depending on context, graduated response approaches are also called "three-strikes" or "six-strikes" policies. Under these systems, the Internet service provider bears responsibility for carrying out intellectual property rights enforcement. This form of enforcement has primarily targeted those using peer-to-peer networks to illegally share movies and music.

A subscriber linked to an Internet address associated with an alleged violation receives a series of warnings after which the subscriber's access is terminated. The following is a generalized example of how a graduated response would work. By joining a peer-to-peer network, a content owner or an entity representing content owners can ascertain the IP address of someone illegally sharing content. The content owner or representative entity can then notify the ISP associated with that IP address. The ISP sends a warning email to the subscriber associated with the Internet address linked to the alleged violation. If a second illegal download occurs over the same subscription line, a certified letter is sent to the subscriber of the Internet access connection involved in the illegal transmission of copyrighted material. If a third violation occurs, the ISP discontinues providing Internet access to the subscriber.

Various incarnations of graduated response policies have been introduced on a nation-by-nation basis and media content industries concerned about copyright infringement have encouraged and backed these efforts. A controversial three-strikes statutory measure called the HADOPI[12] law was introduced in France. The French Constitutional

Council struck down the law as unconstitutional but the legislature passed a comparable statute that added a requirement for judicial review. The United Kingdom introduced a similar graduated response approach to copyright enforcement under the Digital Economy Act.[13]

In the United States, the Motion Picture Association of America (MPAA) and the RIAA helped create the Center for Copyright Information (CCI),[14] a collaboration with Internet access providers such as AT&T, Cablevision, Comcast, Time Warner Cable, and Verizon. The CCI is a graduated system geared toward stopping piracy over P2P file sharing networks. Similar to other graduated response programs, the expectation is that content owners (particularly the organizations that represent content owners) will notify Internet providers when an IP address under their control has been associated with alleged copyright infringement. When an Internet provider has the IP address along with a specific time and date, it can determine which subscriber account was involved in the activity. After a number of warnings to the user, the access providers have agreed to carry out mitigation measures such as reducing access speeds or disconnecting access.

These nascent approaches raise global questions about freedom of expression, due process, the burden on consumers to prove innocence, the long-term efficacy of these measures, the possibility of cutting entire households off from Internet access, and the burden Internet providers bear in carrying out these approaches. Internet service providers must hire personnel to serve as liaisons to the content owners notifying them of subscriber copyright infringement. Personnel must also handle notifications and warnings the company issues to subscribers. They must employ additional attorneys to deal with the underlying legal complexities and gray areas as well as the ensuing lawsuits by subscribers whose services have been terminated. This economic toll is ultimately reflected in inevitable subscription price increases to users.

A United Nations report on human rights and freedom of expression expressly opposed graduated response approaches that disconnect users from the Internet for violations of intellectual property rights law. The Special Rapporteur to the United Nations was "alarmed by proposals to disconnect users from Internet access if they violate intellectual property rights. This includes legislation based on the concept of 'graduated response,' which imposes a series of penalties on copyright infringers that could lead to suspension of Internet service."[15] This is an evolving and contentious area of infrastructure-mediated copyright enforcement.

The Turn to the Domain Name System for Intellectual Property Rights Enforcement

Intellectual property rights owners and enforcement agencies have come to view the DNS as an Internet control point for blocking the online sale of copyrighted content and counterfeit products. Domain name system interventions involve either the seizure of a registered domain name or the redirection of an infringing site to another site, usually one with a law enforcement message. In terms of user perception, the site vanishes. In actuality, the server containing the copyrighted material is not physically or virtually confiscated. The content is also not touched. What has occurred is a blockage of the path to the site, somewhat analogous to the effects of deleting a name from a phone book. In web site redirection, the address resolution process fails to resolve the page to its appropriate virtual location and instead resolves the IP address to an alternative site.

ICE routinely carries out domain name seizures via this address redirection process. With twenty thousand employees and an almost $6 billion budget, ICE has expansive enforcement authority over cross-border issues such as child exportation, firearms, drugs, and smuggling.[16] Many of these activities, which previously were transacted in the physical world or through the mail, are now transacted over the Internet, a phenomenon that has expanded the scope of ICE's jurisdiction.

ICE investigations have led to hundreds of domain name seizures of web sites selling counterfeit goods; illegally distributing movies, television shows, and films; or illegally providing access to pay-per-view type activities such as sporting events.[17] Some of the targeted web sites did not actually house pirated material but provided information indices or links to sites that did provision these materials. The agency's first major effort using domain name seizures to combat piracy and counterfeiting practices occurred in June 2010 under an initiative called "Operation In Our Sites." As the agency announced to the public, "In the first action carried out as part of the initiative, authorities executed seizure warrants against a handful of domain names of Web sites that were offering first-run movies, often within hours of their theatrical release."[18]

If ICE investigations determine that a web site illegally offers copy-righted or trademarked goods without the permission of the rights hold-ers, it requests that a federal magistrate judge issue a criminal seizure warrant for the domain name associated with the web site. In the Opera-tion In Our Sites initiative, ICE had filed for judicial consent to seize nine domain names in the Southern District of New York. Some of the first domain names the agency seized included:

- tvshack.net
- movies-links.tv
- filespump.com
- now-movies.com
- planetmoviez.com
- thepiratecity.org
- zml.com.

Another major seizure occurred five months later.[19] During this en-forcement effort, which Attorney General Eric Holder dubbed "Cyber Monday Crackdown," eighty-two domain names were seized. As evident from the government-published list of domain names seized by ICE, many of the web sites seemed to be online retailers overtly geared to-ward illegally selling counterfeit goods such as sporting equipment, luxury handbags and shoes, and athletic gear; or selling pirated digital content, including music, software, and boxed sets of DVDs. The follow-ing are just a few examples of the seized domain names:

- louisvuittonoutletstore4u.com
- burberryoutlet-us.com
- rapgodfathers.com
- dajaz1.com
- dvdsuperdeal.com
- coachoutletfactory.com
- torrent-finder.com.[20]

If an Internet user entered the domain name of one of the seized sites, the user's query was redirected to a web site depicting a screen with three icons—the seal of the Department of Justice, the seal of the National Intellectual Property Rights Coordination Center, and a Department of Homeland Security special agent badge. Each seized site also included the statement, "This domain name has been seized by ICE—Homeland Security Investigations, pursuant to a seizure warrant issued by a United States District Court." The site also carried a warning about the criminal penalties for first-time copyright infringement, up to five years in prison and a $250,000 fine; and for trafficking in counterfeit goods, up to ten years in prison and a $2,000,000 fine. According to U.S. government documents, the domain name seizures in 2010 redirected almost thirty million people from these web sites to the government seizure banners.[21]

Other rounds of seizures have focused on sites that allegedly stream copyrighted sporting events and pay-per-view events over the Internet. It appears that all of the top-level domains (.org, .com, .net) associated with the seized domain names are operated by U.S. institutions such as Veri-Sign. Indeed, according to ICE, one of "the determinations for the ICE agents and the prosecutors were whether the domain names are of course registered . . . in the United States . . . even if the web site is operated overseas."[22] The court order, once obtained, is served on the domestic domain name registry, which simply redirects the domain name to a page on a different server containing the seizure notice and warning.

The term of art for this Internet governance mechanism is "seizure" but usually the process involves "redirection" or "reassignment." One alternative, and the most decisive approach, is for a law enforcement agency to delegate this redirection to the registry operator, such as Veri-Sign, controlling the authoritative mapping of a domain name into its IP address. The agency simply approaches the registry and indicates the domain name it wants resolved into a different IP address. The registry authoritatively controls the mapping of a top-level domain's resolution of names into numbers and distributes this universally to all domain name resolution servers, essentially creating a universal domain name redirection away from the targeted site. A different alternative is for the law enforcement agency to approach the registrar, such as Go Daddy, that has assigned the targeted domain name and order the registrar to transfer assignment of the entire domain name from the infringing entity to a government authority. Both of these options are possible if the registry or registrar is under the national jurisdiction of the government requesting this redirection or reassignment.

When the infringing web site's domain name is registered in another country or when the registry institution for the associated top-level domain is located in another country, a government agency has little jurisdiction to request a domain name redirection or reassignment. This transnational enforcement complexity explains why there has been so much public policy interest in executing domain name seizures through more local DNS servers within a nation's borders. One of the most controversial aspects of the failed SOPA and PIPA legislative measures in the United States was seeking to do just this.

DNS-based intellectual rights enforcement presents a host of technical questions, particularly if the seizures are carried out through recursive servers. From a technical perspective, these approaches are easily circumvented by the use of an alternative, non-filtered DNS server or by quickly registering the site in another domain. There are often unintended effects of using large technical systems and centralized technologies for purposes completely irrelevant to their designed functionality. The DNS was not originally designed for intellectual property rights enforcement and other types of content gatekeeping. Rather than domain names mapping universally to their actual sites, the resolution process could vary from region to region, changing the universal consistency of the Internet. The number of daily DNS queries that occur is measured in the billions range, and the universal consistency provided by hierarchical governance has been able to handle this volume. It is unclear how the creation of an inconsistent resolution process would affect the operational efficiency of this process. A related concern is how this type of approach would affect the future security of the DNS and, in particular, the ability to use the security protocol DNSSEC.

Others have expressed concern about the effects of domain name seizures on the future of free expression online.[23] Two of the seized sites, RapGodFathers and OnSmash, were popular blogs about hip-hop music. In a statement reacting to the ICE seizures, RapGodFathers explained, "During the whole existence of the website, we always honored any DMCA requests but apparently in US people are guilty before proven innocent."[24] In the case of RapGodFathers, the site's servers were actually seized, not just the domain names that point to the servers. In the case of OnSmash, the seizure involved the domain name pointing to the server. OnSmash.com founder Kevin Hofman has reportedly stated that much of the material they post, such as new songs and videos, is leaked to the site by music labels and artists.[25]

Part of the reason for the interest in local filtering of infringing sites is the ease with which a seized site can quickly reappear, using a different top-level domain, registrar, and registry. As an example, Puerto 80 was the registered owner of two seized domain names, rojadirecta.com and rojadirecta.org. Puerto 80 is a private Spanish company operating out of Arteixo, Spain. Rojadirecta, which could subsequently still be accessed by typing its IP address 209.44.113.146 into the URL bar or at a new domain name rojadirecta.es, is primarily a discussion board geared toward sports and other topics and a site that includes links to streamed sporting events already found on the Internet. Rojadirecta described this indexing as a function similar to what search engines perform. It furthermore argued that the provision of this index does not constitute even contributory infringement because the domain name and associated site provide "substantial non-infringing uses" such as discussion forums and links to authorized sports broadcasts.

Although the seizures serve to immediately take a web site offline, the server itself, the server's physical and virtual connections to the Internet, and the content contained on the server all remain intact. Other than the domain name, the entire infrastructure—physical, logical, institutional—remains *in situ*. Therefore, it is a trivial process to bring a server back online by registering a new domain name, most likely with a registrar in another country or by using a top-level domain such as a country code—or ccTLD—rather than a generic top-level domain such as .com or .net. In the case of Rojadirecta, the infringing content was located on other sites so the seizure did not take down any infringing content but only some links to infringing content.

Circumvention techniques around DNS seizures have also appeared. One early example of circumvention around domain name blocking was the introduction of the MafiaaFire Redirector, freely downloadable software designed to be used in conjunction with the Mozilla Firefox or Google Chrome web browsers to redirect users to web sites whose domain names have been seized by a government. MafiaaFire software code is essentially an add-on, or plug-in, a piece of code added to an application to provide additional functionality, similar to Flash Player adding animation or video viewing functionality to web browsers. The creators of MafiaaFire built this software plug-in in direct response to the domain name seizures.

When a user types in a seized domain name into the URL bar, the plug-in automatically reroutes the user to an alternative domain name that displays the desired site. To keep the software current, the list of seized domains and their new domain name alternatives must be kept current. MafiaaFire allows domain name owners to register an account and input an alternative to their seized domain names. It is easy to envision unintended problems that can arise with this approach, such as spammers redirecting legitimate and nonseized domain names to spam or malware sites. MafiaaFire tries to forestall this type of unintended consequence by attempting to validate that each contributor actually owns the domain name in question, checking each redirect, and offering a form where users can report problems with redirects.

Adding to the governance challenges surrounding domain name seizures, the United States Department of Homeland Security contacted Mozilla and requested that the company remove MafiaaFire as a downloadable add-on.[26] Rather than comply with the request, and to help the company evaluate the agency's request, the company responded with a list of questions for Homeland Security to answer: Have any courts determined that MafiaaFire is in any way illegal; have any courts actually determined that the seized domain names MafiaaFire redirects are liable for infringement or illegal in any other respect; are there any protections in place for MafiaaFire (or domain name holders) if a court decides they were operating lawfully; did any copyright owners first try DMCA takedown notices; were any of the domain name owners forewarned about seizures?[27] Like other uses of infrastructure mediation for content enforcement, the turn to the DNS for IPR enforcement highlights the conflicting values underlying the implementation of Internet governance technologies, in this case law enforcement versus freedom of speech, and the unique role private entities play in governing the Internet.

INTELLECTUAL PROPERTY RIGHTS WITHIN INTERNET GOVERNANCE TECHNOLOGIES

The previous section discussed how content companies and law enforcement have turned to Internet technologies and intermediaries to enforce copyright and trademark laws. Completely distinct from this technologically mediated control of content, intellectual property rights are also embedded within technologies of Internet intermediation themselves.

These embedded rights have a considerable bearing on Internet architecture and the rights of Internet users and developers alike. This section provides three examples of this intersection between Internet governance technologies and intellectual property rights: domain name trademark disputes, standards-embedded patents, and the use of trade secrecy in information intermediaries such as search engines.

Global Governance System for Domain Name Trademark Disputes
The entertainer Madonna owns the trademark registration for the mark "Madonna" for entertainment services and goods.[28] According to the United States Patent and Trademark Office (USPTO), a trademark is a symbol, design, word, phrase or combination thereof that "distinguishes the source of the goods of one party from those of others."[29] Whereas copyright protects an original artistic work such as a song, trademark is designed to protect things such as brand names and logos. For example, the Nike swoosh symbol is universally associated with the company's products. It is a registered trademark that legally prohibits others from associating this logo with non-Nike products. The purpose of trademark is consumer protection as much as brand protection. Consumer recognition of a brand provides a certain assurance of the quality of the brand.

Trademark is an area of information policy tied to national laws, and different countries have different systems for registering trademarks. Domain names can be set up or reached from anywhere in the world. In the Internet environment, domain name trademark protection has required international Internet rulemaking outside the bounds of nation-states in hybridized private and institutional settings.

Domain name trademark disputes have arisen since the development of the World Wide Web. For example, an operator of an adult entertainment site purchased the domain name Madonna.com in 1998 for $20,000 from the registrar Pro Domains. He also registered the trademark "Madonna" in Tunisia. According to legal documents about this case, the individual operated the madonna.com web site as an adult entertainment portal with sexually explicit images. The web site included the disclaimer that "madonna.com is not affiliated or endorsed by the Catholic Church, Madonna College, Madonna Hospital, or Madonna the singer."[30] By 1999, the individual removed the explicit material from the site but still held the domain name registration and kept the site live with only the disclaimer listed above. The individual in question had a history of registering other domain names associated with trademarked terms or business names such as wallstreetjournal.com.

In Internet governance parlance, there are different types of bad faith trademark infringement of domain names. In the Madonna example, this phenomenon is known as "cybersquatting." It often involves registering a domain name with the intent to profit from a trademark owned by someone else or the intent to sell the domain name in question to the trademark holder. Another form of cybersquatting involves the practice of using automated programs to identify when a domain name has expired. Domain name holders sometimes forget to renew names after the fixed period of time after which registrations expire. Cybersquatters exploit this renewal lapse by registering an expired domain name, usually with the intent of profiting financially—possibly even via identity theft—from the registration.

Another bad faith registration involves "typosquatting" in which the registered domain name is nearly identical to a trademark owner's mark only with a minor spelling error. Still another practice is to register a domain name under a different top-level domain, which happened when the same madonna.com registrant registered and operated "whitehouse.com" (easily confused with whitehouse.gov) as an adult entertainment site in the 1990s.

At the time of the madonna.com controversy, ICANN had recently established an arbitration procedure for domain name trademark disputes. Madonna, the entertainer, issued a formal complaint objecting to the domain name registration in question. Shortly after receiving the complaint, the registrant contacted Madonna Rehabilitation Hospital and offered to transfer the domain name to the hospital. Under the dispute resolution system, Madonna, the entertainer, had to prove that (1) the registered domain name was identical or confusingly similar to her trademark; (2) the registrant had no legitimate interest in the domain name; and (3) the domain name had been registered and used in bad faith. A three-member World Intellectual Property Organization arbitration panel found in her favor and ordered the disputed domain name madonna.com to be transferred.

There is no direct connection between the system for registering trademarks, which is territorially nation-bound and publicly administered, and the system for registering domain names, which is privately administered with no *ex ante* consideration of trademark rights. Not surprisingly, trademark disputes have been rampant and have represented a significant policy controversy for the domain name administrative structure. Shortly after the inception of the web, questions emerged about appropriate legal remedies for dealing with trademark-infringing domain name registrations and what responsibility, if any, domain name registrars would assume for infringement. This is a complicated problem of Internet governance. In trademark law, it is possible for two registered trademarks to be identical, just registered as different classes of goods or services. As an example, "Brandname" chocolate and "Brandname" soap could both be validly held trademarks in different classes of goods. This does not at all translate into the Internet environment, where each domain name (for example, www.brandname.com) must be globally unique.

National legal remedies for Internet trademark disputes have not always been effective because of jurisdictional complexities such as where a trademark is registered versus where a server is located versus where a trademark-infringing entity resides. Domain names, because they essentially serve as online markers and business identifiers, have great commercial value. But because they have been obtained via first mover advantage, the legal owners of trademarks are not automatically the owners of associated domain names. Ownership requires registration. Traditional legal intervention in trademark disputes is also too lengthy of a process relative to the quick pace of Internet growth and innovation.

ICANN's Uniform Domain-Name Dispute-Resolution Policy (UDRP) now serves as a mechanism for trademark protection in the sphere of domain names but, like many of ICANN's activities, has itself been controversial. This policy is designed to resolve trademark-related domain name disputes and applies to all generic top-level domains (gTLDs). All ICANN-accredited registrars in gTLDs have agreed to adopt this policy. In effect, the policy exists between a registrar and registrant and is contractually agreed to during the domain name registration process. When a registrant applies for a domain name, it must warrant that the selected domain name does not infringe on the rights of a third party and also must agree to participate in an arbitration process if a third party comes forward with a claim on the name.

Usually, a dispute is required to be resolved by agreement, court decision, or arbitration before the registrar of the domain name will cancel or transfer the domain name in question. However, if the dispute is viewed to be an "abusive registration" such as in the Madonna.com case, there is the option of an expedited review process by submitting a complaint to an entity known as an "approved dispute-resolution service provider."

If a trademark holder believes someone is unlawfully using this trademark in a domain name, the holder has the option of filing a complaint in a jurisdictionally appropriate court against the domain name registrant or, more expeditiously, submitting a complaint to one of ICANN's approved dispute-resolution service providers, the institutions at the center of domain name trademark governance. ICANN publishes an official list of "approved" dispute resolution service providers including the following:

- Asian Domain Name Dispute Resolution Centre
- National Arbitration Forum
- World Intellectual Property Organization (WIPO)
- The Czech Arbitration Court's Arbitration Center for Internet Disputes.

Organizations can become one of these alternative (noncourt) dispute resolution providers by submitting an application to ICANN's Marina del Rey, California headquarters with background on the applicant's capabilities, a list of at least twenty names and qualifications of potential mediation panelists, the criteria for selecting these individuals, a list of supplemental rules it will implement outside of ICANN's rules, and a host of other information. According to ICANN requirements, the panelists are expected to be "highly qualified neutrals" willing to serve as panelists, preferably from multiple countries. Complaints are adjudicated by these "independent panelists" available on each dispute service provider's list.

To provide a sense of scale, in the first eleven years after the inauguration of the UDRP, the WIPO Arbitration and Mediation Center received approximately two thousand cases per year, the majority resulting in termination or transfer of the registrant's domain name.

When a complainant initiates an administrative proceeding with a dispute resolution provider, the complainant must indicate its preference for either a single-member or three-member panel (single member is less expensive), indicate what domain name is the subject of the complaint, and specify the trademark on which the proceeding will address. The complainant also has to, as in the Madonna case, describe the following:

> The manner in which the domain name(s) is/are identical or confusingly similar to a trademark or service mark in which the Complainant has rights; and
>
> Why the Respondent (domain-name holder) should be considered as having no rights or legitimate interests in respect of the domain name(s) that is/are the subject of the complaint; and
>
> Why the domain name(s) should be considered as having been registered and being used in bad faith.[31]

After reviewing the initial complaint, the dispute resolution provider notifies the domain name registrant, who must respond to the provider within twenty days by addressing each allegation and explaining any basis for retaining the disputed domain name. At this point, the one-person or three-person panel makes a determination and, within fourteen days of its appointment, forwards its decision to the dispute resolution provider. If the decision favors the trademark owner, the private registrar where the domain name was registered enforces the ruling by seizing or transferring the domain name from the registrant.

Critics of the UDRP, while acknowledging its efficiency advantage, suggest several shortcomings.[32] The UDRP was not formed through the same type of deliberative international construction that gives legitimacy to other types of international rulemaking procedures, often undergoing ratification by multiple nations' legislative bodies. However, this nation-state deliberative governance approach would have taken years, giving free reign to domain name trademark violations in the interim. The UDRP was quickly implemented and arose initially from a United States Commerce Department proposal and a recommended procedure offered, after international consultation, by WIPO, a United Nations agency addressing global intellectual property protection.[33] Another criticism takes aim at the dispute service provider system, suggesting that trademark holders "forum shop" and use the service providers most likely to rule in their favor.

The UDRP is still a relatively recent and evolving system of trademark governance. Despite the criticisms against its constitution and operations, it has provided much quicker and much less expensive global resolution of trademark disputes than litigation, particularly considering the cross-national complications of such litigation. It is also interesting because it is an example of a globally agreed upon governance system outside of traditional governments.

Standards-Embedded Patents

Internet innovation requires Internet protocols, or standards, that serve as blueprints that product developers follow to achieve compatibility with other products based on the same protocols. The historic standards (for example, TCP/IP) that form the foundation for interoperability over the Internet are generally considered to be "open standards" that enable maximum innovation because standards-setting institutions such as the Internet Engineering Task Force and the World Wide Web Consortium allow anyone to participate in standards development, openly publish these standards, make these written standards available for free, and develop standards that can be implemented by companies in products without these companies having to pay royalties for using these standards.

One can only speculate about whether the Internet would have grown so rapidly and introduced so many new innovations if companies developing products had to pay significant royalties for using these essential standards. In global Internet governance policy debates about standards, an emerging concern involves the increasing extent of royalty-bearing patent claims embedded in standards required for the exchange of information over the Internet. A patent is an intellectual property right granted by a government to legally prohibit others from making, selling, or using this invention for a period of time. The United States government grants patents for twenty years after which the invention becomes publicly disclosed. To be patentable, the invention must be "novel; nonobvious; adequately described or enabled; and claimed by the inventor in clear and definite terms."[34]

Part of the concern over patents in standards emanates from the evolution of more complicated conditions of intellectual property rights under technical standards necessary for routine Internet use. One complication is that the myriad standards-setting institutions that establish Internet-related standards all subscribe to different policies about intellectual property rights. Additionally, a single device connected to the Internet can embed hundreds of different standards.[35] A smartphone is an exemplar of such a device because it provides functions that used to require numerous distinct devices. These functions include making voice calls, videoconferencing, downloading video clips, listening to music, using a GPS to navigate to a location, and connecting to any number of networks including GSM cellular or Wi-Fi. Many of the numerous standards embedded in these devices are royalty-bearing, meaning that device manufacturers have to pay royalties to implement these standards in their products, a phenomenon with potential effects on innovation, economic competition, and costs to end users.[36]

Many democratic governments have policies requiring certain characteristics of standards-based intellectual property in the technologies they procure as large users of the Internet and other goods and services. For example, U.S. federal government policy makes specific reference to intellectual property conditions of standards, stating that the owners of any intellectual property "have agreed to make that intellectual property available on a non-discriminatory, royalty-free or reasonable royalty basis to all interested parties."[37] The objective of the U.S. approach to standards-based intellectual property is to respect the rights of owners of intellectual property rights while promoting the availability of reasonable and nondiscriminatory (RAND) licensing of these intellectual property rights to those interested in using the standards. Other countries, such as India, require that the federal government give preference to the adoption of royalty-free standards.[38] This preference for royalty-free standards is usually called an "open standards" policy, although open standard also refers to other features of a standard such as who is permitted to participate in its development. The rationale for open standards policies includes promoting an economic environment in which there is a level playing field for competition and innovation based on the standard as well as avoiding vendor lock-in and dependence on a single vendor for products or services.

Trade Secrecy and Internet Architecture

The issue of trade secrecy is a separate intellectual property rights area from copyright, trademark, and patents but one that also intersects directly with Internet architecture and governance, particularly in the area of technologies involved in the algorithmic sorting and organizing of information. The formula for Coca Cola is something that easily jumps to mind in the general area of trade secrecy, which protects methods, techniques, and formulas used by a business and that provides a competitive advantage relative to those not able to access the protected trade secret. From a global governance standpoint, the Trade Related Aspects of Intellectual Property Rights (TRIPS) agreement of the World Trade Organization provides minimum agreed upon international standards for trade secrecy protection. Trade secrecy protection is different from patents, which expire after a fixed period of time but which also protect the inventor in cases when someone else independently discovers or invents the patented subject.

Search engine algorithms are an area of Internet governance and architecture that have been protected by trade secrecy and have created public policy concerns about values of transparency and fair treatment. Search engine rankings are not neutral or disembodied. They embed the values and editorial decisions of those who design and operate them. How (and whether) sites are returned and ranked in search engine results raises several policy controversies. To what extent is delegated state censorship being implemented via search engines? Is the search engine biased against sites that compete with the search engine's other business areas?[39] Because of the inherent public interest issues raised by how search engines algorithmically sort and rank online material, there have been calls for greater transparency in how this information ordering occurs and whether this transparency should be legislatively mandated.[40] Trade secrecy offers a cover for search engine companies, particularly during litigation, to refuse to disclose the particulars of how search engine algorithms work.[41] Although greater transparency makes sense from the standpoint of fairness and accountability, it could have unintended consequences such as forestalling the ability of innovative companies to retain their competitive advantage and therefore limiting future innovation and discouraging new entrants. Another consequence would be the facilitation of gaming search engine results. Trade secrecy issues will increasingly complicate the balance of values between protecting business models and creating public accountability.

CHAPTER NINE

The Dark Arts of Internet Governance

THE GOVERNMENT-INDUCED BLACKOUT that severed Internet connectivity in Egypt for several days was a shocking political event in Internet history. Citizens could not access the Internet or use their cell phones. They were blocked from communicating digitally with each other and the rest of the world. The regime of then-president Hosni Mubarak ordered communication outages during a period of political unrest and protests against the government. This communication blackout captured global attention, but unfortunately, totalitarian and autocratic action against technology use is a regular occurrence. In the month following the Egyptian incident, citizens in Libya also experienced Internet disruptions, also reportedly ordered by government authorities during a period of political unrest. The Burmese government blocked Internet access to prevent citizens and journalists from globally broadcasting images and stories about human rights violations and the government's violent response to civic protests.[1] In 2005, the Nepalese government similarly severed international communication during the king's declaration of martial law.[2] In 2009 during the protests in Iran after the country's controversial presidential election, the government selectively disrupted Internet applications including Google's YouTube site. Google's publicly available transparency reports from this time provide graphs vividly depicting the stark and sudden termination of traffic in Iran.

Most people with democratic sensibilities are repulsed by these types of authoritarian communication blackouts and concerned about the associated implications for freedom of expression and basic societal functioning. But these incidents also raise difficult questions about the conditions under which government-ordered intervention in communication networks is permissible or advisable and associated questions about the obligations of private industry to either acquiesce to or resist these demands. If public authorities learned of a planned terrorist attack to be coordinated by cell phone, many would view this as justification for terminating wireless services in the targeted location despite any collateral damage to free expression and commerce. What are the conditions under which governments should (or could) tamper with communication technologies for national security or law enforcement objectives?

One concrete example of this type of service outage occurred in San Francisco in the same year as the Egyptian Internet outage. Bay Area Rapid Transit (BART), a government-run transit system, shut down its in-station cell phone service for three hours to disrupt plans for an in-station protest. Two BART police officers had shot and killed a forty-five-year-old homeless man in a station earlier that summer.[3] The police officers claimed that the man was carrying a knife,[4] whereas witnesses reported that he was unarmed. The reaction to the shooting was racially charged because the BART police officers were Caucasian and the homeless man was African American.

Prior to the cell phone blocking incident, a protest had already occurred. Several demonstrators blocked train doors and one protestor climbed on top of a train.[5] The protest led to the closing of one station and delays of ninety-six BART trains.[6] In the wake of the shooting and demonstrations, and in advance of another anticipated protest, BART management approved a plan to temporarily terminate its in-station cell phone service.[7]

The service blockage impeded communication among protesters but it also blocked all communication. Commuters could not use their smartphones to send text messages or make calls. There was a significant public outcry over BART's actions with many viewing the intentional service disruption as abridging the First Amendment. Even more protests ensued, now against BART's decision to block communication. Public interest groups filed a petition with the Federal Communications

Commission to request a declaratory ruling that BART had violated national communication law by terminating services.[8] The hacker collective Anonymous infiltrated BART servers and obtained personal data about its customers and posted these data online. This episode was the perfect storm of Internet governance issues: security, hacking, freedom of expression, privacy, law enforcement goals, and the right to assemble.

Infrastructure is not a given. Although technologies are political in different ways in different contexts, there are certain mechanisms of Internet governance that, in their first instance, pose dilemmas for the future of Internet freedom. This chapter addresses four of these. The first mechanism is deep packet inspection, a traffic engineering technique in which the content of packets sent over the Internet is inspected, analyzed, and factored into a variety of possible decision processes. The chapter then addresses kill-switch approaches that sever connectivity and explains nine distinct approaches that can block content or access. The third mechanism is the process of delegated censorship in which governments turn directly to private information intermediaries to block or filter information. Finally, the chapter addresses freedom of expression concerns arising from distributed denial of service attacks, which can be directly targeted against civic advocacy groups and generally present collateral damage to free expression by inundating networks with unnecessary traffic.

DEEP PACKET INSPECTION: "INTELLIGENT POLICY ENFORCEMENT" OR THE "DEATH OF PRIVACY"

The introduction of deep packet inspection techniques into the administrative and technological structure of the Internet represents a significant transformation in networked governance as well as a potential floodgate opening methods of potential governance conceivable in the future.

Throughout most of Internet history, network devices have been content agnostic and content neutral. Routers were agnostic in the literal sense of "not knowing" the contents of a packet. They were also disinterested in the sense of homogenously applying routing algorithms (such as minimizing the number of hops) to any packets they handled. Computing devices were neither privy to the content being transmitted nor intrinsically inclined to treat any packet of information differently than any other packet. Each packet transmitted over the Internet contains a header and payload. Network equipment delivers information to its destination by reading a packet's routing and addressing header but has not traditionally intruded into the contents of the packet by inspecting, reading, or manipulating the content or sharing it with a third party. The header contains administrative and routing information that accompanies the content being exchanged and the payload contains the actual content, whether a segment of a YouTube video, an email, or a computer virus.

There was a historical context that shaped this engineering method. Content was homogeneous in that most transmitted information was textual. Alphanumeric text applications such as email, file transfer, and Internet relay chat did not have the bandwidth-consumptive requirements of later multimedia applications such as those involving video and audio transmission. There were few traffic engineering rationales for offering prioritized handling of any packet over any other. A miniscule transmission delay for an email or file transfer was imperceptible to the receiver. Time-sensitive applications such as voice conversations over the Internet call for a different set of performance requirements that need to minimize perceptions of network latency. The differential susceptibility of various applications to network latency represents a technical rationale for the prioritization of some packets over others.

As discussed earlier, the design approach of routing packets without viewing or analyzing content was not actually neutral. It was an expression of the philosophical and technical values of Internet engineers concerned with locating intelligence at endpoints rather than *in medias res*.

Until fairly recently it was also not computationally possible to inspect the entire contents of information exchanged over the Internet because of the enormous processing speeds and computing resources necessary to perform this function. The vast majority of Internet traffic is information payload, versus the small amount of overhead information contained within packet headers. Internet service providers and other information intermediaries have traditionally used packet headers to route packets, perform statistical analysis, and perform routine network management and traffic optimization. Increases in computer processing power have made it viable to inspect the actual content of packets and have facilitated the introduction of DPI techniques.

Deep Packet Inspection for Traffic Management and Security Detection
Agnostic engineering approaches ceased being the norm by the early twenty-first century. Network devices became capable of prioritizing the flow of some packets or blocking or throttling back other packets based on characteristics such as sender, content, type of application, type of protocol, or other feature. Intelligence resides in the middle of the network in a variety of ways and deep packet inspection is one of the technologies entangled in this network governance transformation.

Internet operators routinely use DPI to inspect the contents of transmitted packets of information, at a minimum as part of basic operational functioning around security and traffic management. DPI is capable of scanning each packet, analyzing some characteristic of the packet, and executing a real-time handling decision such as blocking, prioritizing, or throttling. In this sense, DPI is a technology that makes decisions about the allocation of finite bandwidth to the packets of information competing for this scarce resource. As mentioned, those advocating a pure net neutrality position call for legal prohibitions against even this level of network management prioritization geared toward traffic engineering.

As an analogy, consider the postal worker delivering a letter and paying attention only to the destination address, proper postage, and certain contextual conditions such as the weather and the occasional dog. As Bendrath and Mueller vividly describe, imagine a postal worker who "Opens up all packets and letters; Reads the content; Checks it against databases of illegal material and when finding a match sends a copy to the police authorities; Destroys letters with prohibited or immoral content; Sends packages for its own mail-order services to a very fast delivery truck, while the ones from competitors go to a slow, cheap sub-contractor."[9] This is what DPI theoretically enables.

DPI can scrutinize the entire contents of a packet including the payload as well as the packet header. It is a software capability now routinely manufactured into firewalls, routers, and other network devices (some costing hundreds of thousands of dollars) or even embedded within operating systems. The companies that develop these sophisticated devices (for example, Procera, Radisys) frame the functions their products provide as "intelligent policy enforcement," "security intelligence," "traffic intelligence," "adaptive traffic shaping," or "service optimization." The products embedding DPI techniques are so powerful that they can inspect more than a million concurrent connections.

DPI places much more power in the hands of network operators. Some of this capability enhances their ability to efficiently manage traffic on their own networks. DPI serves two obvious traffic management functions. One involves the prioritization and shaping of transmissions based on the performance requirements of the type of traffic, application, or protocol transmitted. An example would be prioritizing the delivery of voice traffic over batch text transmissions because the perceived user experience of voice traffic is so much more sensitive to latency. Over wireless networks in particular, it is not always possible to just add more bandwidth.

Whatever policy decision the network operator makes about traffic shaping can be implemented using the detection techniques within deep packet inspection. It is not the technology that enacts the prioritization but the policy determined by the provider using the technology. Often the decision about what to prioritize is based on the type of traffic being transmitted rather than the actual content of the application. There are certain signature application protocol bit combinations that DPI can identify such as those indicating the transmission of P2P traffic (for example, BitTorrent protocol), web traffic (for example, HTTP), file transfer (for example, FTP), or email (for example, SMTP). DPI can also perform a more granular and technically invasive level of information prioritization. For example, if the detected traffic is video, it can determine whether the source of the video originates from a specific repository such as YouTube.

Network security is another traffic management function DPI addresses. Viruses and other unwanted code are intermixed with or embedded within legitimate information sent over the Internet. Inspecting the contents of a packet can identify viruses because DPI can be programmed to detect certain bit sequences associated with known malicious code. In fact, government statutory interest in compelling network operators to inform their customers when their computers are infected with a virus could almost be construed as a mandate that network operators inspect the actual contents of consumer traffic.

DPI Usage for Political and Economic Rationales—Competition, Advertising, and Censorship

Deep packet inspection techniques have much broader applicability than the security and traffic management functions that fall within the administrative purview of a network operator. This book has consistently highlighted the ways in which control over content has moved into technologies of Internet governance. DPI is another example of this phenomenon. DPI can also be used for censoring content or throttling back traffic that competes with a network operator's primary business. Cable companies and wireless providers offer content services as well as access services. DPI is capable of allowing network providers to prioritize content most closely linked to the services they provide or to throttle back content that competes with their services. The most publicized instances of DPI usage have involved forays into still other areas, such as the ad-serving practices of operators in Europe and the United States that are designed to provide highly targeted marketing based on what a customer views or transacts on the Internet.

Law enforcement and intelligence agencies recognize DPI technologies as another tool in their arsenal of information gathering practices or enforcement of laws prohibiting child pornography or protecting intellectual property rights. Media industries view DPI as a method for detecting and blocking the illegal transmission of copyrighted material such as movies or video games. This piracy detection potential is technically more complicated than it sounds at the content level. For example, if a sample from a movie is detected in transmission, it is difficult for DPI technology to normatively discern whether this media content has been legally purchased or used lawfully under fair use doctrines or whether it has been illegally downloaded. More realistically, copyright owners would ask network operators to block file sharing protocols such as BitTorrent that are closely associated with piracy.

DPI also provides a technically efficient tool for governments wishing to enact surveillance and/or censorship and can be used in a number of international contexts in which repressive governments have instituted tight controls on the ability of citizens to access or share information. For example, the Iranian government and other governments with repressive information policies have allegedly employed DPI.[10]

Governance in the Balance
The two inherent capabilities of DPI—the ability to inspect and the ability to manipulate information—raise quite different questions about values. Most concern about DPI in practice has related to the manipulation and prioritization capability. This concern is very closely tied with the net neutrality question, such as concern over the well-publicized case of Comcast using DPI inspection techniques to throttle back BitTorrent traffic. Notably, the advocacy groups and law professors criticizing Comcast's throttling of BitTorrent traffic based their critique on the desire to preserve basic equality, economic freedom, and freedom of expression.

But there is another obvious value in play when one views throttling from the perspective of how it is actually accomplished using DPI techniques. This concern involves the loss of individual privacy due to the inspection of content during transmission. From a values standpoint, this is a distinct concern from the net neutrality–style objections to discriminatory treatment of some packets over others. It is a concern, however, also directly related to freedom of expression because of the possible chilling effects of these practices.

The inspection and manipulation of information payload for these external content control purposes raise a variety of policy considerations: the extent to which individuals should expect the information they send and receive to remain private and the chilling effects information disclosure can have on individual freedom online; the degree of transparency of private engineering practices that consumers should reasonably expect to see; the net neutrality question about the legality of a network operator possibly prioritizing its own content over competitors' content; the increasing burden placed on private companies to carry out various types of enforcement for third parties such as law enforcement agencies or media content companies; and the question of how to preserve lawful purchases or fair use rights of copyrighted content in mechanized enforcement environments.

DPI is a transformational technology that creates unprecedented regulatory possibilities for controlling the flow of content online. It is a technology that, not surprisingly, is routinely being used by network operators. It is also an area of infrastructure management and Internet governance with almost no transparency. When network providers use DPI to identify and prioritize certain types of traffic on their own networks, no third party becomes systematically aware of this intervention. It is also an area in which there has, to date, been little media attention, public awareness, or policy discussion. Globally, there are few restrictions relegating a network operator's use of deep packet inspection to network management and security practices or prohibitions on retaining or sharing collected data about transmitted content. Rather than drawing attention to or prohibiting DPI, some governments are embracing DPI for their own purposes. Regardless of whether DPI is used for network management and security functions, copyright enforcement, or serving online advertisements, it is a type of surveillance intervention that requires the same amount of scrutiny and examination that other mechanisms of Internet governance have undergone. This is particularly important in light of the implications of this technology for individual rights and economic competition.

TECHNICAL ANATOMY OF A "KILL-SWITCH"

There is no single Internet kill-switch, but there are kill-switches. Numerous infrastructure concentration points provide opportunities for governments and other actors to disrupt communication networks. The design of the Internet's underlying packet switching approach was intended to make networks impervious to a widespread system outage. Concerns about survivable communication networks during the Cold War to a certain extent shaped the development of this approach.[11] Information transmitted over the Internet is broken into packets, which contain the actual content of information to be transmitted along with overhead administrative information contained within the packet header. Routers read the destination address contained within the header of each packet and determine how to most expeditiously route each packet, based on routing algorithms designed to optimize certain characteristics such as minimizing latency, or the delay that a packet experiences from source to destination, or minimizing the number of hops, meaning the number of routers through which a packet traverses. When the packets reach their destination, they are reassembled in the correct order.

This packet switching approach, viewed historically, might seem obvious but it was a completely different approach from the traditional telephone network circuit switching approach which established a physical end-to-end path (or circuit) through a network from the originating caller to the destination receiver and maintained this path for the entirety of the call. The circuit switching approach is inherently centralized and hierarchical, in contrast to the packet switching approach in which network nodes are widely distributed in a mesh network. The distributed, mesh design of the packet switching architecture was motivated in part by the design requirement for the network to continue operating over surviving nodes in the event of a physical attack against other nodes. The Internet's underlying distributed and mesh architecture provides some protection against widespread outages relative to an architectural approach involving centralized and hierarchically organized switching nodes.

Despite the technically distributed nature of the Internet's switching infrastructure, there are other points of vulnerability that can be exploited to carry out Internet outages. Control points can be categorized several ways. Figure 9.1 offers a rough taxonomy illustrating nine categories of concentration points at which Internet outages can be carried out.

Each of these approaches produces different types of outages with varying reach and impacts ranging from highly targeted content blocking to catastrophic outages with sweeping effects on economic and social activity. The most bounded lever for disrupting the flow of information is content-specific filtering, such as blocking a news article on a web site or deleting a social media page. Political expression and economic activity surrounding the specific content is completely blocked but overall connectivity remains intact, web sites can still operate, and financial transactions beyond the affected content can still flow.

Approaches that target an entire Internet site rather than specific content on the site increase the degree of economic and social disruption by an order of magnitude. These approaches include financial and transactional service outages, DNS filtering, and network management-level disruptions. After WikiLeaks released sensitive United States diplomatic cables, financial intermediaries PayPal, MasterCard, and Visa chose to terminate the flow of funds to the WikiLeaks web site. This is an example of a targeted economic disruption of a specific web site, al-

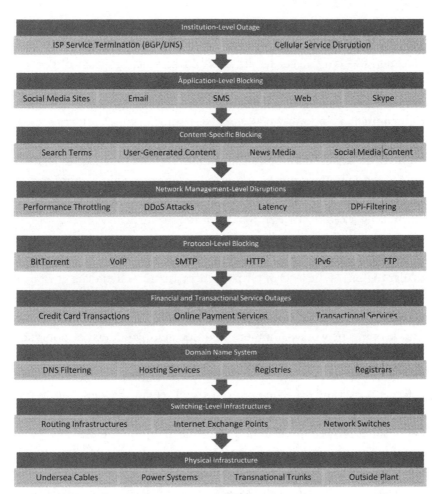

FIGURE 9.1: Internet Control Points Susceptible to Intentional or Unintentional Disruptions

beit in a highly politicized context. IP address blocking and DNS filtering similarly target a web site. As the previous chapter explained, DNS filtering can occur via domain name seizures or DNS redirection carried out by a domain name register. Network management and security level disruptions produce a similar site-specific effect. For example, DDoS attacks usually target a particular web site, bombarding it with requests to the extent that it effectively cuts off the flow of information and transactions surrounding the site. Blocking or throttling back traffic via DPI produces a similar disruption to a targeted site.

More widespread disruptions emanate from approaches that target specific services, such as application-level blocking or protocol-level blocking. Blocking a specific protocol blocks an entire class of service. Blocking FTP prohibits file downloads using this protocol; blocking P2P protocols seeks to block applications associated with illegal sharing of copyrighted media; blocking SMTP targets email; blocking VoIP affects services such as Skype. These approaches target broad categories of network services, having economic and political effects on the transactions made via these applications but not severing an entire network. Application-level blocking is similar in that it targets a particular service, such as prohibiting access to Twitter in parts of the world.

Interconnection and infrastructure disruptions can have much more catastrophic consequences including extensive access outages in a particular region. At the level of physical infrastructure, there is a great deal of redundancy of physical paths and a wide geographical distribution of physical equipment. But there still are concentration points. The power grid keeping network equipment and servers operational is one such physical infrastructure vulnerability. An intentional or unintentional disruption of the power grid would provide a near-complete severing of Internet access and the economic and social activity that depends on this access. The transoceanic cable system that serves as much of the Internet's global physical backbone is a similar point of vulnerability. Most international communications are routed via submarine fiber optic cables as opposed to satellites. This submarine infrastructure is susceptible to natural or human-made outages because of its physical vulnerability lying on the ocean floor and concentrated vulnerability where it emerges from the ocean at points of ingress into nation-bound terrestrial systems. Ship anchors sometimes damage these cables, but natural occurrences, such as earthquakes, tsunamis, volcanic eruptions, and icebergs, have also caused outages.

The magnitude 7.1 Hengchun earthquake that struck the coast of Taiwan in 2006 broke nine fiber optic cables, a catastrophic occurrence for the Internet's submarine infrastructure.[12] The impact of this natural disaster on communications was profound, temporarily affecting Internet and phone service and cutting off critical infrastructure flows including financial markets. Taiwan's largest telecommunications provider, Chunghwa Telecom Co., reported that the submarine cable breaks cut off 98 percent of its communication with Hong Kong, Malaysia, Singapore, and Thailand.[13] China Telecom also reported faults in several international undersea cable links including the so-called FLAG North Asia Loop, which disrupted communications between Asia and the United States.

Massive transoceanic cable outages have primarily resulted from natural occurrences but, because these links provide concentrated points of ingress into and egress out of a country, they are vulnerable to intentional outages, particularly if a government wished to retain communications within its country but sever communications between its country and the international community. This type of catastrophic disruption would prevent citizens and the media from communicating with the outside world and impede all global electronic trade with the affected nation.

The most effective so-called kill-switch approach is institutional as much as technological. Governments wishing to disrupt its citizens' Internet access can "order" service providers to shut down their networks. Based on the statements of network operators and the sequence of network service terminations that occurred during the 2011 Egyptian Internet outages, this appears to have been the route taken by the Egyptian government. Rather than all major Egyptian networks terminating service at once, there was more of a sequential series of outages that one would expect when a government official systematically made calls to service providers. The outages also affected cell phone services, supporting the notion that they were directed by the government and carried out by a variety of private institutions provisioning mobile phone and Internet access. An efficient way for a service provider to carry out an order to terminate its network's Internet presence is to target both the interior gateway protocol that determines how traffic is routed within its autonomous system and the exterior routing protocol, Border Gateway Protocol, that advertises to the rest of the world a set of Internet address prefixes indicating how to reach web sites and other services. Terminating these routes makes everything essentially disappear.

The Egyptian outage did not happen instantaneously. On January 25, citizens experienced application-specific outages such as an inability to reach Twitter. But by January 27 citizens experienced a near-total network outage. These outages were detectable to the outside world because each network operator's advertised BGP routes were suddenly with-drawn. For example, Renesys's analysis of the blackout sequence showed Telecom Egypt shutting down its services at 22:12; Raya at 22:13; Link Egypt at 22:17; Etisalat Misr at 22:19; and Internet Egypt at 22:25.[14] The outage not only involved the termination of inter-network connections but, as experienced by Egyptian citizens within the country, communica-tions within each network as well.

BGPmon produced a revealing table that indicated the number of Internet address prefixes that were advertised via Border Gateway Proto-col to the outside world on January 27 versus what had been advertised earlier that week. In some cases, networks completely disappeared to the outside world. For example, Vodafone previously announced forty-one Internet address prefixes but on January 27 advertised none of these collections of IP addresses previously accessible via its network (ASN 36935).[15]

Vodafone was one of the network operators directed to terminate services and obligated under Egyptian law to do so. Their press releases helped provide an account of how private companies were directed to carry out government instructions. Vodafone issued the following press release on January 28, 2011:

> All mobile operators in Egypt have been instructed to suspend
> services in selected areas. Under Egyptian legislation the
> authorities have the right to issue such an order and we are
> obliged to comply with it. The Egyptian authorities will be
> clarifying the situation in due course.[16]

The following day, Vodafone announced that it was able to restore Inter-net service and was "actively lobbying to reactivate SMS services as quickly as possible for our customers."[17] The company suggested that it had no legal alternative but to acquiesce to the demands of government authorities to suspend its services. This type of institutionally demarcated approach has a high socioeconomic toll because it results in a complete and catastrophic blackout of communications networks and severs all economic activity over these infrastructures.

This account clarifies that, although the monolithic term "kill-switch" is a misnomer, there are numerous points of concentration where out-ages and disruptions can occur. Countries that impose tight controls over content and access usually implement a collection of methods rather than a single approach. The system of censorship and access restrictions imposed by China is usually referred to as "The Great Firewall of China." There is no single firewall but rather a collection of technologies and institutional mechanisms that block certain words, web sites, IP addresses, and applications.

DELEGATED CENSORSHIP
Governments seeking to block or remove Internet content are usually not capable of directly removing information from the Internet unless the content deemed objectionable is housed on a government server, which is seldom the case. Instead, government agencies and courts approach the private companies housing or providing access to the information and request that they remove or block access to the information, at least for those citizens living under the initiating country's laws. These corporations are not passive intermediaries mechanically acquiescing to court orders and other government injunctions but rather actively adjudicate which requests to oblige and which to refuse.

Government Content Removal Requests and National Law
State requests to remove online content often originate in attempts to enforce compliance with national laws on defamation, state secrets, hate speech, blasphemy, child protection, pornography, privacy, lèse-majesté (insulting a monarch), and various restrictions on political speech under electoral and campaign finance laws. In other cases, governments seek to censor online content to silence political opposition or suppress the media.

Private companies responding to these government requests face a difficult and complicated decision process. Each national context has a unique statutory and constitutional framework of regulations and it is an intractable task to try to independently confirm the legitimacy of each appeal. A number of countries, including Austria, Belgium, Germany, and Israel have laws that prohibit the dissemination of Nazi propaganda and Holocaust denials. Dutch laws include hate-speech prohibitions against language that offends a group of people based on characteristics such as race, religion, sexual orientation, or disability. United States law provides strong protections for freedom of speech, protecting language that countries such as Brazil would characterize as legally prohibited hate speech. Thailand has a strong set of lèse-majesté laws criminalizing disparaging comments about the monarch. As an illustration of the gravity of these laws, a Thai citizen was sentenced to twenty years in prison for allegedly sending "four text messages to a government official about Thailand's royal family."[18] Communication laws vary considerably depending on national context. Commensurately, government requests for private companies to delete online content vary widely.

Google's Transparency Report presents a narrow but helpful snapshot of the types of state requests made to information intermediaries. Every six months, the company voluntarily releases data about the types of content removal requests it receives from governments and other entities. These requests target the removal of posts from its blog hosting site Blogger, videos hosted on YouTube, postings on its Orkut social media platform, links in Google search, and data and images in Street View, Google Earth, Google Maps, Google+, Google Groups, Google AdWords, and its other online properties.

In the last half of 2011, Brazil issued the highest number of content removal requests, at 194. The number of individual items targeted in these requests totaled 554. The United States had the highest number of total items targeted for removal at 6,192 items distributed within a total of 187 content removal requests. Looking into country-specific data helps demonstrate the types of content governments are targeting for removal. For example, Figure 9.2 visually depicts the distribution of rationales cited for the U.S. government's requests for content removal (data by request, not by item). The majority of requests related to either "defamation" or "privacy and security." The requests originating even in democratic societies are no means homogenous and reflect the values prioritized in each society. For example, in the same time period, the majority of Brazil's 194 requests, as depicted in Figure 9.3, fell into categories of "defamation" and "impersonation."

There are a few additional factors that would expand these depictions and the data more generally. For example, as discussed in the previous chapter, Google receives many requests to remove content allegedly violating copyright and trademark law. These requests often emanate from the private sector rather than governments so copyright removal is not adequately factored into these government numbers. It also does not

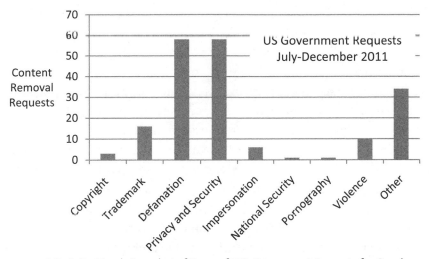

FIGURE 9.2: A Six-Month Snapshot of Types of U.S. Government Requests for Google to Remove Content

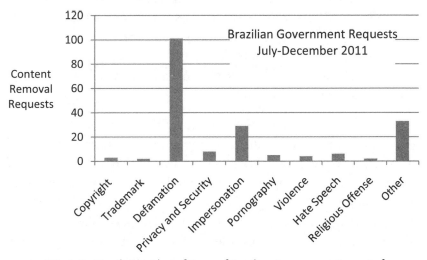

FIGURE 9.3: A Six-Month Snapshot of Types of Brazilian Government Requests for Google to Remove Content

sufficiently account for the number of child pornography takedown requests, which Google receives and quickly responds to in numerous ways. The statistics shared in this data store also do not reflect the many instances of content removals Google processes because of user-reported terms of service violations in its various online properties such as hate-speech restrictions in its Blogger platform. Such requests are not made by governments or court order. They arise from Google's own policies, as addressed in the Chapter 7 analysis of the public policy role of information intermediaries. Most notably, content removal statistics do not reflect outages and extensive service blockages due to government-ordered outages. For example, in the time period depicted in Figures 9.2 and 9.3, no Google products were accessible in Libya.

Government requests to take down information extend far beyond compliance with national statutes and concern with issues such as defamation, public decency, and privacy. Government intervention also reaches into even more clearly demarcated areas of political speech. Google's assessment of Internet freedom since it first began disclosing these data in 2010 sounds an alarm about the prevalence of government censorship of political content:

> This is the fifth data set that we've released. And just like every other time before, we've been asked to take down political speech. It's alarming not only because free expression is at risk, but because some of these requests come from countries you might not suspect—Western democracies not typically associated with censorship.[19]

As examples, Google singled out requests that it denied: The Spanish government requested the removal of 270 search returns linking to news or blog sites referencing public officials; and a Polish public institution requested the removal of search results linking to a web site critical of this institution.

By voluntarily publishing even these limited data about government takedown requests, however, Google is singling itself out relative to other intermediaries in demonstrating the importance it places on democratic values of transparency and openness. The larger question is why democratic governments are themselves not disclosing data about content removal requests.

Private Industry Adjudication of Government Censorship Requests
In the online public sphere, private corporations exert a great deal of power as arbiters of what does and does not get censored in the face of mounting government pressure. Without published data about corpo-

Table 9.1
Snapshot of Google's Rate of Compliance with Government Content-Removal Requests

COUNTRY	PERCENTAGE OF REMOVAL REQUESTS "FULLY OR PARTIALLY COMPLIED WITH"
Brazil	54
Canada	63
Germany	77
India	29
Pakistan	50
Spain	37
Thailand	100
Turkey	56
United Kingdom	55
United States	42

rate compliance with government censorship requests, it would be very difficult to characterize the public–private relationship surrounding takedown requests. Do corporations serve as a check on government power; a conciliatory force simply carrying out government requests; or something in between? Looking at narrow data provided by Google about government removal requests, the company complies with 65 percent of court orders (globally) and 47 percent of more informal government requests (globally). Expressed differently, Google refuses 35 percent of court orders and 53 percent of informal requests. Table 9.1 shows how the compliance percentage rate breaks down by some selected countries.

Looking at some specific examples of what the company has removed, or refused to remove, provides further insight into intermediary governance. Each example obviously exists in different circumstances and national legal frameworks and cultural norms. Table 9.2 provides representative examples of government content requests with which Google did and did not comply.[20]

Private intermediary decisions to remove online material, whether delegated from government or voluntarily executed, are shaped by many

Table 9.2

Government Content-Removal Requests with Which Google
Complied or Did Not Comply

AREA OF LAW OR CULTURE	REQUESTING COUNTRY & YEAR	GOVERNMENT REQUEST AND GOOGLE'S RESPONSE
Lèse-majesté laws	Thailand 2012	The Thai government requested the removal of 14 YouTube videos allegedly insulting the monarchy. Google restricted 3 from view in Thailand.
Defamation	United States 2012	At U.S. government request, Google removed 1,110 items from Google Groups over ongoing defamation of a man and his family.
Impersonation	Brazil 2012	Google complied with a court order to remove 860 Orkut profiles for impersonation.
Government criticism	Vietnam 2010	Google declined a Vietnamese government request to remove search results on a particular word containing a supposedly unflattering depiction of former Vietnamese leaders.
Police brutality	United States 2011	Google refused a local law enforcement agency request to delete YouTube videos portraying police brutality.
Privacy	Spain 2011	The Spanish Data Protection Authority requested the removal of 270 search links to sites referencing individuals or public figures and 3 blogs and 3 videos. Google did not remove this content.

variables. One factor is the framework of a company's own terms of service, which are both an expression of corporate values and a mechanism of private contractual agreements with users. Global public relations is another consideration. Private intermediaries must walk a fine line between taking down content that is "highly objectionable" to the majority of users and pushing back against unreasonable government censorship requests. In global markets with wide-ranging moral, religious, and political norms and varied histories, navigating this terrain is difficult. Corporations also obviously have to consider the local laws in which their services and products are used, as well as the governing laws in the country in which they are incorporated. The publication of transparency data demonstrates the nuanced power individual companies have in performing this mediation function.

In some contexts, though, technology companies have little discretionary power over government content-removal requests. The Chinese government requires Chinese search engine giant Baidu to carry out requests to censor various types of information. Eight Chinese residents of New York filed a $17 million lawsuit against Baidu in a U.S. district court after the company removed links to online material they posted about the democratic movement in China.[21] Cases like these will rarely have any bearing because of the court's lack of jurisdiction over Chinese policies.

Although private information intermediaries incorporate in a particular country, their reach is global rather than territorial. They are the digital public sphere mediating between governments and citizens and the spaces where communication occurs. Whether private industry is a "check on government power," "a rogue force," or something in between depends on context and specific circumstances. The data residing in the Google Transparency Report indicate disconnects between what governments demand and what private industry delivers and therefore supports the theme of the privatization of Internet governance.

DENIAL OF SERVICE ATTACKS AS HUMAN RIGHTS SUPPRESSION

Distributed denial of service software is an example of a technology that serves no purpose other than to suppress the flow of information. Chapter 4 explained the technology of DDoS attacks, techniques that hijack computers and instruct them to incapacitate a targeted computer by simultaneously flooding it with requests. Although these techniques are often presented as a form of dissent or political action against governments or other dominant social forces, they are equally mechanisms of government action against citizens. Either way, there is a tremendous collateral damage to freedom of expression. In parts of the world, governments have used DDoS techniques to silence alternative media, citizen journalists, and human rights organizations. For example, a Chinese-language web site in the United States was temporarily incapacitated by a DDoS attack. Boxun had been reporting on a political scandal in China and reportedly received an email threatening a DDoS attack unless it disabled its site.[22]

Responses that mitigate these attacks create a dilemma. One strategy for human rights organizations and alternative media to be more resistant to DDoS attacks is to shift the hosting of these sites from their own servers to a professional intermediary company such as Google's Blogger platform because these hosting sites tend to have greater defenses (for example, site mirroring and caching) against DDoS attacks than an entity hosting its own site. Ironically, greater intermediation can help promote security but also creates an additional institutional control point through which governments can attempt to enact delegated censorship.

RETHINKING FREEDOM OF EXPRESSION IN DIGITAL CONTEXTS

Attempts to control and stifle the circulation of ideas are a hallmark of closed societies. Censorship has always been a primary tool for prohibiting the dissemination of information construed as unfavorable to prevailing power structures. China censors a variety of media ranging from literature and newspapers to television and online applications. The ruling party censors information as varied as religious texts and pro-Tibetan material. Governments are not historically alone in suppressing information. The Roman Catholic Church for centuries maintained a List of Prohibited Books (Index Librorum Prohibitorum) which included scientific works by astronomers such as Johannes Kepler.

As Manuel Castells has explained, "Throughout history communication and information have been fundamental sources of power and counter-power, of domination and social change."[23] This battle has moved into online contexts and is increasingly being mediated by infrastructure and technologies of Internet governance. Those wishing to censor information can co-opt the tools of Internet governance—whether DPI, the DNS, interconnection protocols, or systems of information intermediation. This phenomenon provides insights into the nature of dissent in the digital context.

Freedom of expression is not merely about the content of expression but about the ability to use technological tools that are themselves an expression or that circumvent information controls. Dissentient expression in opposition to government policies has historically involved the dissemination of information such as news, flyers, or government-suppressed literature. Today it requires technological tools that circumvent technically mediated censorship or create the context for free expression. Security measures against DDoS attacks are necessary for freedom of expression to flourish. Because the Internet's technical architecture beneath the layer of content is largely unseen to Internet users, it would be easy to view expression as only about the dissemination of content. In the Internet governance context, freedom of expression is not only about speech and the dissemination of information—it can be praxis. Architecture includes control points. Circumventing control points requires technological tools and the ability to create innovative platforms for producing, sharing, and distributing content. Hardware and software governance are now inextricably connected to expression. And individual civil liberties online can no longer be sustained without paying attention to Internet governance policies.

CHAPTER TEN

Internet Governance and Internet Freedom

THE INTERNET IS GOVERNED. Internet governance control points are not legal control points, nor are they confined within nation-state boundaries. They are often manifested through the design of technical architecture, the decisions of global institutions of Internet governance, or the policies of private companies, all globally transcending forces in constant flux and in constant tension with national legal systems, intergovernmental treaties, and regional cultural norms. This book has explained more than a hundred levers of control through which Internet governance is enacted. Some of these are virtual and quite invisible to the Internet public, such as the allocation of critical Internet resources and the development of protocols. Others are infrastructure control points, such as Internet interconnection and last-mile Internet access. Still other forms of governance are much closer to Internet users, such as the privacy policies established by social media companies. All of these coordinating functions cumulatively keep the Internet operational.

Internet governance is a contested space reflecting broader global power struggles. It is also a twenty-first century reality that Internet governance has expanded beyond operational governance functions. Internet governance technologies are recognized as powerful forces to control the flow of content—for intellectual property rights enforcement, for example. They are also being co-opted for censorship, for surveillance, for kill-switch interventions, and for making political statements via technical mechanisms such as DDoS attacks.

Internet governance is also mercurial. Many emerging administrative questions will have to be resolved in the coming years. This final chapter presents some of these open governance areas and explains what is at stake. Depending on how they are resolved, many of these issues pose a threat to the stability of the Internet's architecture and to individual freedom. How these concerns are addressed (or not) will have implications for individual civil liberties in areas such as anonymity, security, and freedom of expression. These issues have common thematic questions at their root. What should be the balance between nation-state governance and nonterritorial modes of governance? What should be the appropriate role of corporate social responsibility in determining communicative contexts of political or cultural expression? What is the appropriate equilibrium between values related to sustaining Internet innovation and profitable business models versus individual autonomy and access to knowledge?

Unresolved issues at the intersection of Internet governance and Internet freedom include attempts to introduce government regulation at Internet interconnection points; broader tensions between multistakeholder governance and greater government control; online advertising as a Faustian bargain in which users trade privacy for free Internet goods; the trend away from online anonymity at the technical architecture level; the erosion of Internet interoperability; and the co-opting of the DNS into the Internet's primary content-control mechanism.

INTERNATIONAL PRESSURE TO REGULATE INTERNET INTERCONNECTION

Calls for direct government regulation of Internet interconnection have been present since the commercialization of the Internet's backbone in the 1990s. Those advocating for interconnection regulation have cited various rationales such as incentivizing the global spread of connection points or mediating equitable payment structures for the exchange of traffic between network operators. Despite these discussions, Internet interconnection has remained one of the most privatized areas of the Internet. The agreements network operators negotiate to interconnect bilaterally or at shared Internet exchange points are private contractual arrangements. The Internet is a self-formulated ecosystem of private networks. Historically, *ex post* regulation of these agreements has arisen only when there was an antitrust concern or a legal dispute related to a peering disagreement.

In the midst of this privatization, infrastructure interconnection raises a number of public interest concerns, many of them examined already in this book. Shared interconnection points can serve as central-ized points of control for government surveillance and censorship or con-centrated targets for Internet disruptions. The global distribution of IXPs, while growing rapidly, is asymmetrically concentrated in the developed world, raising interconnection equality concerns in emerging markets. Individual market incentives often trump issues of technical efficiency, with disincentives for incumbent global network operators to engage in settlement-free peering with newer entrants, viewed instead as potential customers. It is not surprising that policymakers have continued to ques-tion the adequacy of incentives for network operators to interconnect without regulatory constraints.

Governance questions about regulating Internet interconnection usually address issues of compensation and pricing. For example, the European Telecommunications Network Operators' Association (ETNO) submitted a proposal in advance of the 2012 International Telecommu-nication Union (ITU) World Conference on International Telecommu-nications (WCIT) that suggested three global policy alterations pertinent to Internet interconnection: expansion of the International Telecommu-nication Regulations (ITRs) to include Internet connectivity; involve-ment of nation states in "facilitating" interconnection; and the prospect of compensation between providers based on the policy of "sending party network pays."

The ITRs are an international treaty dating back to the late 1980s and addressing cross-border operation of telecommunications carriers. This pre-web treaty was directed at the international exchange of tradi-tional circuit-switched voice traffic. Many of the providers addressed by the treaty were either state-owned or monopoly- or oligopoly-oriented pri-vate national operators. The treaty is overseen by the International Tele-communication Union, a specialized subagency of the United Nations.

Interconnection proposals such as ETNO's, which did not gain trac-tion at the world conference, would transform Internet governance in profound and potentially disconcerting ways. Telecommunications carriers are concerned that "fair compensation is received for carried traffic" by network operators and are interested in the prospect of United Nations member states facilitating "the development of international IP interconnections."[1] The proposal interjects a traditional telecommunications regulatory philosophy into interconnection. Nation-state governance of interconnection points would be a significant change in itself but the expansion of ITRs to include Internet connectivity would also place Internet interconnection somewhat under the jurisdiction of the United Nations. The ITU itself has done a great deal to promote access to knowledge and bridge the digital divide around the world but U.N. member state oversight of Internet infrastructure would ascribe a great deal of influence to countries—such as Russia and China—with poor records on freedom of expression online. An open question is what their influence over global connection points would mean.

Global discussions about interconnection also raise the possibility of "sending party network pays" in international interconnection. This term conceptually originates in the traditional way that voice providers have connected, such as in international phone calls where the payment burden rests primarily with the originating caller and network. Translating this into Internet interconnection would amount to a transmission tax on large content providers such as Netflix and Hulu and conceivably even large media companies such as the BBC and CNN. In practice, if a user in South Africa chose to download a video from a YouTube server, the idea is presumably that Google would be compelled to pay the local carrier in South Africa to deliver the content to the requesting user.

As the Center for Democracy and Technology (CDT) has suggested, such a shift would "urge fundamental changes to the way the Internet works" and would increase the cost of Internet access, hinder access to knowledge in the developing world, and slow Internet economic development.[2] If content providers had to pay every time citizens requested their content, one can envision these content providers making market choices to not disseminate their content to parts of the world imposing this additional pricing obligation. The prospect of having to pay carriers to deliver content would also discourage the rise of new content companies, including those in emerging markets. Content origination pricing structures would have significant implications for both content innovation and access to knowledge.

But this form of interconnection pricing regulation could also have direct implications for Internet infrastructure. Interconnection points, including IXPs, would be the most viable point of enforcement for any new pricing regulation among network operators and content companies. Reductions in the number of content companies willing to connect in areas imposing content interconnection payments would reduce the financial viability of these localized sites (because of reductions in paying members) or discourage the development of new shared interconnection points. Either one of these technical and economic constraints on interconnection could affect populations in local emerging markets by ultimately reducing incentives for networks to connect directly to each other rather than at junctures outside the country. This would constrain traffic delivery optimization and increase latency by pushing media content away from these local markets.

Internet interconnection, because of its enormous public interest role, is a critical part of privatized Internet governance with implications for access to knowledge, participation in the digital public sphere, maximizing Internet growth and economic competition, and preserving a universal rather than balkanized Internet. Interest in interconnection regulation and proposals for government oversight of pricing structures will likely continue to be a central Internet governance concern between content companies, incumbent telecommunications providers, and governments with an interest in particular forms of interconnection monetization.

THE POLITICS OF "MULTISTAKEHOLDERISM"

As this book has sought to explain, Internet governance is not a monolithic system with keys that can be handed over to one group or another. It is a multi-layered system of administration and operational oversight that spans areas as diverse as standards setting, cybersecurity, and interconnection agreements. Therefore, a question such as "who should control the Internet, the United Nations or some other organization" makes no sense whatsoever. The appropriate question involves determining what is the most effective form of governance in each specific context. A constantly shifting balance of powers between private industry, international technical governance institutions, governments, and civil society has characterized contemporary Internet governance approaches. This balance of powers is often called "multistakeholderism."

It is important to view multistakeholderism not as a value in itself applied universally but as a question of what form of administration is necessary in any particular context. Certain areas of Internet governance should jurisdictionally be overseen by national governments or via international treaties. Other areas are effectively administered by the private sector or non-profit institutions. In these cases, transparency and accountability are values necessary to create the legitimacy for these groups to establish public policy for the Internet.

Still other areas require the direct involvement of many stakeholders. In these cases, the question often reduces to one of the appropriate balance between national regulation and private governance. This is a contentious issue in many areas and certainly remains so in the distribution of political power around the functions ICANN performs, although this agonistic condition might actually help preserve aspects of critical Internet resource governance that already work. The functions performed under the auspices of ICANN are narrow but important components of Internet governance, such as overseeing IP addresses and a variety of functions related to the DNS. Many of these functions are among the most centralized in Internet governance. Because of the importance and visibility of the functions ICANN oversees, the institution has been heavily scrutinized since its inception.

Three primary discourses epitomize power struggles over procedural and jurisdictional aspects of ICANN. The first is a general critique about accountability and procedures. ICANN has adopted a number of participatory governance structures emphasizing multistakeholderism, some viewed by Internet governance experts as too diffuse to be effective or adequately accountable.[3] The second critical discourse involves international concern about its historic relationship with the U.S. Department of Commerce. Although ICANN has moved from unilateral U.S. oversight to a more international structure, its IANA function that carries out many of the most critical Internet governance responsibilities is still under contract with the Commerce Department. For more than a decade, member states of the United Nations have applied pressure to end this U.S. administrative relationship with ICANN. This effort has a long history, perhaps best epitomized by a recommendation out of the 2005 U.N. Working Group on Internet Governance calling for a diminishment of what it viewed as U.S. hegemony over domain names and numbers. The U.N. definition of Internet governance emerged out of this process: "Internet governance is the development and application by Governments, the private sector and civil society, in their respective roles, of shared principles, norms, rules, decision-making procedures, and programmes that shape the evolution and use of the Internet."[4] Note the prominent listing of governments in this multistakeholder definition.

The third discourse responds to the second, with concern by private industry, technologists, and American policymakers that the United Nations will capture authority over crucial aspects of the Internet. Instead, these stakeholders emphasize the need for multistakeholder rather than centralized coordination. For example, the U.S. government's 2009 "Affirmation of Commitments" with ICANN emphasized private sector–led multistakeholderism: "DOC (Department of Commerce) affirms its commitment to a multi-stakeholder, private sector led, bottom-up policy development model for DNS technical coordination that acts for the benefit of global Internet users. A private coordinating process, the outcomes of which reflect the public interest, is best able to flexibly meet the changing needs of the Internet and of Internet users."[5]

The basic principle underlying all of these concerns is multistakeholder governance, albeit three different forms of multistakeholderism: widely diffused, government led, and private sector led. "Multistakeholder governance" of the Internet has become a dominant theme taken up by the United Nations, political leaders, advocacy organizations, and scholars, many of whom have been involved in the institutional U.N. process of the World Summit on the Information Society (WSIS), the Working Group on Internet Governance (WGIG), and the later U.N. Internet Governance Forum (IGF), a series of international conferences on Internet governance that began in Athens, Greece in 2006.

At the 2011 G-8[6] meeting in Deauville, France, leaders agreed "on a number of key principles, including freedom, respect for privacy and intellectual property, multi-stakeholder governance, cybersecurity, and protection from crime, that underpin a strong and flourishing Internet."[7] Advocates of multistakeholder governance, though not necessarily advocating for this form of governance as a replacement for nation-state governance, have presented the concept as essential for cross-border circumstances, such as the Internet, and as an impetus for prompting more democratic processes around the world: "Multistakeholder governance can foster democracy, enrich existing representative frameworks and empower citizens in our interconnected and interdependent world."[8]

Acknowledging the positive intentions of multistakeholder advocacy, there are also reasons to be cautious about the implementation of such approaches and the underlying agendas sometimes masked in these framings. The multistakeholder Zeitgeist has elevated the concept to a value in itself or an end in itself without critically examining what this concept can obfuscate. Multistakeholderism directed in a top-down manner or directed broadly rather than at a specific administrative function is usually a proxy for a broader political power struggle. For example, in international discussions, the term "multistakeholderism" began as a proxy for the ongoing concern about the traditional tie between the United States and ICANN. The U.N. Internet Governance Forum itself arose from the impasse over U.N. calls for a diminishment of U.S. control of the root and American resistance to these recommendations. The purpose of the IGF was to create a formal space for multistakeholder dialogue about global Internet policy.[9] There has been a great emphasis on the IGF in Internet governance scholarship, a phenomenon that may be overdone considering that the IGF is not an Internet governance body. It is a series of conferences with no policymaking authority whatsoever. Even as a space for global discourse, some have criticized the IGF for avoiding controversial subject matter such as government censorship or intellectual property rights.[10] The practice of Internet governance has continued to occur outside of this dialogue in institutions, in private decision making, and in government Internet policies. The focus on multistakeholder discussions of the IGF has therefore had little relevance to multistakeholderism in Internet governance as actually practiced.

Another concern about formal mechanisms of multistakeholderism is the risk of inherent centralization. Multistakeholder approaches, to be effective, tend to become centralized governance processes requiring organization, procedural mechanisms, and even hierarchy to ensure that all stakeholder voices are heard. Who should serve as this gatekeeper and enforcer? The Internet's success has traditionally emanated from bottom-up involvement whereby no one entity is in control of Internet governance in its entirety. The presumption behind the enforcement of multistakeholderism is government centralization because government has the necessary legitimacy to create the processes to foster and enforce multistakeholder approaches. This question of legitimacy creates an infinite regress of having to have an enforcer of multistakeholderism. When multistakeholderism elevates the role of private industry in enforcing Internet policymaking, this also raises legitimacy questions.

A similar concern about multistakeholder governance is raised with the following question: Whose democratic values? Multistakeholder approaches that seek to promote democracy can be a race to the lowest common denominator of what is an acceptable democratic value. For example, China is centrally involved in multistakeholder discussions in U.N. groups and fora. China's conception of democratic values on the Internet is not a conception of democracy that would promote Internet freedom at all, but one concerned with restricting the flow of information through filtering and blocking technologies. A final caveat is that multistakeholderism is inherently focused on traditional governments. Multistakeholderism, as explained above, can be a proxy for efforts to diminish the power, real or perceived, of the United States government over central Internet governance functions such as the distribution of Internet names and numbers. Underlying these efforts is the desire to have power sharing by many governments, rather than one. The risk is that the role of civil society, the input of corporations, and the contributions of new global institutional forms are omitted.

Multistakeholder models of Internet governance in the most distributed and general sense of decentralization and diversity can avoid the pitfalls of these formalized mechanisms of multistakeholderism that, ironically, tip the scale toward governmental control and centralization. This book has explained the many points of governance control over the Internet. It is exactly this decentralized and distributed balance of power that is likely responsible for the ongoing resilience, stability, and adaptability of the Internet. The difference is between a top-down imposition of multistakeholderism and the way actual multistakeholder approaches organically grow in practice.

ONLINE ADVERTISING AS FAUSTIAN BARGAIN
TRADING PRIVACY FOR FREE INTERNET GOODS

Internet privacy concerns permeate many areas of Internet governance, including the design of protocols, the privacy settings in social media, and the deep packet inspection practices of ISPs. The evolving practice of online advertising models may become an even greater privacy dilemma.

Whether one views it this way or not, the business model supporting much of the Internet industry is predicated on users relinquishing individual privacy in exchange for free information and software.[11] Material and financial barriers to the ability of individuals to produce and distribute information have radically fallen, a phenomenon that has helped to advance possibilities for freedom of expression and creativity.[12] But one of the enablers of these new possibilities is the preponderance of free software platforms, in turn made possible by extensive industrial systems of online advertising.

Whether news articles or online videos, much digital information is basically "free." This evolution of access to free knowledge and entertainment has created new Internet industries even as the disruptive momentum of this evolution has eroded revenue streams of dominant media forces. Money still changes hands, but this exchange centers around online advertising revenue rather than the exchange of payments for information and information goods. The flow of currency has not stopped; it has just shifted to a predominantly advertiser-supported model. Scholars and policymakers have directed much attention to how these new market mechanisms and generational expectations about free information have challenged traditional media business models. This appropriate focus on the transformative economic and social implications of access to free digital *content* has deflected attention from the accompanying transformation from *software* as a basic consumer expenditure to a completely free good.

Consumers are so accustomed to free social media applications that it might not even register that these software programs are free. Those involved in the "free software movement" advocate for free as in free speech (Latin: *libre*) rather than free as in free beer (Latin: *gratis*). What has occurred in practice is a preponderance of software as free as in free beer. The public does not pay for the use of social media platforms Orkut or Twitter or Internet search engines Google, Yahoo!, or Bing. Adding a video to an information repository such as YouTube is not a market exchange. Email software and storage is free. Online GPS maps can be freely downloaded. This transformation from *ad valorem* to *gratis* software is as groundbreaking as the evolution to free information. This transformation does not imply that the overall software market has eroded whatsoever or is part of an altruistic or pro bono software development culture. Developing and maintaining social media software is expensive. Software companies like Google and Facebook require massive annual operating budgets. The cost to operate Google in the second quarter of 2012 alone was more than $6 billion.[13] What it does mean is that revenue sources have shifted from consumers to third parties.

Rather than goods and services economically changing hands between producers and consumers, these commodities are exchanged for free and financial compensation for goods and services has shifted almost entirely from consumer to advertising intermediary. This third-party system requires two forms of economic currency: "eyeballs" and personal data. It is broadly referred to as an attention economy in which the number and quality of individuals exposed to advertisements is quantifiable, and a personalization economy in which systems of advertising value subscriber data collected, retained, and aggregated across platforms.

From an Internet governance perspective, this transformation to advertisement-supported Internet intermediation raises questions about the extent to which the *libre* has been relinquished for the *gratis*. As Internet privacy scholar Michael Zimmer explains, "a kind of Faustian bargain emerges: Search 2.0 promises breadth, depth, efficiency, and relevancy, but enables the widespread collection of personal and intellectual information in the name of its perfect recall."[14]

Chapter 7 discussed the privacy implications of several forms of online advertising including behavioral, contextual, locational, and social advertising. In all of these approaches, it is increasingly standard practice for an individual's behavior to be tracked over numerous unrelated web sites by a private third party that has no direct relationship or contractual agreement with this individual.

The Internet's original architectural approach was dependent on addressing and routing information based on a virtual IP address. This type of virtual identification itself raises privacy issues, although primarily through traceable identification when tied to another piece of information about an individual's identity. But it is quite far removed from the enormous system of personal and administrative information collected via contemporary social networking platforms, cell phones, and search engines.

The published privacy policies of online service providers offer a sense of the types of individual data that are collected and how this information is used and shared. Individuals using a social media platform or smartphone app might feel that their online transactions are private but, in practice, a great deal of information is collected during these activities. Much of this information is not related to content but to associated information such as administrative and logistical identifiers. The following are some of the types of information collected about individuals:

- device information, including unique hardware identifiers
- mobile phone number, if accessing the Internet from a phone
- IP address
- time and date of phone calls
- actual location based on GPS, Wi-Fi, or cellular signal from a mobile device.[15]

The collection and sharing of data about individuals is at the heart of both online advertising and new forms of government surveillance. This type of data collection poses a host of problems for individual privacy, the protection of children online, and the possibility of social and economic harm from the sharing, intentional or not, of these data. For individuals aware of this extensive system of data collection, this can change the conditions of free speech by having a chilling effect on what citizens are willing to say or do online. Conversely, extensive limitations to these practices could destroy business models providing free software platforms and the possibilities for free expression these platforms have afforded. The question of how to balance the protection of individual privacy with the ability of these new business models to flourish is the difficult Internet policy question.

Government statutes about online privacy often focus on industry-specific transactions in areas such as health care or finance. Other efforts have tried to focus specifically on the protection of children online or regulations related to surveillance, such as limiting the capture of street view pictures for use in online maps. Privacy laws have struggled to keep up with changes in technology and different regions have different philosophical views about the extent of privacy that is reasonable or feasible to expect. The European Union has relatively strong privacy protections, viewing the protection of personal data as a basic human right and reflecting this philosophy in its "Data Protection Directive."

How the balance between privacy and industry models based on online advertising will unfold is not at all settled. As in other areas of Internet governance, interventions in online advertising privacy practices can occur in several ways ranging from legal approaches such as intergovernmental agreements, national laws, and private contractual agreements between end users and platforms to more informal mechanisms such as voluntary industry standards for privacy protection choices in online advertising and technological circumvention methods that give individuals the choice about what data are collected, retained, or exchanged with other third parties. At a minimum, what has normatively worked in other Internet governance arenas would suggest that industry disclosures about privacy practices and the user freedom to decide what information is shared are quite reasonable to expect. These practices of disclosure and individual choice could forestall laws that would potentially provide a homogenous privacy approach for everyone and interject regulatory burdens on emerging industries.

THE EROSION OF ANONYMITY

Shortly after the invention of the World Wide Web in the early 1990s, a famous cartoon in *The New Yorker* depicted an Internet-surfing dog along with the caption "On the Internet, nobody knows you're a dog." The initial end-to-end architecture and other technical affordances of the Internet seemed to normatively promote possibilities for anonymous communication, including the simple ability to anonymously surf the web from a browser. At a minimum, there was traceable anonymity, meaning a certain expectation for privacy unless law enforcement obtained from a service provider additional personal identity information associated with the IP address linked with the online information. As the Internet and intermediary platforms have developed, there is a significant fissure between perceptions of online anonymity and the reality of hidden identity infrastructures beneath the layer of content.

During the Middle East uprisings that would later be called the "Arab Spring," media outlets around the globe became captivated with the personal blog postings of Amina Abdallah Arraf. Her postings were set in the historical context of revolutionary protests against governments in Tunisia, Egypt, Lebanon, Syria, and other Arab states with the rest of the world watching video footage of street protests and marches, sometimes with violent responses from government forces. The world was also captivated by the use of social media such as Twitter, Facebook, and YouTube both to organize social resistance efforts and to disseminate information about these social movements to the rest of the world. It was in this political context that this blogger's voice offered riveting accounts of the efforts of the Syrian government to crack down on protestors.

The blogger—of the "Gay Girl in Damascus" blog—described herself as an American-born lesbian living in Damascus, Syria. Her postings described her personal experiences protesting on the streets of Damascus. She offered accounts of her eyes burning from tear gas as she witnessed other protesters vomiting from the tear gas.[16] She also offered a vivid picture of Syria's oppressive climate for gays and lesbians, describing a frightening visit from Syrian security forces to her own home.[17] Her accounts ceased abruptly after someone described as Amina's cousin posted an announcement on the blog claiming that Syrian government security forces had abducted Amina. The cousin's posting provided vivid details of Amina's location and activities prior to her abduction and stated that her friend had witnessed Amina's seizure by three men in their early twenties. Her abduction attracted wide attention from prominent global media sources including the *Washington Post*, which reported that "Arraf, 35, a Syrian American who was born in Staunton, VA., joined the more than 10,000 people who have been plucked from their homes or from the streets of cities since the Syrian uprising began 11 weeks ago."[18]

But the story and the person herself were fabrications. After a barrage of media attention and the inception of an inquiry by the U.S. Department of State, the young lesbian blogger in Syria was revealed to be a straight, middle-aged, American man studying in Scotland. After a week of media concern over Amina's disappearance, Tom MacMaster released a statement publicly confessing that he had fabricated the character of Amina and that the blog postings were his fictitious creations. Prior to his confession, a London woman had seen the media attention over Amina's abduction and claimed that the photos widely broadcast over the Internet were actually photos of her. When her claim surfaced, the media began questioning the veracity of the "Gay Girl in Damascus" circumstances.[19]

This saga raises obvious questions related to content, such as problems with journalistic practices and proper vetting of stories, particularly when a story "goes viral" and there is little time to fact-check or contact witnesses. But from an Internet governance standpoint, it raises issues about the authentication of identities and the question about whether policies should ever prohibit online anonymity. This is not a hypothetical question. Bans on anonymity are entering policy discourses around the globe. But these discussions focus on the content level and what Internet users, including the media, perceive.

There can at least be the perception of anonymity at the content level. Anyone can create a blog under a *nom de plume* or establish a Twitter account with a handle that does not reveal the individual's offline identity. But at the layer of infrastructure, anonymity is no longer readily feasible. Anyone can gain information about who has registered a domain name by looking this up in the WHOIS (pronounced "who is") database, which includes the domain name registrant's name, mailing address, and email address. The WHOIS database, under revision as of this writing, keeps track of who has registered a domain name.[20] Even though it is possible to anonymize this information by proxy, many registrants have not thought to do this because of unfamiliarity with both the WHOIS database and the anonymization process.

Some social media policies and news commentary spaces require individuals to use real-name identifiers. Facebook's policy requires that "Facebook users provide their real names and information" and "will not provide any false personal information on Facebook."[21] It is easy to cite social rationales for the use of real identifiers. Real identification requirements are believed to discourage anonymous cyberbullying, although there is ample cyberbullying in social media platforms requiring real identification. The use of real identification is also thought to promote civility in news and blog comment areas and to foster digital citizenship.[22] Looked at from a more global perspective, these real identification requirements in social media platforms can present problems for activists, and citizens generally, in areas of the world with repressive governments wanting to crack down on dissent. Uncritical accounts linking social media and political revolutions fail to acknowledge the ways in which these same forms of social media are used by governments to monitor plans for future protests, to suppress speech, and to identify those who participated in government protests from photographs posted in social media. Individuals have free choice about whether to join social media platforms, but even someone who has never joined these platforms can be photographed and identified online.

Global regulatory interest in requiring real identification has increasingly emerged. It is common practice in parts of the world to require the presentation of an identification card to gain access to the Internet in a cybercafé. India requires cybercafé owners to determine, and track for a year, the identity of their patrons by requesting some official form of identification card such as a driver's license, passport, or voter identification card.[23] In early 2013, Chinese authorities were contemplating a policy to prohibit digital anonymity, even at the content level. The policy would require real name registration in exchange for Internet use. Internet scholar Michael Froomkin cautions, "The next wave of Internet regulation is now in sight: the abolition of online anonymity."[24] This trend away from anonymity is emerging on several fronts: national statutory mandates for real identification for online access or speech, platform requirements for real identification, and cultural pressure for real identification over concerns about the role of anonymity in cyberbullying and online hate speech. The extent and direction of these moves is an open question of global Internet governance and one that has to balance conflicting social values such as the desire to promote civil discourse versus the desire to protect individual privacy.

Apart from requirements for real identification at the content and application level, traceable anonymity and technical identifiers are much more embedded. In terms of easy traceable anonymity, Internet subscriptions, whether home Internet access or a mobile phone service, usually require a billing arrangement and the presentation of an identification card. Technical identifiers that can link information sent over the Internet to an individual exist at the level of hardware (a globally unique binary number on a physical Ethernet card); via an IP address or unique combination of software attributes on a computer; or locationally, via cell phone location, Wi-Fi antenna location, or GPS.

Table 10.1 depicts some of these layers of technical identity infrastructure. These identifiers, in combination with the personal information gathered when subscribing to an Internet service, readily enable

Table 10.1

Routes to Traceable Identity

Government-Level
- Proposals for Mandatory National Identification Systems

Service Provider-Level
- ID Requirements at Cybercafés
- ID Requirements for Mobile Subscription
- ID Requirements for Fixed Internet Access
- Any Access Tied to Billing Arrangement
- Globally Unique Phone Number

Locational Identification
- Wi-Fi Antenna Position
- Network Segment of IP Address
- Cellular Base Station Triangulation
- GPS Triangulation

Application-Level Identification
- Real Identification Requirements for Social Media Accounts
- Real Name Requirements for Media and Blog Comments

Logical/Virtual Identification
- Internet Protocol Address
- Unique Software Attributes on Computers
- Cookies

Unique Hardware Identification
- Unique Hardware Address on Ethernet Card
- Mobile Phone Hardware Device Identifiers

---

traceable anonymity. A law enforcement agent, armed with a unique technical identifier or combination of identifiers, can approach a network or application provider to find out the real identity of the person associated with that technical identifier. Traceable anonymity, via a court order, is probably sufficient for balancing some individual privacy versus law enforcement goals. But real identification requirements extend much farther than traceable anonymity, eliminating the possibility for anonymity even at the content level. The existence of such an entrenched identity infrastructure beneath the layer of content might actually make it quite challenging to move toward greater affordances for anonymity online. The great question is what implications movements away from anonymous or at least pseudonymous speech will have for freedom of expression, for the online political sphere, and for Internet culture.

CHALLENGES TO INTERNET INTEROPERABILITY

Another emerging Internet governance challenge relates to interoperability, the fundamental principle on which the Internet was originally designed.[25] As explained in Chapter 3, the Internet works because of the standards that provide universal order to the stream of os and 1s that represent emails, movies, audio, and other types of information. Internet use requires the basic TCP/IP protocols underlying the Internet as well as the deployment of countless formats that standardize how music should be encoded and compressed (for example, MP3); how video and image should be formatted (for example, MPEG and JPEG); how information should be transmitted between a web browser and web server (for example, HTTP); or how voice should be transmitted over the Internet (for example, VoIP). Interoperability is not a given and is still a fairly recent phenomenon from the era in which proprietary networking protocols prevented computing devices made by Apple from communicating with computers made by IBM.

Some Internet applications are drifting back to the era where interoperability was not a valued principle; this is not a positive development for the Internet's technical architecture or for innovation. For example, social media approaches erode interoperability in four distinct ways: lack of inherent compatibility among platforms; lack of Uniform Resource Locator (URL) universality; lack of data portability; and lack of universal searchability. In all of these cases, standard approaches are available but companies have explicitly designed interoperability out of their systems. Internet governance approaches, especially via the design of technical architecture, have historically embedded principles of compatibility, data portability, universal searchability, and URL accessibility. This approach is no longer the de facto technical norm for Internet applications.

For example, Skype, though excellent and serving an important social function, includes proprietary specifications that technologically constrain compatibility with other voice systems. Skype is an instant messaging application that allows individuals to communicate with other Skype users by voice, video, or text. The application has become widely popular as a video calling service not only because it works well but because the software can be downloaded for free and the cost of Skype-to-Skype long distance calling over an existing Internet connection is free. Skype, purchased by Microsoft in 2011, has become popular with hundreds of millions of users. Skype is also a protocol: a somewhat proprietary protocol. It uses an unpublished, closed signaling standard that is not natively compatible with other VoIP services.

Proprietary protocols force a certain type of business model. Someone with a Skype application wishing to make an off-Skype call has to subscribe to unlock this interconnectivity feature. This proprietary approach has gained a great deal of market traction, but is quite a departure from traditional Internet applications such as web browsers and email clients that are natively compatible with other browsers and email clients without having to unlock interoperability or pay an additional fee. For example, someone using a Yahoo! email address can automatically reach someone using a Gmail address. If email had remained proprietary, this would obviously not be the case.

There is a similar technical and business model retreat from universality in URLs. The web was designed explicitly to provide a universally consistent way of reaching a web site from any browser in any part of the world. Social media approaches have traded this open approach for more siloed nomenclature in which hypertexts among information sources remain relegated within this silo and are not necessarily accessible from other platforms or applications. As web inventor Tim Berners-Lee cautions,

The isolation occurs because each piece of information does not have a URI (URL). Connections among data exist only within a site. So the more you enter, the more you become locked in. Your social-networking site becomes a central platform—a closed silo of content, and one that does not give you full control over your information in it. The more this kind of architecture gains widespread use, the more the Web becomes fragmented, and the less we enjoy a single, universal information space.[26]

More proprietary platforms are what the market has selected but this selection has consequences. There is not the interoperability among social networking platforms, for example, that exists for other web platforms or email applications. This is a very real shift from an open, unified web to a more balkanized Internet. In an open, universal web, standards are published. This open publication of standards has contributed to rapid Internet innovation because any company can use the standard to develop new products and features. In an open, universal web, standards are developed, for the most part, in openly participatory groups like the W3C or the IETF. In realms that are partitioned, protocols are controlled by individual companies and the only applications permitted are those authorized by these gatekeepers. These gatekeeping approaches have enormous market inertia but, from the standpoint of Internet governance, they are diminishing universal interoperability.

This de-prioritization of interoperability is likely to extend into emerging Internet architectures such as cloud computing and eHealth systems. For example, approaches to cloud computing by different software companies are not yet settling on industry-wide compatibility standards. This lack of *ex ante* standardization for cloud computing and other emerging information models will likely present challenges to consumers such as vendor lock-in and lack of data portability.

THE TRANSFORMATION OF THE DOMAIN NAME SYSTEM INTO CONTENT ENFORCEMENT MECHANISM

The Internet's Domain Name System is one of the foundational technical systems of Internet governance necessary for making the Internet usable and universal. Although the task of translating between alphanumeric names that humans use and binary numbers that routers use is straightforward, the fantastically massive scale and institutional oversight complexity of this system is daunting. A consistent translation of names into numbers is what makes a web site consistently available anywhere in the world. The DNS is part of what makes the Internet universal. This book has described several ways in which the DNS has been co-opted for content control uses beyond its principal address resolution function, including nation-specific censorship of objectionable content. It has also described efforts to use the DNS to address the problem of global piracy. A looming governance question is whether this type of blocking will move from authoritative registries into local recursive DNS servers. The latter could further transform the Internet from a universal to a balkanized digital sphere in which the content that can be accessed is dependent on the local operator through which an individual accesses the web. Before making such a significant move to potentially fragmenting the Domain Name System, and as this book has emphasized, it is crucial for policymakers and the public alike to understand how such a shift would affect the Internet's security, stability, and universality.

PROSPECTS FOR THE FUTURE OF INTERNET GOVERNANCE

The only constant in Internet governance is the condition of constant change, creating the omnipresent uncertainty of rivalrous alternative futures. Internet governance is a potent and complicated form of governance because it involves the technical mediation of the public sphere and the privatization of conditions of civil liberties. Although the Internet is governed, this governance is not fixed any more than Internet technical architecture is fixed. Authority over the Internet is constantly evolving to address new business models, emerging technologies, and shifting cultural contexts. At one point in Internet history, a single individual served as a central coordinator of several key Internet governance systems. As the Internet's architecture and public interest entanglements expanded over the years, policymaking evolved to predominantly U.S. institutions and then to the contemporary multistakeholder model whereby governance is enacted by private entities, new global institutions, the design of technical architecture, and governmental bodies. Vinton Cerf has explained, "The Net prospered precisely because governments—for the most part—allowed the Internet to grow organically, with civil society, academia, private sector and voluntary standards bodies collaborating on development, operation and governance."[27]

Coordination and administration necessary to keep the Internet operational require huge financial investments and commitments. Private industry not only performs many aspects of Internet governance, it also funds much of Internet governance, whether Internet exchange points, infrastructure security, network management, and the business models that sustain standardization and critical resource administration.

From a global twenty-first century perspective, Internet freedom is not yet achieved. The same exact technologies that increase possibilities for economic and communicative freedom are also used by governments and private industry to restrict these freedoms. No matter how strenuously media narratives associate social media and other Internet technologies with global political change, there is as much government Internet repression as there are possibilities for Internet political expression. In many parts of the world totalitarian regimes enact surveillance networks of control that limit possibilities for individual privacy and freedom. Even in democratic countries, degrees of Internet freedom related to privacy, expression, and individual autonomy are constantly negotiated against conflicting values of national security and law enforcement.

As goes Internet governance, so goes Internet freedom. Much is at stake in how Internet governance continues to unfold. As Vinton Cerf warned, "If all of us do not pay attention to what is going on, users worldwide will be at risk of losing the open and free Internet that has brought so much to so many."[28] Public awareness and engagement in these issues are critical considering the public interest issues in the balance.

AD   Area Director
AfriNIC   African Network Information Centre
APNIC   Asia Pacific Network Information Centre
ARIN   American Registry for Internet Numbers
ARPANET   Advanced Research Projects Agency Network
AS   Autonomous System
ASCII   American Standard Code for Information Interchange
ASN   Autonomous System Numbers
BGP   Border Gateway Protocol
BIT   Binary Digit
CA   Certificate Authority
ccTLD   Country-Code Top-Level Domain
CDA   Communications Decency Act
CDN   Content Delivery Network or Content Distribution Network
CDT   Center for Democracy and Technology
CERT   Computer Emergency Response Team
CFAA   Computer Fraud and Abuse Act
CIR   Critical Internet Resource
CIX   Commercial Internet eXchange
CNNIC   China Internet Network Information Center
CRPD   Convention on the Rights of Persons with Disabilities
CSIRT   Computer Security Incident Response Team

DARPA	Defense Advanced Research Projects Agency
DBMS	Database Management System
DDoS	Distributed Denial of Service
DEC	Digital Equipment Corporation
DMCA	Digital Millennium Copyright Act
DNS	Domain Name System
DNSSEC	Domain Name System Security Extensions
DPI	Deep Packet Inspection
DSL	Digital Subscriber Line
EFF	Electronic Frontier Foundation
ETNO	European Telecommunications Network Operators' Association
EU	European Union
FAA	Federal Aviation Administration
FCC	Federal Communications Commission
FTC	Federal Trade Commission
FTP	File Transfer Protocol
Gbps	Gigabits Per Second
GNI	Global Network Initiative
GPS	Global Positioning System
HTML	HyperText Markup Language
HTTP	Hypertext Transfer Protocol
IAB	Internet Architecture Board or Internet Activities Board
IANA	Internet Assigned Numbers Authority
IBM	International Business Machines
ICANN	Internet Corporation for Assigned Names and Numbers
ICCPR	International Covenant on Civil and Political Rights
ICE	Immigration and Customs Enforcement
ICESCR	International Covenant on Economic, Social, and Cultural Rights
ICMP	Internet Control Message Protocol
ICT	Information and Communication Technologies
IEEE	Institute of Electrical and Electronics Engineers
IESG	Internet Engineering Steering Group
IETF	Internet Engineering Task Force
IGF	Internet Governance Forum
IP	Internet Protocol
IPR	Intellectual Property Rights
IPv4	Internet Protocol Version 4
IPv6	Internet Protocol Version 6

ISO	International Organization for Standardization
ISOC	Internet Society
ISP	Internet Service Provider
ITRs	International Telecommunication Regulations
ITU	International Telecommunication Union
IXP	Internet Exchange Point
JPEG	Joint Photographic Experts Group
LACNIC	Latin America and Caribbean Network Information Centre
LAN	Local Area Network
LIR	Local Internet Registry
MAE	Metropolitan Area Exchanges
MP3	MPEG-1 or MPEG-2 Audio Layer 3
MPAA	Motion Picture Association of America
MPEG	Moving Picture Experts Group
NAP	Network Access Point
NDA	Nondisclosure Agreement
NIC	Network Information Center
NSFNET	National Science Foundation Network
NTIA	National Telecommunications and Information Administration
P2P	Peer-to-Peer
P3P	Platform for Privacy Preferences Project
PIPA	PROTECT IP Act, or Preventing Real Online Threats to Economic Creativity and Theft of Intellectual Property Act
QoS	Quality of Service
RAND	Reasonable and Nondiscriminatory
RFC	Request for Comments
RIAA	Recording Industry Association of America
RIPE NCC	Réseaux IP Européens Network Coordination Centre
RIR	Regional Internet Registry
RPKI	Resource Public Key Infrastructure
RTP	Real-time Transport Protocol
SAC	Standardization Administration of China
SCADA	Supervisory Control and Data Acquisition
SIDR	Secure Inter-Domain Routing
SIP	Session Initiation Protocol
S/MIME	Secure Multipurpose Internet Mail Extensions
SMTP	Simple Mail Transfer Protocol
SNA	Systems Network Architecture

SOPA	Stop Online Piracy Act
SRI NIC	Stanford Research Institute's Network Information Center
STS	Science and Technology Studies
TBT	Technical Barriers to Trade
TCP	Transmission Control Protocol
TCP/IP	Transmission Control Protocol/Internet Protocol
TLD	Top-Level Domain
TLS	Transport Layer Security
TRIPS	Trade Related Aspects of Intellectual Property Rights
TTP	Trusted Third Party
UDHR	Universal Declaration of Human Rights
UDRP	Uniform Domain-Name Dispute-Resolution Policy
URI	Uniform Resource Identifier
URL	Uniform Resource Locator
US-CERT	United States Computer Emergency Readiness Team
USC-ISI	University of Southern California, Information Sciences Institute
USPTO	United States Patent and Trademark Office
USTR	United States Trade Representative
VoIP	Voice over Internet Protocol
W3C	World Wide Web Consortium
WAI	Web Accessibility Initiative
WCAG	Web Content Accessibility Guidelines
WCIT	World Conference on International Telecommunications
WGIG	Working Group on Internet Governance
WIDE Project	Widely Integrated Distributed Environment Project
Wi-Fi	Wireless Fidelity
WiMAX	Worldwide Interoperability for Microwave Access
WIPO	World Intellectual Property Organization
WSIS	World Summit on the Information Society
WTO	World Trade Organization
XML	Extensible Markup Language

1. THE INTERNET GOVERNANCE OXYMORON

1. See official Go Daddy press release, "Go Daddy No Longer Supports SOPA: Looks to Internet Community & Fellow Tech Leaders to Develop Legislation We All Support," December 23, 2011. Accessed at http://www.godaddy.com /newscenter/release-view.aspx?news_item_id=378.

2. Alexis Ohanian on Bloomberg Television's "In Business with Margaret Brennan," January 4, 2012.

3. House Judiciary Chairman Lamar Smith quoted in *Roll Call* in Jonathan Strong, "Online Piracy Measure Brings Out Hard Feelings," January 2, 2012. Accessed at http://www.rollcall.com/news/online_piracy_measure_brings _out_hard_feelings-211304-1.html.

4. "An Open Letter from Internet Engineers to the US Congress," published on the web site of the Electronic Frontier Foundation, December 15, 2011. Accessed at https://www.eff.org/deeplinks/2011/12/internet-inventors-warn -against-sopa-and-pipa.

5. Official White House response issued by Victoria Espinel, Aneesh Chopra, and Howard Schmidt, "Combating Online Piracy While Protecting an Open and Innovative Internet," January 14, 2012. Accessed at https://wwws.white house.gov/petition-tool/response/combating-online-piracy-while-protecting -open-and-innovative-internet.

6. Geoffrey Bowker and Susan Leigh Star, "How Things (Actor-Net)Work: Classification, Magic and the Ubiquity of Standards," URL November 18, 1996. Accessed at http://www.sis.pitt.edu/~gbowker/actnet.html.

7. Langdon Winner, "Do Artifacts Have Politics?" in *The Whale and the Reactor: A Search for Limits in an Age of High Technology,* Chicago: University of Chicago Press, 1986, p. 19.

8. Sheila Jasanoff, "The Idiom of Co-Production," in Sheila Jasanoff, ed., *States of Knowledge: The Co-Production of Science and Social Order,* London: Routledge, 2004, p. 3.

9. For an overview of actor-network theory, see Bruno Latour, *Reassembling the Social: An Introduction to Actor-Network Theory,* Oxford: Oxford University Press, 2007.

10. See Bruno Latour, "On Technical Mediation," in *Common Knowledge* 3, no. 2 (1994): 29–64.

11. As a starting point into this literature, see Andrew Crane et al., eds., *The Oxford Handbook of Corporate Social Responsibility,* Oxford: Oxford University Press, 2008.

12. See Global Network Initiative, "Principles on Freedom of Expression and Privacy." URL (last accessed July 2, 2012) https://globalnetworkinitiative.org/principles/index.php#20.

13. McKinsey Global Institute Report, "Internet Matters: The Net's Sweeping Impact on Growth, Jobs, and Prosperity," May 2011. Accessed at http://www.mckinsey.com/Insights/MGI/Research/Technology_and_Innovation/Internet_matters.

14. The term "obligatory passage points" is borrowed from Michel Callon's "Elements of a Sociology of Translation," in John Law, ed., *Power Action and Belief: A New Sociology of Knowledge?* London: Routledge, 1986, p. 196.

15. For a history of the origins of Internet architecture and governance, see Janet Abbate, *Inventing the Internet,* Cambridge, MA: MIT Press, 1999.

16. Milton Mueller, *Networks and States: The Global Politics of Internet Governance,* Cambridge, MA: MIT Press, 2010, p. 9.

17. From the introduction of William Dutton, ed., *Oxford Handbook of Internet Studies,* Oxford: Oxford University Press, 2013, p. 1.

18. Excellent examples of Internet scholars who address more content-oriented topics include Yochai Benkler's work on new modes of knowledge production in *The Wealth of Networks: How Social Production Transforms Markets and Freedom,* New Haven, CT: Yale University Press, 2006; Manuel Castell's work on the networked public sphere in "The New Public Sphere: Global Civil Society, Communication Networks, and Global Governance," *Annals of the American Academy of Political and Social Science* 616(1): 79–93, 2008; and scholarship on online political campaigns produced by communication scholars such as Daniel Kreiss, *Taking Our Country Back: The Crafting of Networked Politics from Howard Dean to Barack Obama,* Oxford: Oxford University Press, 2012 and David Karpf, *The MoveOn Effect: The Unexpected Transformation of American Political Advocacy,* Oxford: Oxford University Press, 2012.

2. CONTROLLING INTERNET RESOURCES

1. House Energy and Commerce Committee hearing, "International Proposals to Regulate the Internet," May 31, 2012.

2. Congressional testimony of Vinton Cerf before the House Energy and Commerce Committee, Subcommittee on Communications and Technology, May

31, 2012. Written testimony accessed at http://googlepublicpolicy.blogspot.ca /2012/05/testifying-before-us-house-of.html.

3. "Recommendations" of the IBSA Multistakeholder Meeting on Global Internet Governance, held September 1–2, 2011, in Rio de Janeiro, Brazil.

4. Steve Crocker, RFC 1, "Host Software," April 1969.

5. For more information about the original specification, see Jon Postel, RFC 791, "Internet Protocol, DARPA Internet Program Protocol Specification Prepared for the Defense Advanced Research Projects Agency," September 1981.

6. Milton Mueller's book *Ruling the Root: Internet Governance and the Taming of Cyberspace*, Cambridge, MA: MIT Press, 2002, provides an excellent history and analysis of the rise of the DNS and associated governance controversies.

7. Paul Mockapetris, RFC 882, "Domain Names—Concepts and Facilities," November 1983.

8. See Paul Mockapetris, RFC 882, "Domain Names—Concepts and Facilities," November 1983; RFC 883, "Domain Names—Implementation and Specification," November 1983; RFC 1034, "Domain Names—Concepts and Facilities," November 1987; and RFC 1035, "Domain Names—Implementation and Specification," November 1987.

9. Jon Postel and Joyce Reynolds, RFC 920, "Domain Requirements," October 1984.

10. See Quaizar Vohra and Enke Chen, RFC 4893, "BGP Support for Four-Octet AS Number Space," May 2007.

11. ARIN publishes a list of registered ASNs at URL (last accessed July 11, 2012) ftp://ftp.arin.net/info/asn.txt.

12. Internet Architecture Board, RFC 2826, "IAB Technical Comment on the Unique DNS Root," May 2000.

13. Vinton Cerf, RFC 2468, "I Remember IANA," October 1998.

14. United States Department of Commerce, National Telecommunications and Information Administration, *Management of Internet Names and Addresses*, June 5, 1998. Accessed at http://www.ntia.doc.gov/ntiahome/domainname /6_5_98dns.htm.

15. Milton Mueller's *Ruling the Root* (2002) provides an analysis of the evolution of ICANN and the DNS and associated governance debates.

16. United States Department of Commerce Cooperative Agreement No. NCR 92–18742. Agreement and Amendments available online at URL (last accessed July 13, 2012) http://www.ntia.doc.gov/page/verisign-cooperative -agreement.

17. NTIA press release, "Commerce Department Awards Contract for Management of Key Internet Functions to ICANN," July 2, 2012. Accessed at http://www.ntia.doc.gov/press-release/2012/commerce-department-awards -contract-management-key-internet-functions-icann.

18. IANA publishes the list of root servers on its web site at URL (last accessed July 12, 2012) http://www.iana.org/domains/root/servers.

19. Lars-Johan Liman et al., "Operation of the Root Name Servers," presentation at the ICANN meeting in Rio de Janeiro, Brazil, March 24, 2003.

20. For a more detailed history and explanation of Internet address allocation, see Chapter 5, "The Internet Address Space," in Laura DeNardis, *Protocol Politics: The Globalization of Internet Governance,* Cambridge, MA: MIT Press, 2009.

21. Accreditation criteria for RIRs are outlined in ICANN's "ICP-2 Criteria for Establishment of New Regional Internet Registries." URL (last accessed March 14, 2012) http://www.afrinic.net/docs/billing/afcorp-fee200703.htm.

22. For more detailed pricing information, see the AfriNIC fee schedule available at URL (last accessed March 4, 2012) at http://www.afrinic.net/docs/billing /afcorp-fee200703.htm.

23. Yahoo! privacy policy available online at URL (last accessed March 14, 2012) http://info.yahoo.com/privacy/us/yahoo/details.html.

24. Google privacy policy available online at URL (last accessed March 14, 2012) http://www.google.com/policies/privacy/.

25. Letter from Assistant Secretary Michael Gallagher to Vinton Cerf, August 11, 2005. Accessed at http://www.icann.org/correspondence/gallagher-to-cerf -15aug05.pdf.

26. See "Reveal Day 13 June 2012—New gTLD Applied-for Strings," June 13, 2012, containing the list of applicants for new gTLDs, published on ICANN's web site at http://newgtlds.icann.org/en/program-status/application-results /strings-1200utc-13jun12-en.

27. See ICANN's "gTLD Applicant Guidebook," Version 2012-06-04. Accessed at http://newgtlds.icann.org/en/applicants/agb.

28. U.S. Department of Commerce, National Telecommunications and Information Administration, "US Principles on the Internet's Domain Name and Addressing System," June 30, 2005. Accessed at http://www.ntia.doc.gov /other-publication/2005/us-principles-internets-domain-name-and -addressing-system.

3. SETTING STANDARDS FOR THE INTERNET

1. Yochai Benkler, *The Wealth of Networks: How Social Production Transforms Markets and Freedom,* New Haven, CT: Yale University Press, 2006, p. 131.

2. Ken Alder, "A Revolution to Measure: The Political Economy of the Metric System in France," in M. Norton Wise, ed., *The Values of Precision,* Princeton, NJ: Princeton University Press, 1995, p. 39.

3. As reported in *Fast Company* magazine. See Austin Carr, "BitTorrent Has More Users than Netflix and Hulu Combined—Doubled," January 4, 2011. Accessed at http://www.fastcompany.com/1714001/bittorrent-swells-to-100 -million-users.

4. Geoffrey C. Bowker and Susan Leigh Star, "How Things (Actor-Net)Work: Classification, Magic and the Ubiquity of Standards," *Philosophia,* November 18, 1996.

5. David Clark et al., RFC 1287, "Towards the Future Internet Architecture," December 1991.

6. Janet Abbate, *Inventing the Internet,* Cambridge, MA: The MIT Press, 1999.

7. Thomas Hughes, *Rescuing Prometheus: Four Monumental Projects That Changed the Modern World*, New York: Vintage Books, 1998, pp. 255–300.

8. Vinton Cerf and Robert Kahn, "A Protocol for Packet Network Intercommunication," in *IEEE Transactions on Communications* COM-22, no. 5 (May 1974): 637–648.

9. Internet Society Mission Statement. URL (last accessed July 17, 2012) http://www.internetsociety.org/who-we-are.

10. Steve Crocker, RFC 1, "Host Software," April 1969.

11. RFC Editor, RFC 2555, "30 Years of RFCs," April 1999.

12. David Waitzman, RFC 1149, "A Standard for the Transmission of IP Datagrams on Avian Carriers," April 1990.

13. The RFC process is succinctly described in Paul Hoffman and Susan Harris, RFC 4677, "The Tao of IETF," September 2006.

14. For formal details about the Internet standards process, see Scott Bradner, RFC 2026, "The Internet Standards Process," October 1996.

15. For details about the invention of the web, see Tim Berners-Lee, *Weaving the Web*, New York: HarperBusiness, 2000.

16. See W3C "History." URL (last accessed July 18, 2012) http://www.w3.org/Consortium/facts#history.

17. From the W3C's "Membership Fees" web page. URL (last accessed July 18, 2012) http://www.w3.org/Consortium/fees/.

18. World Wide Web Consortium, "W3C Patent Policy," February 5, 2004. Accessed at www.w3.org/Consortium/Patent-Policy-20040205/.

19. The entire text of the United Nations' "Convention on the Rights of Persons with Disabilities" is available online at URL (last accessed July 19, 2012) http://www2.ohchr.org/english/law/disabilities-convention.htm.

20. W3C Recommendation "Web Content Accessibility Guidelines," WCAG 2.0, December 11, 2008. Accessed at http://www.w3.org/TR/WCAG20/.

21. Alissa Cooper, RFC 6462, "Report from the Internet Privacy Workshop," January 2012.

22. Tom Narten et al., RFC 3041, "Privacy Extensions for Stateless Address Autoconfiguration in IPv6," September 2007.

23. W3C, "The Platform for Privacy Preferences 1.1 Specification," November 13, 2006.

24. W3C press release, "W3C Announces First Draft of Standard for Online Privacy," November 14, 2012. Accessed at http://www.w3.org/2011/11/dnt-pr.html.en.

25. IANA IPv4 Address Space Registry accessed at URL (last accessed March 15, 2012) http://www.iana.org/assignments/ipv4-address-space/ipv4-address-space.xml.

26. See, for example, Benkler, *The Wealth of Networks*, and Rishab Ghosh, "An Economic Basis for Open Standards," December 2005. Accessed at http://flosspols.org/deliverables/FLOSSPOLSD04-openstandards-v6.pdf.

27. See the WTO Agreement on Technical Barriers to Trade. Accessed at http://www.wto.org/english/tratop_e/tbt_e/tbtagr_e.htm.

28. For a lengthy explanation of global debates about open standards, see Laura DeNardis, ed., *Opening Standards: The Global Politics of Interoperability*, Cambridge, MA: MIT Press, 2011.

4. CYBERSECURITY GOVERNANCE

1. An F-Secure Security Labs analyst received a series of emails from an Iranian scientist making this claim. Reported on July 23, 2012, on the company blog. Accessed at http://www.f-secure.com/weblog/archives/00002403.html.
2. United States Industrial Control Systems Cyber Emergency Response Team, ICS-CERT Advisory "Primary Stuxnet Indicators," September 29, 2010.
3. See, for example, David E. Sanger, "Obama Order Sped up Wave of Cyberattacks against Iran," *New York Times*, June 1, 2012.
4. Gadi Evron, "Battling Botnets and Online Mobs: Estonia's Defense Efforts during the Internet War," *Georgetown Journal of International Affairs* (Winter/Spring 2008), pp. 121–126.
5. Tony Smith, "Hacker Jailed for Revenge Sewage Attacks," *The Register*, October 31, 2001.
6. A technical account of the attack is available in Marshall Abrams and Joe Weiss, "Malicious Control System Cyber Security Attack Case Study—Maroochy Water Services, Australia," 2008. Accessed at http://csrc.nist.gov/groups/SMA/fisma/ics/documents/Maroochy-Water-Services-Case-Study_report.pdf.
7. Peter Yee, Usenet Discussion Posting on comp.protocols.tcp-ip, November 2, 1988.
8. The commonly cited number of infected computers is six thousand, derived in part because MIT professor and vice president of information systems James Bruce estimated to reporters from a Boston CBS affiliate that the attack affected 10 percent of MIT's computers. Reporters extrapolated this 10 percent estimate to the entire sixty thousand computers then connected to the Internet to derive the number six thousand. See M. Eichin and J. Rochlis, *With Microscope and Tweezers: An Analysis of the Internet Virus of November 1988*, Massachusetts Institute of Technology (November 1988).
9. *U.S. v. Robert Tappan Morris*, Case Number 89-CR-139, U.S. District Judge Howard G. Munson, United States District Court, Northern District of New York, May 16, 1990.
10. Theodore Eisenberg, "The Cornell Commission on Morris and the Worm," *Communications of the ACM* 32, no. 6 (June 1989): 706–709.
11. CERT Advisory CA-1999-04 "Melissa Macro Virus," March 31, 1999. Accessed at http://www.cert.org/advisories/CA-1999-04.html.
12. US-CERT Alert TA12-024A, "'Anonymous' DDoS Activity," last revised April 23, 2012. Accessed at http://www.us-cert.gov/cas/techalerts/TA12-024A.html.
13. Whitfield Diffie and Martin Hellman, "New Directions in Cryptography," *IEEE Transactions on Information Theory*, 22, no. 6 (1976): 644–654.
14. Ed Felten, "Web Certification Fail: Bad Assumptions Lead to Bad Technology," blog posting on Freedom to Tinker, February 23, 2010. Accessed at

https://freedom-to-tinker.com/blog/felten/web-certification-fail-bad
-assumptions-lead-bad-technology/.

15. Brenden Kuerbis and Milton L. Mueller, "Negotiating a New Governance
Hierarchy: An Analysis of the Conflicting Incentives to Secure Internet
Routing," in *Communications & Strategies* 81, 1st Q. (2011): 125.

16. Paul Vixie, Gerry Sneeringer, and Mark Schleifer, "Events of 21-Oct-2002,"
ISC/UMD/Cogent Event Report, November 24, 2002. Accessed at http://d.root
-servers.org/october21.txt.

17. Twitter blog posting on August 6, 2009. Accessed at http://status.twitter.com
/post/157191978/ongoing-denial-of-service-attack.

18. For a more detailed description of SYN-TCP flooding, see U.S. Department of
Homeland Security, U.S. Computer Emergency Readiness Team (US CERT)
Advisory CA-1996-21, "TCP SYN Flooding and IP Spoofing Attacks," last
revised November 29, 2000. Accessed at http://www.cert.org/advisories/CA
-1996-21.html.

19. CERT Advisory CA-1998-01, "Smurf IP Denial-of-Service Attacks," last revised
March 13, 2000. Accessed at http://www-cert.org/advisories/CA-1998-01.html.

20. Lee Garber, "Denial-of-Service Attacks Rip the Internet," in *IEEE Computer
Magazine* (April 2000): pp. 12–17.

21. Federal Bureau of Investigation press release, "Mafiaboy Pleads Guilty,"
Washington, DC, January 19, 2001. Accessed at http://www.fbi.gov/news
/pressrel/press-releases/mafiaboy-pleads-guilty.

22. The Berkman Center for Internet and Society at Harvard University conducted a study addressing the phenomenon of silencing independent media
and human rights groups. See Ethan Zuckerman et al., "Distributed Denial
of Service Attacks against 'Independent Media and Human Rights Sites,'"
December 2010. Accessed at http://cyber.law.harvard.edu/publications/2010
/DDoS_Independent_Media_Human_Rights.

23. PayPal press release, "PayPal Statement Regarding WikiLeaks," December 3,
2010. Accessed at https://www.thepaypalblog.com/2010/12/paypal-statement
-regarding-wikileaks/.

24. 18 U.S.C.A § 1030.

25. Aaron Smith, Pew Internet Report, "Government Online," April 27, 2010.

26. Ellen Nakashima et al., "U.S., South Korea Targeted in Swarm of Internet Attacks," *Washington Post,* July 9, 2009.

27. Nato News Release, "NATO Opens New Centre of Excellence on Cyber Defense," May 14, 2008. Accessed at http://www.nato.int/docu/update/2008/05
-may/e0514a.html.

28. For example, the U.S. government's Defense Advanced Research Projects
Agency (which funded the Internet's predecessor network) launched its Plan
X Program "to create revolutionary technologies for understanding, planning,
and managing cyberwarfare in real-time, large-scale, and dynamic network
environments." See DARPA-SN-12-51 Foundational Cyberwarfare (Plan X)
Proposer's Day Workshop (September 27, 2012) Accouncement.

29. Robert M. Metcalfe, "From the Ether" column, *InfoWorld,* December 4, 1995.

5. GOVERNANCE AT THE INTERNET'S CORE

1. Source of data: AS relationship table for AS number 3356 (Level 3) drawn from Border Gateway Protocol routing data as tracked by the Cooperative Association for Internet Data Analysis. Accessed at http://as-rank.caida.org /?table-number-as=100&ranksort=number%20of%20ASes%20in %20customer%20cone&as=3356&mode0=as-info.

2. Mark Winther, IDC White Paper, "Tier 1 ISPs: What They Are and Why They Are Important," May 2006. Accessed at http://www.us.ntt.net/downloads /papers/IDC_Tier1_ISPs.pdf .

3. Ian Cooper, Ingrid Melve, and Gary Tomlinson, RFC 3040, "Internet Web Replication and Caching," January 2001.

4. For a taxonomy of CDNs, see Al-Mukaddim Khan Pathan and Rajkumar Buyya, "A Taxonomy and Survey of Content Delivery Networks." URL (last accessed December 27, 2011) http://www.cloudbus.org/reports /CDN-Taxonomy.pdf.

5. Facts about Akamai as reported on the company web site. URL (last accessed December 27, 2011) http://www.akamai.com/html/about/facts _figures.html.

6. "The 32-bit AS Number Report," maintained daily by Internet engineer Geoff Huston. URL (last accessed December 19, 2011) http://www.potaroo.net/tools /asn32/.

7. John Hawkinson and Tony Bates, RFC 1930 "Guidelines for Creation, Selection, and Registration of an Autonomous System (AS)," March 1996.

8. For a history of Internet exchange points, see Lyman Chapin, "Interconnection and Peering among Internet Service Providers: A Historical Perspective," Interisle White Paper, 2005. Accessed at www.interisle.net/sub/ISP %20Interconnection.pdf.

9. Background information about DE-CIX accessed at https://www.de-cix.net/.

10. The entire list of full members of the London Internet Exchange is available at the URL (last accessed December 28, 2011) https://www.linx.net/pubtools /member-techlist.html.

11. "London Internet Exchange (LINX) Memorandum of Understanding Version 11.01–22nd November 2011." Accessed at https://www.linx.net/govern/mou .html#s7.

12. Peyman Faratin, David Clark, et al., "The Growing Complexity of Internet Interconnection," in *Communications & Strategies*, no. 72, 4th Q. (2008): 51–71.

13. Bill Woodcock and Vijay Adhikari, "Survey of Characteristics of Internet Carrier Interconnection Agreements," Packet Clearing House Summary Report, May 2, 2011, p. 2. Accessed at http://www.pch.net/resources/papers/peering -survey/PCH-Peering-Survey-2011.pdf.

14. "AT&T Global IP Network Settlement-Free Peering Policy," last updated May 2011. Accessed at http://www.corp.att.com/peering/.

15. Ibid.

16. "Comcast Settlement-Free Interconnection (SFI) Policy," last updated July 2011. Accessed at http://www.comcast.com/peering/?SCRedirect=true.

17. "Verizon Business Policy for Settlement-Free Interconnection with Internet Networks," 2011. Accessed at http://www.verizonbusiness.com/terms /peering/.

18. "AT&T Global IP Network Settlement-Free Peering Policy," last updated May 2011. Accessed at http://www.corp.att.com/peering/.

19. "Comcast Settlement-Free Interconnection (SFI) Policy," last updated July 2011. Accessed at http://www.comcast.com/peering/?SCRedirect=true.

20. For a description of donut peering, see Greg Goth, "New Internet Economics Might Not Make It to the Edge," in *IEEE Internet Computing* 14, no. 1 (January 2010): 7–9.

21. Karen Rose, "Africa Shifts Focus from Infrastructure to Interconnection," *IEEE Internet Computing* (November/December 2010): p. 56.

22. Internet Society, "Internet Exchange Points." URL (last accessed February 9, 2012) http://www.internetsociety.org/internet-exchange-points-ixps.

23. Phil Weiser, "The Future of Internet Regulation," University of Colorado Law Legal Studies Research Paper No. 09-02, 2009. Accessed at http://ssrn.com /abstract=1344757.

24. As reported by Scott Wooley, "The Day the Web Went Dead," Forbes.com, December 12, 2008. Accessed at http://www.forbes.com/2008/12/01/cogent -sprint-regulation-tech-enter-cz_sw_1202cogent.html.

25. Ibid.

26. Ibid.

27. Michael Kende, "The Digital Handshake: Connecting Internet Backbones," FCC Office of Plans and Policy Working Paper No. 32. URL (last accessed August 15, 2012) http://www.fcc.gov/Bureaus/OPP/working_papers/oppwp32.pdf.

28. Jay P. Kesan and Rajiv C. Shah, "Fool Us Once Shame on You—Fool Us Twice Shame on Us: What We Can Learn from the Privatizations of the Internet Backbone Network and the Domain Name System," *Washington University Law Quarterly* 79 (2001): 89. Accessed at http://papers.ssrn.com /sol3/papers.cfm?abstract_id=260834.

29. J. Scott Marcus et al., "The Future of IP Interconnection: Technical Economic, and Public Policy Aspects," Study for the European Commission, January 29, 2008. Accessed at http://ec.europa.eu/information_society/policy/ecomm/ doc/library/ext_studies/future_ip_intercon/ip_intercon_study_final.pdf.

6. INTERNET ACCESS AND NETWORK NEUTRALITY

1. Adam Liptak, "Verizon Blocks Messages of Abortion Rights Group," *New York Times*, September 27, 2007.

2. Adam Liptak, "Verizon Reverses Itself on Abortion Messages," *New York Times*, September 27, 2007.

3. Jack M. Balkin, "Media Access: A Question of Design," *George Washington Law Review* 76 (2007–2008): 935.

4. See, for example, the Associated Press wire by Peter Svensson, "Comcast Blocks Some Internet Traffic," New York (AP), October 19, 2007.

5. Daniel J. Weitzner, "Net Neutrality . . . Seriously This Time," in *IEEE Internet Computing*, May/June 2008.

6. FCC 05-151 FCC Policy Statement on Broadband Internet Access, adopted August 5, 2005.

7. FCC 08-183 *in re* "Formal Complaint of Free Press and Public Knowledge against Comcast Corp. for Secretly Degrading Peer-to-Peer Applications," 23 F.C.C.R. 13,028 (2008).

8. AT&T News Release, "An Update for Our Smartphone Customers with Unlimited Data Plans," Dallas, Texas, July 29, 2011. Accessed at http://www.att .com/gen/press-room?pid=20535&cdvn=news&newsarticleid=32318& mapcode=corporate.

9. Ibid.

10. Consumer quote from AT&T online forum. Posting on December 9, 2011, at http://forums.att.com/t5/forums/forumtopicprintpage/board-id/Billing /message-id/78427/print-single-message/false/page/1.

11. AT&T's "Wireless Customer Agreement" accessed on the company's web site at http://www.wireless.att.com/learn/articles-resources/wireless-terms.jsp.

12. Greg Risling, "Judge Awards iPhone User $850 in Throttling Case," Associated Press, February 25, 2012.

13. Reuters, "VoIP providers call on EU to ensure free access," April 3, 2009. Accessed at http://www.reuters.com/article/2009/04/03/skype-iphone -idUSL354621020090403.

14. "At SBC, It's All about 'Scale and Scope,'" *Businessweek* Interview with SBC CEO Edward Whitacre, November 7, 2005. Accessed at http://www .businessweek.com/magazine/content/05_45/b3958092.htm.

15. For an engineering description of quality of service issues over the Internet, see Pelin Aksoy and Laura DeNardis, *Information Technology in Theory*, Boston: Thompson 2007, p. 348.

16. Marvin Ammori, "Net Neutrality and the 21st Century First Amendment," blog posting on Balkinization, December 10, 2009. Accessed at http://balkin .blogspot.com/2009/12/net-neutrality-and-21st-century-first.html.

17. Barbara van Schewick, "What a Non-Discrimination Rule Should Look Like," Paper presented at the 38th Research Conference on Communication, Information and Internet Policy, October 1–3, 2010, Arlington, VA, p. 1. Accessed at http://papers.ssrn.com/sol3/papers.cfm?abstract_id=1684677. Emphasis added.

18. FCC 05-151 FCC Policy Statement on Broadband Internet Access, adopted August 5, 2005.

19. Sandra Harding, *Is Science Multicultural? Postcolonialisms, Feminisms, and Epistemologies (Race, Gender, and Science)*, Bloomington: Indiana University Press, 1998, p. 133.

20. Sandra Harding, *Science and Social Inequality: Feminist and Postcolonial Issues*, Urbana: University of Illinois Press, 2006.

21. FCC 10-21 Report and Order, "In the Matter of Preserving the Open Internet Broadband Industry Practices," released December 23, 2010. Accessed at http://hraunfoss.fcc.gov/edocs_public/attachmatch/FCC-10–201A1_Rcd.pdf.

22. Verizon-Google Legislative Framework Proposal, August 2010. Accessed at https://docs.google.com/viewer?url=http://www.google.com/googleblogs /pdfs/verizon_google_legislative_framework_proposal_081010.pdf.

23. Lawrence Lessig, "Another Deregulation Debacle," *New York Times,* August 10, 2010.

24. Jim Harper, "A Capture of the Industry," *New York Times,* February 3, 2011.

7. THE PUBLIC POLICY ROLE OF PRIVATE INFORMATION INTERMEDIARIES

1. NBC Sports press release, "NBC Olympics and Twitter Announce Partnership for London 2012 Olympics Games," London, July 23, 2012.

2. Alex Macgillivray, Twitter official blog posting, "Our Approach to Trust & Safety and Private Information," July 31, 2012. Accessed at http://blog.twitter .com/2012/07/our-approach-to-trust-safety-and.html.

3. See, generally, Brian Carpenter, ed., RFC 1958, "Architectural Principles of the Internet," June 1996; and J. Saltzer, D. P. Reed, and D. D. Clark, "End-to-End Arguments in System Design," in *ACM Transactions on Computer Systems* 2 (November 1984): 27–288.

4. Tarleton Gillespie, "The Politics of 'Platforms,'" *New Media & Society, 12, No. 3* (2010): 3.

5. From Google's mission statement. URL (last accessed October 28, 2011) http://www.google.com/about/corporate/company/.

6. See "J. Christopher Stevens," *New York Times,* September 16, 2012.

7. Claire Cain Miller, "As Violence Spreads in Arab World, Google Blocks Access to Inflammatory Video," *New York Times,* September 13, 2012.

8. Rachel Whetstone, "Free Expression and Controversial Content on the Web," Google official blog, November 14, 2007. Accessed at http://googleblog .blogspot.co.uk/2007/11/free-expression-and-controversial.html.

9. Ibid.

10. Jonathan Zittrain, *The Future of the Internet and How to Stop It,* New Haven, CT: Yale University Press, 2008, p. x.

11. Anti-Defamation League press release, "ADL Praises Apple for Removing Hezbollah TV App from iTunes Stores," July 31, 2012. Accessed at http://archive .adl.org/PresRele/Internet_75/6353_75.htm.

12. Amazon press release. [Amazon Statement Regarding WikiLeaks], 2010. Accessed at http://aws.amazon.com/message/65348/.

13. Ibid.

14. PayPal press release. "PayPal Statement Regarding WikiLeaks," December 3, 2010. Accessed at https://www.thepaypalblog.com/2010/12/paypal-statement -regarding-wikileaks/.

15. "Updated Statement about WikiLeaks from PayPal General Counsel John Muller," Official PayPal blog posting, December 8, 2010. Accessed at

https://www.thepaypalblog.com/2010/12/updated-statement-about-wikileaks
-from-paypal-general-counsel-john-muller/.

16. For one of the many news accounts of this disclosure, see Ellen Nakashima, "Feeling Betrayed, Facebook Users Force Site to Honor Their Privacy," *Washington Post*, November 30, 2007.

17. Facebook press release, "Leading Websites Offer Facebook Beacon for Social Distribution," November 6, 2007. Accessed at http://www.facebook.com /press/releases.php?p=9166.

18. Facebook press release, "Announcement: Facebook Users Can Now Opt Out of Beacon Feature," December 5, 2007. Accessed at http://www.facebook.com /press/releases.php?p=11174.

19. *Lane et al. v. Facebook, Inc. et al.*, class-action lawsuit filed in the U.S. District Court for the Northern District of California, San Jose Division, August 12, 2008.

20. Data obtained from the Google Transparency Report for the six-month period ending December 31, 2011. Accessed at http://www.google.com /transparencyreport/userdatarequests/.

21. Ibid.

22. Chris Jay Hoofnagle et al., "Behavioral Advertising: The Offer You Cannot Refuse," *Harvard Law and Policy Review* 6 (2012): 273.

23. From the text of Title 47, Section 230, United States Code, enacted as part of the Communications Decency Act, in turn a component of the Telecommunications Act of 1996.

24. Facebook Statement of Rights and Responsibilities, URL (last accessed August 22, 2012) http://www.facebook.com/legal/terms.

8. INTERNET ARCHITECTURE AND INTELLECTUAL PROPERTY

1. See the ABC news story and video interview "Teen Transplant Candidate Sued over Music Download," WTAE.com Pittsburgh. URL (last accessed September 7, 2011) at http://www.wtae.com/news/18160365/detail .html.

2. Statistic taken from the Recording Industry Association of America web site. URL (last accessed June 9, 2011) http://www.riaa.com/physicalpiracy.php ?content_selector=piracy-online-scope-of-the-problem.

3. Office of the United States Trade Representative, "2011 Special 301 Report," 2011, p. 11. Accessed at http://www.ustr.gov/webfm_send/2841.

4. James Boyle, "The Second Enclosure Movement and the Construction of the Public Domain," in *Law and Contemporary Problems* 66 (Winter–Spring 2003): 33–74.

5. Joe Karaganis, ed., "Media Piracy in Emerging Economies," Social Science Research Council, 2011, p. 1. Accessed at http://piracy.ssrc.org.

6. Google's Terms of Service, last modified March 1, 2012. Accessed at http://www .google.com/intl/en/policies/terms/.

7. Section 9, "Copyright," of Twitter's Terms of Service. URL (last accessed September 15, 2012) http://twitter.com/tos.

8. Google's Terms of Service, last modified March 1, 2012. Accessed at http://www.google.com/intl/en/policies/terms/.

9. Source, Google Transparency Report, last updated September 15, 2012.

10. Official Google Search blog posting on August 10, 2012. Accessed at http://insidesearch.blogspot.com/2012/08/an-update-to-our-search-algorithms.html.

11. Ibid.

12. HADOPI is an acronym for Haute Autorité pour la Diffusion des Œuvres et la Protection des Droits sur Internet, a French government agency. The English translation is the High Authority for Transmission of Creative Works and Copyright Protection on the Internet.

13. See Section 9 of the Digital Economy Act of 2010. Accessed at http://www.legislation.gov.uk/ukpga/2010/24/section/9?view=plain.

14. See the Memorandum of Understanding establishing the Center for Copyright Information, July 6, 2012. Accessed at http://www.copyrightinformation.org/sites/default/files/Momorandum%20of%20Understanding.pdf

15. United Nations General Assembly, Submission to the Human Rights Council, "Report of the Special Rapporteur on the Promotion and Protection of the Right to Freedom of Opinion and Expression," May 16, 2011, p. 14. Accessed at http://www2.ohchr.org/english/bodies/hrcouncil/docs/17session/A.HRC.17.27_en.pdf.

16. According to public remarks by John Morton, director of U.S. Immigration and Customs Enforcement, at the State of the Net Conference in Washington, DC, on January 18, 2011. Accessed at http://www.ice.gov/doclib/news/library/speeches/011811morton.pdf.

17. See, for example, the Immigration and Customs Enforcement press release, issued November 29, 2010, announcing a list of eighty-two domain name seizures. Accessed at http://www.ice.gov/doclib/news/releases/2010/domain_names.pdf.

18. U.S. Immigration and Customs Enforcement press release, " 'Operation In Our Sites' Targets Internet Movie Pirates," June 30, 2010. Accessed at http://www.ice.gov/news/releases/1006/100630losangeles.htm.

19. See the Department of Justice press release, "Federal Courts Order Seizure of 82 Website Domains Involved in Selling Counterfeit Goods as Part of DOJ and ICE Cyber Monday Crackdown," November 29, 2010. Accessed at http://www.justice.gov/opa/pr/2010/November/10-ag-1355.html.

20. For a lengthier list of seized domain names, see the U.S. Immigration and Customs Enforcement (of the Department of Homeland Security) news release, "List of Domain Names Seized by ICE," November 29, 2010. Accessed at http://www.ice.gov/doclib/news/releases/2010/domain_names.pdf.

21. U.S. Intellectual Property Enforcement Coordinator, "2010 U.S. Intellectual Property Enforcement Coordinator Annual Report on Intellectual Property Enforcement," February 2011. Accessed at http://www.whitehouse.gov/sites/default/files/omb/IPEC/ipec_annual_report_feb2011.pdf.

22. According to public remarks by John Morton, director of U.S. Immigration and Customs Enforcement, at the State of the Net Conference in Washington,

DC, on January 18, 2011. Accessed at http://www.ice.gov/doclib/news/library/speeches/011811morton.pdf.

23. Wendy Seltzer, "Exposing the Flaws of Censorship by Domain Name," in *IEEE Security and Privacy* 9, no. 1 (2011): 83–87.

24. RapGodFathers statement, "RapGodFathers Servers Seized by U.S. Authority." URL (last accessed July 5, 2011) http://www.rapgodfathers.info/news/14591-rapgodfathers-servers-seized-by-us-authorities.

25. Reported by Ben Sisario in "Piracy Fight Shuts Down Music Blogs," *New York Times,* December 13, 2010.

26. Harvey Anderson, vice president of business affairs and general counsel at Mozilla, blog posting, "Homeland Security Request to Take Down MafiaaFire Add-on," May 5, 2011. Accessed at http://lockshot.wordpress.com/2011/05/05/homeland-security-request-to-take-down-mafiaafire-add-on/.

27. April 19, 2011, email from Mozilla to U.S. Department of Homeland Security, "To help us evaluate the Department of Homeland Security's request to take-down/remove the MAFIAAfire.com add-on from Mozilla's websites." Accessed at http://www.scribd.com/doc/54218316/Questions-to-Department-of-Homeland-Security-April-19-2011.

28. Trademark Registration No. 1,473,554 and 1,463,601.

29. United States Patent and Trademark Office, "Basic Facts about Trademark," October 2010. Accessed at http://www.uspto.gov/trademarks/basics/BasicFacts_with_correct_links.pdf.

30. WIPO Arbitration and Mediation Center, Administrative Panel Decision, "Madonna Ciccone, p/k/a Madonna v. Dan Parisi and 'Madonna.com,'" Case No. D2000-0847, October 12, 2000.

31. Excerpt from ICANN's "Rules for Uniform Domain Name Dispute Resolution Policy (the 'Rules')," effective March 1, 2010. Accessed at http://www.icann.org/en/help/dndr/udrp/rules.

32. For a critique of the UDRP system, see Lawrence R. Helfer, "International Dispute Settlement at the Trademark-Domain Name Interface," *Pepperdine Law Review* 29, no. 1 (2002): Article 6.

33. WIPO, "The Management of Internet Names and Addresses: Intellectual Property Issues," Final Report of the First WIPO Internet Domain Name Process, April 30, 1999. Accessed at http://www.wipo.int/amc/en/processes/process1/report/finalreport.html.

34. United States Patent and Trademark Office web site. URL (last accessed August 15, 2012) http://www.uspto.gov/inventors/patents.jsp.

35. See Brad Biddle, Andrew White, and Sean Woods, "How Many Standards in a Laptop? (And Other Empirical Questions)," September 10, 2010. Accessed at http://papers.ssrn.com/sol3/papers.cfm?abstract_id=1619440.

36. See, generally, Bruce H. Kobayashi and Joshua D. Wright, "Intellectual Property and Standard Setting," George Mason Law and Economics Research Paper No. 09-40, 2009.

37. OMB Circular No. A-119 Revised, Memorandum for Heads of Executive Departments and Agencies, "Federal Participation in the Development and Use of Voluntary Consensus Standards in Conformity Assessment Activities," February 10, 1998. Accessed at http://www.whitehouse.gov/omb/circulars_a119.

38. Government of India, Ministry of Communications and Information Technology, Actual Text of Policy on Open Standards. Accessed at http://egovstandards.gov.in/notification/Notification_Policy_on_Open_Standards_-_12Nov10.pdf/view.

39. Eric Goldman, "Search Engine Bias and the Demise of Search Engine Utopianism," *Yale Journal of Law and Technology*, 2005–2006. Accessed at http://papers.ssrn.com/sol3/papers.cfm?abstract_id=893892.

40. Frank Pasquale, "Rankings, Reductionism, and Responsibility," Seton Hall Public Law Research Paper No. 888327, 2006. Accessed at http://ssrn.com/abstract=888327.

41. James Grimmelmann, "The Structure of Search Engine Law," *Iowa Law Review* 93 (2007).

9. THE DARK ARTS OF INTERNET GOVERNANCE

1. See the account of Burma Internet shutdown in OpenNet Initiative Bulletin, "Pulling the Plug: A Technical Review of the Internet Shutdown in Burma." URL (last accessed March 21, 2011) http://opennet.net/sites/opennet.net/files/ONI_Bulletin_Burma_2007.pdf.

2. See OpenNet Initiative's dispatch "Nepal: Internet Down, Media Censorship Imposed." URL (last accessed March 21, 2011) http://opennet.net/blog/2005/02/nepal-internet-down-media-censorship-imposed.

3. Elinson Zusha and Shoshana Walter. "Latest BART Shooting Prompts New Discussion of Reforms," *New York Times*, July 16, 2011. Accessed at http://www.nytimes.com/2011/07/17/us/17bcbart.html?pagewanted=all.

4. Linton Johnson, "BART—July 4 News Conference on Officer Involved Shooting at Civic Center Station," *BART—Bay Area Rapid Transit*, July 4, 2011. Accessed at http://www.bart.gov/news/articles/2011/news20110704a.aspx.

5. "A Letter from BART to Our Customers," August 20, 2011. Accessed at http://www.bart.gov/news/articles/2011/news20110820.aspx.

6. Ibid.

7. Zusha Elinson, "After Cellphone Action, BART Faces Escalating Protests," *New York Times*, August 21, 2011. Accessed at http://www.nytimes.com/2011/08/21/us/21bcbart.html?pagewanted=all.

8. See Emergency Petition for Declaratory Ruling of Public Knowledge et al., before the Federal Communications Commission, August 29, 2011. Accessed at http://www.publicknowledge.org/files/docs/publicinterestpetitionFCCBART.pdf.

9. Ralf Bendrath and Milton Mueller, "The End of the Net as We Know It? Deep Packet Inspection and Internet Governance," in *New Media and Society* 13, no. 7 (2011): 1148.

10. Rebecca MacKinnon, *Consent of the Networked: The World-Wide Struggle for Internet Freedom,* New York: Basic Books, 2012, p. 59.

11. For a detailed historical account of the development of packet switching, see Janet Abbate, "White Heat and Cold War: The Origins and Meanings of Packet Switching," in *Inventing the Internet,* Cambridge, MA: MIT Press, 1999.

12. See "Submarine Cables and the Oceans: Connecting the World," UNEP-WCMC Biodiversity Series No. 31, 2009, p. 9. Accessed at http://www.iscpc .org/publications/ICPC-UNEP_Report.pdf.

13. Reported by Chris Williams, "Taiwan Earthquake Shakes Internet," in *The Register,* December 27, 2006. Accessed at http://www.theregister.co.uk/2006 /12/27/boxing_day_earthquake_taiwan/.

14. Renesys blog announcement about Egypt outage, January 27, 2011. Accessed at http://www.renesys.com/blog/2011/01/egypt-leaves-the-internet.shtml.

15. BGPmon data accessed at URL (last accessed August 29, 2012) http:// bgpmon.net/blog/?p=450.

16. Vodafone press release, January 28, 2012. Accessed at http://www.vodafone .com/content/index/media/press_statements/statement_on_egypt.html.

17. Vodafone press release, January 29, 2012. Accessed at http://www.vodafone .com/content/index/media/press_statements/statement_on_egypt.html.

18. The story of Ampon Tangnoppakul's arrest is described in the *Economist* in "An Inconvenient Death: A Sad Story of Bad Law, Absurd Sentences and Political Expediency," May 12, 2012. Accessed at http://www.economist.com /node/21554585.

19. Official Google blog posting by Senior Policy Analyst Dorothy Chou, "More Transparency into Government Requests," June 17, 2012. Accessed at http:// googleblog.blogspot.com/2012/06/more-transparency-into-government.html.

20. Google Transparency Report Government "Removal Requests" page. URL (last accessed June 20, 2012) http://www.google.com/transparencyreport /removals/government/.

21. *Zhang et al. v. Baidu.com, Inc. et al.,* U.S. District Court, Southern District of New York, No. 11-03388.

22. BBC News, "US Website Covering China's Bo Xilai Scandal Hacked," April 21, 2012. Accessed at http://www.bbc.co.uk/news/world-asia-china-17796810.

23. Manuel Castells, "Communication, Power and Counter-Power in the Network Society," in *International Journal of Communication* 1 (2007): 238. Accessed at http://ijoc.org/ojs/index.php/ijoc/article/view/46/35.

10. INTERNET GOVERNANCE AND INTERNET FREEDOM

1. European Telecommunication Network Operators' Association, CWG-WCIT12 Contribution 109, Council Working Group to Prepare for the 2012 World Conference on International Telecommunications, June 6, 2012.

2. Center for Democracy and Technology, "ETNO Proposal Threatens to Impair Access to Open, Global Internet," June 21, 2012. Accessed at https://www.cdt .org/report/etno-proposal-threatens-access-open-global-internet.

3. For details, see Milton Mueller, *Networks and States, The Global Politics of Internet Governance,* Cambridge, MA: MIT Press, 2010, p. 248.
4. Report of the United Nations Working Group on Internet Governance, Chateuau de Bossey, June 2005, p. 4. Accessed at http://www.wgig.org/docs/WGIGREPORT.pdf.
5. ICANN, "Affirmation of Commitments by the United States Department of Commerce and the Internet Corporation for Assigned Names and Numbers," September 30, 2009.
6. G-8 stands for the "Group of 8," a forum created by France in the 1970s (initially as the G-6) for meetings of the heads of state of major economies. At the time of the Deauville Declaration, the G-8 included Canada, France, Germany, Italy, Japan, Russia, the United Kingdom, and the United States.
7. "The Deauville G-8 Declaration," May 27, 2011. Accessed at www.whitehouse.gov/the-press-office/2011/05/27/deauville-g-8-declaration.
8. Bertrand de La Chapelle, "Multistakeholder Governance: Principles and Challenges of an Innovative Political Paradigm," in Wolfgang Kleinwachter, ed., MIND [Multistakeholder Internet Dialogue] Collaboratory Discussion Paper Series No. 1, September 2011. Accessed at http://dl.collaboratory.de/mind/mind_02_neu.pdf.
9. See, for example, Jeremy Malcolm, *Multi-Stakeholder Governance and the Internet Governance Forum,* Perth: Terminus Press, 2008.
10. See, for example, William H. Dutton, John Palfrey, and Malcolm Peltu, "Deciphering the Codes of Internet Governance: Understanding the Hard Issues at Stake," Oxford Internet Institute Forum Discussion Paper No. 8, 2007.
11. See, generally, Chris Anderson, *Free: The Future of a Radical Price,* New York: Hyperion, 2009.
12. Yochai Benkler, *The Wealth of Networks: How Social Production Transforms Markets and Freedom,* New Haven, CT: Yale University Press, 2006.
13. Google Investor Relations, "Google Announces Second Quarter 2012 Financial Results," July 19, 2012. Accessed at http://investor.google.com/earnings/2012/Q2_google_earnings.html. Google's operating expenses for the quarter were $4 billion; other cost of revenue (e.g., data center operational expenses) totaled $2.41 billion.
14. Michael Zimmer, "The Externalities of Search 2.0: The Emerging Privacy Threats When the Drive for the Perfect Search Engine Meets Web 2.0," *First Monday* 13, no. 3 (March 3, 2008).
15. See, for example, Yahoo! privacy policy available at URL (last accessed March 14, 2012) http://info.yahoo.com/privacy/us/yahoo/details.html; and Google privacy policy available at URL (last accessed March 14, 2012) http://www.google.com/policies/privacy/.
16. The Gay Girl in Damascus blog posting "Making Sense of Syria Today," posted on April 19, 2011, but subsequently taken offline.
17. The Gay Girl in Damascus blog posting "My Father the Hero," posted on April 29, 2011, but subsequently taken offline.

18. Liz Sly, " 'Gay Girl in Damascus' Blogger Detained," *Washington Post,* June 7, 2011. Accessed at http://www.washingtonpost.com/world/middle-east/gay -girl-in-damascus-blogger-detained/2011/06/07/AGoTmQLH_story.html ?nav=emailpage.

19. See, for example, Isabella Steger's article "Photos of Syrian-American Blogger Called into Question," *Wall Street Journal,* June 8, 2011.

20. The WHOIS protocol is specified in Leslie Daigle, RFC 3912, "WHOIS Proto-col Specification," September 2004.

21. See Facebook's Terms of Service, "Statement of Rights and Responsibilities," revision date June 18, 2012. Accessed at http://www.facebook.com/legal/ terms.

22. See Danielle Keats Citron and Helen Norton, "Intermediaries and Hate Speech: Fostering Digital Citizenship for the Information Age," *Boston University Law Review* 91 (2011): 1435.

23. See Government of India, Ministry of Communications and Information Technology, "Guidelines for Cyber Cafes," 2011. Accessed at http://mit.gov.in /content/notifications.

24. A. Michael Froomkin, "Lessons Learned Too Well," paper presented at the Oxford Internet Institute's "A Decade in Internet Time: Symposium on the Dynamics of the Internet and Society," September 22, 2011.

25. This section is expanded further in Laura DeNardis, "The Social Media Chal-lenge to Internet Governance," forthcoming in William Dutton and Mark Graham, eds., *Society and the Internet: How Information and Social Networks Are Changing Our Lives,* Oxford: Oxford University Press.

26. Tim Berners-Lee, "Long Live the Web: A Call for Continued Open Standards and Neutrality," *Scientific American,* December 2010.

27. Vinton Cerf, "Keep the Internet Open," *New York Times,* May 24, 2012. Ac-cessed at http://www.nytimes.com/2012/05/25/opinion/keep-the-internet -open.html.

28. Testimony of Vinton Cerf before the House Energy and Commerce Commit-tee Subcommittee on Communications and Technology, Hearing on "Inter-national Proposals to Regulate the Internet," May 31, 2012.

Authentication—In computer networking, the verification of an individual's identity for access to a network resource; or the verification of the identity of an online site.

Autonomous System (AS)—A collection of routing prefixes indicating IP addresses reachable within a network's domain.

Autonomous System Number (ASN)—A unique binary number assigned to each autonomous system.

Binary—A language code, made up of two numbers, o and 1, that can be used to encode any type of information in a digital system.

Biometric Identification—Authentication of an individual based on a unique physical attribute, such as DNA, facial feature, fingerprint, voice pattern, or retinal pattern.

BitTorrent—A peer-to-peer file sharing protocol or client designed to efficiently share large digital files over a network.

Bluetooth—A wireless standard, using an unlicensed frequency range, for transmission over very short distances such as between a phone and a wireless earpiece.

Border Gateway Protocol (BGP)—An exterior routing protocol instructing routers how to exchange information among autonomous systems.

Buffering—The introduction of a slight timing delay and temporary storage so that video or audio appears to be continuously streamed.

Cell—In cellular telephony, a small geographical area served by a base station antenna.

Certificate Authority (CA)—A trusted third party that assigns and vouches for digital certificates.

Circuit Switching—A network switching approach that establishes a dedicated, end-to-end path maintained for the duration of a transmission.

Coaxial Cable—A copper transmission medium consisting of a core cylindrical conductor surrounded by an insulating material and a braided copper shield.

Compression—The mathematical manipulation of digitally encoded information to decrease file size for more efficient transmission or storage.

Computer Emergency Response/Readiness Team (CERT)—A governmental or nongovernmental institution that addresses Internet security problems.

Deep Packet Inspection—A capability built into routers for inspecting the payload of a packet as well as its header information.

Digital Certificate—An encrypted binary attachment to information; used for authenticating an individual or a site.

Distributed Denial of Service (DDoS) Attack—An attack that incapacitates a targeted computer by inundating it with requests that originate simultaneously from thousands of distributed computers.

Domain Name System—An enormous, distributed database management system that translates domain names into IP addresses.

Dotted Decimal Format—Shorthand code for representing a 32-bit IPv4 address in decimal.

Electromagnetic Spectrum—The entire range of electromagnetic frequency waves, such as radio waves, light waves, X-rays, and gamma rays.

Encode—To transform an analog signal into a digital format.

Encryption—The mathematical scrambling of data to make it unreadable to unauthorized parties.

Encryption Key—A cipher (number) that encodes or decodes information during the encryption or decryption process.

Ethernet—The dominant local area network standards.

Fiber Optics—A glass transmission medium.

Frequency—Number of cycles per second.

Global Positioning System (GPS)—A collection of satellites and their supporting systems that provide three-dimensional location information.

Graduated Response—A system of intellectual property rights enforcement in which an infringing user's Internet access is cut off after repeated warnings.

Handoff—In cellular telephony, the seamless transfer of a call from one base station (and frequency) to an adjacent base station (and frequency).

Header—A packet's administrative overhead information, containing addressing and other information, which accompanies a packet's payload.

Hexadecimal—A numbering system representing information using the following sixteen characters: 0, 1, 2, 3, 4, 5, 6, 7, 8, 9, A, B, C, D, E, and F. Also called the Base-16 numbering system.

Hop—An instance of a packet traversing a router.

HyperText Markup Language (HTML)—A standard language for encoding web information.

International Organization for Standardization (ISO)—A prominent international standards-setting organization composed of national standards-setting bodies.

International Telecommunication Union (ITU)—A specialized United Nations agency focusing on information and communication technologies and standardization.

Internet Address—A 32- or 128-bit binary number that serves as a unique Internet identifier, either assigned permanently or for a session.

Internet Address Space—The collection of all available Internet addresses.

Internet Assigned Numbers Authority (IANA)—The Internet governance institution overseeing unique Internet numbers such as IPv4 addresses, IPv6 addresses, Autonomous System Numbers, and various protocol numbers.

Internet Corporation for Assigned Names and Numbers (ICANN)—Internet governance institution responsible for the administration of the critical Internet resources of Internet names and numbers.

Internet Engineering Task Force (IETF)—Standards-setting body that has established many of the core Internet protocols.

Internet Exchange Point (IXP)—A shared point of interconnection at which multiple networks conjoin to exchange packets.

Internet Protocol (IP)—Standard for two crucial networking functions: formatting and addressing packets for transmission over the Internet.

Interoperability—The ability for different devices to exchange information because they adhere to common formats and standards.

IPv4—Internet Protocol version 4 is the prevailing Internet address standard assigning a unique 32-bit identifier.

IPv6—Internet Protocol version 6 is the newer Internet address standard assigning a unique 128-bit identifier.

Key Length—The number of bits contained in an encryption key.

Kill-Switch—A euphemism for any number of mechanisms for disrupting a communication system.

Latency—The delay experienced between the transmission and receipt of a packet over a network.

Local Area Network (LAN)—A network that spans a limited geographical area, such as within a building.

Moore's Law—In its current form, the theory predicting that the number of transistors that can be integrated on a circuit will double every eighteen months.

MP3—A formatting standard used to compress audio files.

Multimedia—Information that integrates various types of content including alphanumeric text, audio, video, and images.

Net Neutrality—A principle advocating for the nondiscriminatory treatment of traffic over an access network.

Packet—In packet switching, a small segment of information to be individually addressed and routed over a network to its destination.

Packet Switching—A network switching approach in which information is broken into small units, called packets, which are sequenced, transmitted individually over a network, and reassembled at their destination.

Payload—The content of a packet.

Peer-to-Peer (P2P)—Refers to a file sharing protocol in which files are distributed in segments over multiple peer computers rather than contained entirely on a single centralized computer.

Regional Internet Registry (RIR)—A private, nonprofit entity that allocates and assigns IP addresses in its respective region.

Registrar—An entity that assigns domain names to individuals and institutions requesting these names.

Registry Operator—An institution responsible for maintaining an authoritative database of names and associated IP addresses for every domain name registered within a top-level domain.

Request for Comments (RFCs)—The publications and standards that collectively provide blueprints for the basic operation of the Internet.

Root Zone File—The definitive list of names and IP addresses of all the authoritative DNS servers for top-level domains, including country-code TLDs. More accurately called the root zone database.

Router—A switching device that directs a packet to its destination based on the packet's destination IP address and the algorithmic routing tables contained within the device.

Routing Table—A database a router consults to determine how to direct a packet over a network to its destination.

Session Initiation Protocol (SIP)—A Voice over Internet Protocol signaling protocol.

Simple Mail Transfer Protocol (SMTP)—An electronic mail standard.

Spoof—To forge an IP address, usually to carry out an unauthorized activity.

Throttle—To intentionally slow down traffic over a network.

Top-Level Domain (TLD)—The top suffix in the domain name hierarchy. Examples include .com, .org, and .edu.

Transmission Control Protocol/Internet Protocol (TCP/IP)—The core family of protocols used for Internet connectivity.

Triangulation—The approach of pinpointing physical location by calculating a device's distance from three points of reference.

Twisted Pair—A copper transmission medium in which two wires are twisted around each other.

Uniform Resource Locator (URL)—A string of alphanumeric characters identifying a web resource.

Virus—Malicious computer code embedded in a legitimate program which is activated only when a user takes some action such as clicking on an email attachment.

Voice over Internet Protocol (VoIP)—A family of communication standards for the digital transmission of voice over an Internet Protocol network.

Wi-Fi, or Wireless Fidelity—A family of standards, based on the Institute of Electrical and Electronics Engineers' 802.11 specifications, for wireless local transmission.

WiMAX—An acronym for Worldwide Interoperability for Microwave Access, a high-speed metropolitan area wireless standard.

World Wide Web Consortium (W3C)—The institution that sets technical standards for the Web.

Worm—Malicious computer code designed to be autonomous and self-propagating without any action by a user.

XML—Extensible (or eXtensible) Markup Language, a contemporary information formatting and encoding standard for the web.

RECOMMENDED READING

There is an impressive amount of scholarship on both the history of Internet governance and contemporary policy problems. An interdisciplinary body of scholarship has coalesced around the international community of scholars known as the "Global Internet Governance Academic Network," or GigaNet. This work represents some of the leading scholarship and thinking around the topic of Internet governance, some of it cited in this book. Other leading works of Internet governance have come from legal scholars, historians of technology, and other disciplines. The following is a list of recommended books addressing Internet governance subjects.

Abbate, Janet. *Inventing the Internet*. MIT Press, 1999.

Antonova, Slavka. *Powerscape of Internet Governance—How Was Global Multistakeholderism Invented in ICANN?* VDM Verlag, 2008.

Benedek, Wolfgang, Veronika Bauer, and Matthias C. Kettemann, eds. *Internet Governance and the Information Society: Global Perspectives and European Dimensions*. Eleven International Publishing, 2008.

Braman, Sandra. *Change of State: Information, Policy, and Power*. MIT Press, 2009.

Brousseau, Eric, Meryem Marzouki, and Cécile Méadel, eds. *Governance, Regulation, and Powers on the Internet*. Cambridge University Press, 2012.

Bygrave, Lee A., and Jon Bing, eds. *Internet Governance: Infrastructure and Institutions*. Oxford University Press, 2009.

Dany, Charlotte. *Global Governance and NGO Participation: Shaping the Information Society in the United Nations*. Routledge, 2012.

Deibert, Ronald, John Palfrey, Rafal Rohozinski, and Jonathan Zittrain, eds. *Access Contested: Security, Identity, and Resistance in Asian Cyberspace*. MIT Press, 2011.

———, eds. *Access Controlled: The Shaping of Power, Rights, and Rule in Cyberspace.* MIT Press, 2010.

———, eds. *Access Denied: The Practice and Policy of Global Internet Filtering.* MIT Press, 2008.

DeNardis, Laura, ed. *Opening Standards—The Global Politics of Interoperability.* MIT Press, 2011.

———. *Protocol Politics: The Globalization of Internet Governance.* MIT Press, 2009.

Drake, William J. *Reforming Internet Governance: Perspectives from the Working Group on Internet Governance.* United Nations Publications, March 2005.

Drake, William J., and Ernest J. Wilson. *Governing Global Electronic Networks: International Perspectives on Policy and Power.* MIT Press, 2008.

Dutton, William H., ed. *The Oxford Handbook of Internet Studies.* Oxford University Press, 2013.

Flyverbom, Mikkel. *The Power of Networks: Organizing the Global Politics of the Internet.* Edward Elgar, 2011.

Galloway, Alexander R. *Protocol: How Control Exists after Decentralization.* MIT Press, 2004.

Gillespie, Tarleton. *Wired Shut: Copyright and the Shape of Digital Culture.* MIT Press, 2007.

Goldsmith, Jack, and Tim Wu. *Who Controls the Internet? Illusions of a Borderless World.* Oxford University Press, 2008.

Greenstein, Shane, and Victor Stango, eds. *Standards and Public Policy.* Cambridge University Press, 2007.

Komaitis, Konstantinos. *The Current State of Domain Name Regulation: Domain Names as Second Class Citizens in a Mark-Dominated World.* Routledge, 2010.

Kulesza, Joanna. *International Internet Law.* Routledge, 2012.

Lessig, Lawrence. *Code: Version 2.0.* Basic Books, 2006.

MacKinnon, Rebecca. *Consent of the Networked: The Worldwide Struggle for Internet Freedom.* Basic Books, 2012.

MacLean, Don, ed. *Internet Governance: A Grand Collaboration.* United Nations Publications, July 2004.

Malcolm, Jeremy. *Multi-Stakeholder Governance and the Internet Governance Forum.* Terminus Press, 2008.

Mansell, Robin, and Marc Raboy, eds. *The Handbook of Global Media and Communication Policy.* Wiley-Blackwell, 2011.

Marsden, Christopher T. *Internet Co-Regulation: European Law, Regulatory Governance and Legitimacy in Cyberspace.* Cambridge University Press, 2011.

———. *Net Neutrality: Towards a Co-Regulatory Solution.* Bloomsbury, 2010.

Mathiason, John. *Internet Governance: The New Frontier of Global Institutions.* Routledge, 2008.

Mueller, Milton. *Networks and States: The Global Politics of Internet Governance.* MIT Press, 2010.

———. *Ruling the Root: Internet Governance and the Taming of Cyberspace.* MIT Press, 2002.

Musiani, Francesca. *Cyberhandshakes: How the Internet Challenges Dispute Resolution (. . . And Simplifies It)*. EuroEditions, 2009.

Palfrey, John, and Urs Gasser. *Interop: The Promise and Perils of Highly Interconnected Systems*. Basic Books, 2012.

Paré, Daniel J. *Internet Governance in Transition: Who Is the Master of This Domain?* Rowman & Littlefield, 2003.

Pavan, Elena. *Frames and Connections in the Governance of Global Communications*. Lexington Books, 2012.

Post, David G. *In Search of Jefferson's Moose: Notes on the State of Cyberspace*. Oxford University Press, 2009.

Raboy, Marc, Normand Landry, and Jeremy Shtern. *Digital Solidarities, Communication Policy and Multi-Stakeholder Global Governance: The Legacy of the World Summit on the Information Society*. Peter Lang Publishing, 2010.

Saleh, Nivien. *Third World Citizens and the Information Technology Revolution*. Palgrave Macmillan, 2010.

Singh, J. P. *Negotiation and the Global Information Economy*. Cambridge University Press, 2008.

Stauffacher, Daniel, and Wolfgang Kleinwächter, eds. *The World Summit on the Information Society: Moving from the Past into the Future*. United Nations Publications, January 2005.

Thierer, Adam, and Clyde Wayne Crews Jr., eds. *Who Rules the Net? Internet Governance and Jurisdiction*. Cato Institute, 2003.

Vaidhyanathan, Siva. *The Googlization of Everything: (And Why We Should Worry)*. University of California Press, 2011.

van Shewick, Barbara. *Internet Architecture and Innovation*. MIT Press, 2010.

Weber, Rolf H. *Shaping Internet Governance: Regulatory Challenges*. Springer, 2010.

Wu, Tim. *The Master Switch: The Rise and Fall of Information Empires*. Vintage, 2011.

Zittrain, Jonathan. *The Future of the Internet and How to Stop It*. Yale University Press, 2008.

INDEX

3Com, 106
802.11 wireless standards, 133, 270
access (broadband), 131–134
accessibility standards, 77–78
actor-network theory, 12, 250
AD. *See* Area Director (of the IETF)
advertising (online), 3, 8, 12, 29, 31, 58, 111,
    157, 162, 166–167, 205, 231–234
African Network Information Centre
    (AfriNIC), 53–54
AfriNIC. *See* African Network Informa-
    tion Centre
Ahmadinejad, Mahmoud, 103
Akamai Technologies, 109, 112, 116
Alcatel-Lucent, 45
Amazon, 12, 61, 69, 102, 104, 142,
    161, 169
American Registry for Internet Numbers
    (ARIN), 53
America Online, 69
Ameritech, 115
Ames Research Center, 50, 88
Ammori, Marvin, 146
AMS-IX, 113
Angie's List, 168
anonymity, 234–239
Anonymous, 91, 104, 201
Anti-Defamation League, 160

Anycast, 51
APNIC. *See* Asia Pacific Network
    Information Centre
app censorship, 159–161
Apple, Inc., 60, 68, 81, 158, 160, 239
AppleTalk, 68
App Store (Apple), 158, 160
Arabic language characters (in domain
    names), 56
Area Director (of the IETF), 69
ARIN. *See* American Registry for Internet
    Numbers
ARPANET, 18, 38, 39, 42, 69, 70, 72,
    245
AS. *See* autonomous system
ASCII, 38, 56, 245
Asia Pacific Network Information Centre
    (APNIC), 53
ASNs. *See* Autonomous System Numbers
assistive device (for the disabled), 77
asynchronous (communication), 144
AT&T, 109–110, 116; and intellectual
    property, 183; peering policies, 118–121;
    usage plans, 137–139
AT&T Mobility v. Concepcion, 139
authentication, 21, 24, 79, 88, 104, 236,
    267; of DNS queries, 97–98; of
    routing, 95–97; of web sites, 93–95